THE NT

THE NTH DOCTOR

Jean-Marc Lofficier

First published in Great Britain in 1997 by
Doctor Who Books
an imprint of Virgin Publishing Ltd
332 Ladbroke Grove
London W10 5AH

ISBN 0 426 20499 9

Cover illustration by Colin Howard

Typeset by Galleon Typesetting, Ipswich
Printed and bound in Great Britain by
Mackays of Chatham PLC

Contents

Dedication

To my sister-in-law, Gwennis, for her unflagging support, Chris Heer for his valuable advice and notes, and Lou Anders, Lee Harlin Bahan, Jon Blum, Neil Hogan, Corey Klemow, David McKinnon, Jason Miller, Siobhan Morgan, Kate Orman, Debi Smolenske, Shannon Patrick Sullivan, Joe Wesson, Gary Zielinski and all the other ragweed-free folks whom I've had the pleasure of meeting on the Internet.

J.-M. L.

Acknowledgements

I am grateful to the following people who helped me in the compilation of the information included in this book: Johnny Byrne, Robert DeLaurentis, Denny Martin Flinn, Tony Harding, John Leekley, Peter Litten, Rebecca Levene, Leonard Nimoy and Philip Segal.

J.-M. L.

Introduction

'Life is not a sum of what we have been, but what we yearn to be.'

José Ortega y Gasset

The purpose of this book is to offer a fairly comprehensive and somewhat scholarly look at the *Doctor Who*s that might have been, outside the realm of the original BBC television series. Not the 1st, or the 8th, or the 9th, or even the 13th Doctor, but the . . . Nth Doctor.

Hypothetical Doctors. Doctors pulled out of what Hollywood poetically calls 'development limbo'. Doctors whose existences are less than 'canon', and yet more legitimate than that, for example, of the stage plays or comics. Doctors whose existence may still affect the future of *Doctor Who*. Nth Doctors.

As I have done in the past, I have written this Introduction in order to clear some potential misunderstandings concerning the approach that I took in writing this book, and to explain some of the rules that I followed and assumptions that I made. If you happen to disagree with any of the following editorial decisions, then you will probably find faults with this book.

Selection of material

In agreement with my editors at Virgin, I have decided to cover only seven unproduced scripts, all intended to be a film or television continuation of the original BBC television series.

I have purposely not delved into the various scripts or treatments which were, at one time or another, commissioned by, or written for, the original BBC television series, but never produced. First, these have been adequately documented in various fan magazines. One, Anthony Coburn's *The Masters of Luxor*, was even published, and reviewed in the updated version of my *Doctor Who Programme Guide*. Besides, I feel that a book of this nature ought to be written by someone based in England, with full access to the BBC archives.

Instead, I have concentrated on the one major area that has not been extensively researched and that has been, until now, the subject of rumours and half-baked, often erroneous, information: the attempts, by the BBC and others, to resurrect *Doctor Who* after its cancellation in 1989.

These unproduced scripts each represent a vital link in the chain that bridges the gap between the BBC's final story, *Survival* (7P), and the 1996 made-for-television *Doctor Who* feature, starring Paul McGann.

Titles

With the exception of *The Dark Dimension* these scripts, including that of the Paul McGann made-for-television feature, were all officially entitled *Doctor Who* with some minor variations, which is both confusing in a book of this nature and, frankly, not terribly imaginative.

I have therefore taken the liberty of labelling these scripts with more distinctive titles, although in every instance I have sought to confirm these titles with the writer (or the producer) themselves. For your information, here is an accurate 'scorecard' of the material covered in this book:

- *The Return of Varnax* is the first screenplay developed by a company called Daltenreys Ltd (a.k.a. Greenlight and Coast to Coast) in order to launch *Doctor Who* as a full-length feature film. It was written in 1987 by Mark Ezra, based on a story by Daltenreys' principals, Peter Litten and George Dugdale. Its official title was simply *Doctor Who – The Movie*.
- *The Time Lord* was written in 1988 by Johnny Byrne, who also penned the original BBC television series stories *The Keeper of Traken* (5T), *Arc of Infinity* (6E) and *Warriors of*

the Deep (6L). Byrne was hired by Daltenreys to rewrite Ezra's screenplay. Its official title was *Doctor Who – The Time Lord* and its story was still credited to Litten and Dugdale. *The Time Lord* went through at least four major versions.

- *Last of the Time Lords* (a.k.a. *The Last Time Lord*) is a substantially different version of *The Time Lord*, also penned by Johnny Byrne in 1991, before Daltenreys/ Greenlight/Coast to Coast passed the torch to Lumière. The script itself was never completed – only 75 pages were written. Two versions of the story exist, plus yet one more attempt at creating a third story (*Chameleon*), which never made it past outline stage.

- *The Jewels of Time* is a screenplay written in 1993 by Denny Martin Flinn for Lumière. It was intended to be directed by Leonard Nimoy, before the rights reverted to the BBC. Its official title was *Doctor Who – The Movie*, but this title was fully approved by Flinn.

- *The Dark Dimension* is a screenplay written by Adrian Rigelsford, also in 1993, as part of an attempt by BBC Enterprises (now BBC Worldwide) to produce a direct-to-video *Doctor Who* feature, to capitalise on the then upcoming 30th anniversary of the programme.

- *Fathers and Brothers* is a screenplay written by John Leekley in 1994. It was the first script commissioned by executive producer Philip Segal on behalf of Amblin Television, Universal Television and BBC Enterprises. Its official title was *Doctor Who*, but this title was fully approved by Leekley.

- *The Time of My Life* is a screenplay written by Robert DeLaurentis, also in 1994. It was the second script commissioned by executive producer Philip Segal on behalf of Amblin Television, Universal Television and BBC Enterprises. Its official title was *Dr. Who?* (with a question mark); this title is the one chosen by DeLaurentis.

- Finally, *Enemy Within* – which is not covered but is often mentioned in this book, since every other script eventually led to it – is the screenplay written in 1995 by Matthew

Jacobs. It was the third script commissioned by executive producer Philip Segal on behalf of Universal Television and BBC Worldwide (Amblin was no longer involved at that stage), and the one which eventually became the made-for-television feature starring Paul McGann. Its official title was *Doctor Who*. *Enemy Within* is the title given to it by Segal.

Background

I have tried to interview at least one person connected with each of the scripts reviewed in this book, so that readers can hear their voices as well.

Speaking of voices, it will not escape readers' attention that a good portion of this book is written from first-hand experience, and that the Appendix even includes me, to a minor extent, as a participant in the process.

This is because several times over the years I have found myself approached by producers who wanted to pick my brains about the series. My wife Randy and I met with Leonard Nimoy to discuss *The Jewels of Time*, and we acted as 'fan liaisons' for Philip Segal for about a year, a time of turmoil and changes for the new show. This has given us a unique insiders' perspective on the various attempts at reworking *Doctor Who*, one which I hope readers will enjoy.

Notes

Readers of *The Terrestrial Index* and *The Universal Data-bank* already know that I have always enjoyed 'retconning' (a fan term derived from 'retroactive continuity') the *Doctor Who* universe, that is to say, trying to fit all the pieces – even the ones that were realistically not meant to fit – within a greater, coherent fictional tapestry.

Argument about each 'Nth Doctor' script's degree of 'canonicity' will ultimately depend on each reader's own evaluation. Readers who wish to disregard any or all of the scripts reviewed here are, naturally, free to do so. Since these scripts were not produced, their status as regards their 'canonicity' is highly subjective.

However, one should bear in mind that these scripts were fully licensed and approved by the BBC. The new elements that they proposed to introduce in the *Doctor Who* universe may often seem fairly radical to the readers, but they are no less a break with the past than, say, *The Deadly Assassin* (4P) was when compared to *The War Games* (ZZ), or *Genesis of the Daleks* (4E) to *The Daleks* (B). Change – often radical change – has always been a respected tradition of *Doctor Who*.

For these reasons I feel justified in treating the 'Nth Doctor' scripts as, at the very least, something closely related to main *Doctor Who* continuity, not unlike the *New Adventures* or the *Missing Adventures*. John Leekley's *Fathers and Brothers*, in particular, deserves special consideration, since many of the revelations it contained about the Doctor's past appear to have been carried over into Matthew Jacobs' *Enemy Within*, and would have become part of series continuity had there been a series. What we have here is a 'Segal Masterplan', different yet no less valid than the previously established 'Cartmel Masterplan'.

The question that I therefore asked myself in analysing each of these scripts was, if they had been produced, how would we have reconciled them with the rest of the existing *Doctor Who* universe?

The surprising answer I found was that, in fact, it would not have taken much to make these scripts fit in with continuity, which, if anything, is a glorious tribute to the strength and flexibility of the *Doctor Who* concept.

While 'retconning' the scripts, I came up with a number of theories that throw new light on the Doctor, his past, and various other elements of the Whoniverse. Clearly all the theories expressed in this book are, in the end, just that – the product of my personal opinions. Other fan scholars, such as John Peel, David Banks, Paul Cornell, Martin Day, Keith Topping and Lance Parkin, have presented their own conflicting, if equally worthy, interpretations.

It is fairly safe to state, however, that if you do not care for

Doctor Who continuity, you might want to skip the footnotes entirely.

Reviews

I have included a brief general review of each script – all in my humble opinion, of course. However, readers should keep in mind that the quotes provided in this book represent (on average) only about 7 per cent of the scripts themselves, and furthermore that these quotes have been selected for their relevance to the *Doctor Who* universe rather than for their literary merits.

As it would be unfair to judge a painting by looking at less than 10 per cent of its canvas, readers should not presume to pass judgment on these scripts – other than in matters pertaining to continuity.

Also, none of these scripts ever reached the final shooting stage. They were all 'drafts', and would probably have been further rewritten before being shot. (I have, in fact, included some speculation as to what changes might have been made.) So, these scripts should be considered 'works in progress', and not definitive statements of their respective writers' intentions.

Finally, as everyone who has studied the art of film-making knows, even a good script can be mangled beyond recognition by poor execution, and a mediocre script can sometimes be improved by skilled direction and great acting. Therefore, it would also be a mistake to prejudge what these productions might have been and looked like on the basis of these scripts alone.

In conclusion, as I write this (in July 1996) it has become clear that *Enemy Within* was not the huge commercial success hoped for by its producers. As a result, the very future of *Doctor Who* in film and television is, once again, uncertain. The 'Nth Doctor' scripts, taken together, may give us a glimpse of what lies ahead, should the good Doctor some day return to grace our screens.

Lastly, I would be remiss if I did not thank here my wife and writing partner, Randy (hence the 'we' which sometimes replaces the 'I' in this work), who has helped write and polish this book.

Jean-Marc Lofficier

Prologue (pre-1987)

The first time I was approached to discuss the concept of a *Doctor Who* movie was in 1981, as I was working on the first draft of what eventually became *The Doctor Who Programme Guide*.

The series had just made a critical splash in America with the syndication of a package comprised of the episodes from *Robot* (4A) to *Invasion of Time* (4Z), featuring odd introductions delivered by American actor, Howard DaSilva, sold to a number of independent television stations. A first dedicated *Doctor Who* convention had been held in Los Angeles in December 1980, which Randy and I had attended. We had also arranged for the guest appearances of Terrance Dicks and, through Terrance's good offices, Tom Baker and then-producer Graham Williams. I had also just finished working on an article about *Doctor Who* for the French cinema magazine, *L'Écran Fantastique*, an article which, for Randy and me, started it all.

The convention was a massive success and, since it had been held on its doorstep, Hollywood took notice. This was also the time when the American editions of some of the Target novelisations, republished by Pinnacle with a brilliant introduction by Harlan Ellison, had hit the bookshops, giving the show added visibility. *Doctor Who* and Tom Baker were therefore, in Hollywood lingo, 'hot'.

They started to come out of the woodwork soon after that, 'they' being, of course, the wannabe producers who, always looking for a locomotive to which they could hitch their wagon, knew a good thing when they saw one.

There were rumours in England of a feature film project, *Doctor Who Meets Scratchman*, being arranged by Tom Baker and Ian Marter. In America I was briefly contacted by the producers who later released an unsuccessful *Lone Ranger* remake.

Tom Baker left and was replaced by Peter Davison. In Hollywood the iron was no longer hot and *Doctor Who* had started to be considered a little like yesterday's news. Yet short-lived attempts continued to surface.

There was talk of an animated series to be produced by Nelvana for CBS whose then-executive, Michael Chase-Walker, liked *Doctor Who*. Around 1986 producer Bob Kosberg expressed an interest in the property. (Randy and I ended up briefly working with Bob on what eventually became *Twelve Monkeys*, but that, as they say, is another story.) But, in typical Hollywood fashion, nothing ever happened for our favourite Time Lord. It did not matter much, anyway, because the show was still on the air, year after year, like clockwork.

Then in 1989, after a couple of premonitory hiccups, the unthinkable happened. *Doctor Who* was cancelled.

But, to quote *Logopolis* (5V), 'the moment had been prepared for . . .'

1

THE RETURN OF VARNAX

by

Mark Ezra

from a story by
Peter Litten & George Dugdale

Background

The saga of the producing team that became known to fans variously as 'Daltenreys', 'Greenlight' and 'Coast to Coast' began in 1986, soon after the original *Doctor Who* television series was put on hold by the BBC.

Special effects wizards Peter Litten, George Dugdale and John Humphreys, who had previously worked on various BBC shows including *Doctor Who*, decided that the time was ripe to launch the Doctor on the silver screen as a big-budget, special effects-laden motion picture.

In a remarkable feat of entrepreneurial spirit, Litten, Dugdale and Humphreys succeeded in raising the not inconsiderable sum of money requested by BBC Enterprises (later renamed BBC Worldwide), the commercial arm of the BBC, for the sale of the motion picture rights to *Doctor Who*. With financial backing from various entertainment industry personalities, such as Brian Ferry, John Illsley, etc., they formed an entity called Daltenreys Limited to make the deal.

When rights to a property like *Doctor Who* are sold to a producer they are usually sold for a certain period of time – called 'term' and measured in years – during which time the said producer must make a movie. If no film is produced the rights eventually revert to their original owner at the expiration of the term.

Daltenreys' efforts were ultimately doomed when they did not succeed in commencing principal photography on a *Doctor Who* feature film before the expiration of the term granted by BBC Enterprises, who then refused to grant any further time.

The definition of the rights sold by BBC Enterprises are crucial to understanding the reasons for this failure, and BBC Enterprises' refusal to grant the extension. Since at the time the deal was struck the BBC intended to continue production on the television series, the television rights, which would normally have been sold together with the motion picture rights, were retained by BBC Enterprises.

Later when, at Philip Segal's behest, BBC Enterprises eventually decided to join forces with Amblin Television and

Universal Television to produce a new *Doctor Who* television series, it discovered that splitting up the motion picture and television rights had become an impediment to its efforts. In effect, having both a film and television series with the same name and the same hero, who would undoubtedly be played by two different actors, was deemed too confusing for audiences. It also created potentially serious problems with respect to the exploitation of merchandising rights.

Ultimately BBC Enterprises was forced to make a choice between its co-production with Amblin Television/Universal Television, and the extension of the term granted to Daltenreys and its associates; it chose the former.

Returning to 1986: having secured the rights, Daltenreys then moved on to commission a script from writer Mark Ezra, with whom Litten and Dugdale had worked before. In August 1987 Ezra turned out a script officially entitled *Doctor Who – The Movie*, based on a story developed by Litten and Dugdale. (The title *The Return of Varnax* is a made-up title used here for convenience purposes.)

Story

We open on warlord ZARGON's massive warship, orbiting the planet Trufador. Zargon issues an ultimatum to the Trufadons to surrender or be destroyed. A prisoner is dragged into the room, handcuffed and his face covered with a hood. It is the DOCTOR, and we see his TARDIS (in the shape of the familiar London Police Box) standing nearby. [1]

The Doctor pleads with Zargon to renounce his megalomaniacal dreams of conquest, but his pleas fall on deaf ears. The evil warlord has seized the Doctor's Time Rotor – a mechanical device something like a cross between an egg-timer and the symbol for infinity with a control knob on top – without which the TARDIS cannot travel in time. [2]

A gloating Zargon orders the Doctor to be unmasked ('revealing a very famous face' [3]) to watch the destruction of Trufador by his Doomsday Weapon, a super-powerful, evil-looking missile. The Doctor warns that the Trufadons will

13

retaliate and both parties will be annihilated. But Zargon believes that his weapon is powerful enough to prevent any counter-strike. He orders it to be launched.

At that very moment the Doctor breaks free of his chains, seizes the Time Rotor and uses it to create a TIME WARP – a pitch-black hole in space and time which swallows Zargon's missile.[4] It is a measure that is strictly forbidden by the Time Lords.

A now powerless Zargon watches in horror as the Trufadons launch their own missile attack. The Doctor, still holding the Time Rotor, escapes into the TARDIS, leaving Zargon and his men to face their deserved destruction.

After CREDITS have rolled, the TARDIS rematerialises on Gallifrey, where the Doctor is immediately placed under arrest.

We cut to the bleak world of Centros, a doomed planet facing impending annihilation from its belching red sun. The Earth probe Voyager is recovered by two humanoids who take the plaque showing Earth's co-ordinates to their over-lord, the evil (and yet unseen) VARNAX. The merciless villain orders them killed by his two companions, the beauti-ful but deadly MORGANA and the bulky cyborg warrior NEGLOS.

Meanwhile, native rebels led by young ONYX and his friend KALCIS set up some explosives in preparation for their assault on Varnax's seemingly impregnable citadel. But things appear to go a little too smoothly. Indeed, this is part of Varnax's devious scheme. He exhorts his men:

Varnax *My faithful warriors, long have I promised you that one day we should leave this dying planet and return to our true and rightful home, Gallifrey. I tell you now that time is near at hand. The sun is dying. Soon it will explode, taking this world of Centros with it into oblivion. But do not fear. By then we shall be long gone. We will be gone, never to return again. I will lead you to our new home. Another world where we shall conquer the population as we once did here. Our Empire will reign supreme once again![5]*

14

Varnax wants the rebels to capture a cosmic transmitter and summon help from Gallifrey, acting as bait for the fish he wishes to capture. But the insurgents prove deadlier than even he anticipated. Having seized a cache of weapons, Onyx and his men burst into Varnax's throne room and battle is joined between the rebels, Morgana and Neglos. During the battle we discover that Varnax is a cyborg too – 'a vile travesty of a human being – more machine than man; his deformed, twisted frame is supported by a complex arrangement of tubes, cables and pistons that give life to his otherwise useless body.'

Morgana and Neglos repel the rebels, who are allowed to capture the transmitter. Kalcis sacrifices his life so that Onyx and his friends can escape from the citadel.

Meanwhile on Gallifrey the High Council, comprised of three TIME LORDS, is passing judgment on the Doctor:

Time Lord 2 *My honourable Time Lord is too generous to the defendant. He has interfered with the course of Time itself by opening a Time Warp – in direct contravention of every rule . . . and has placed the entire stability of the universe at risk.*

Time Lord 3 *Our own ancestors meddled with the fifth dimension in similar manner . . . And I need not recount the evil to which it was put.*

Time Lord 1 *Our early history is an embarrassment to us all.* [6] *However, there is no suggestion that the defendant had any but the least selfish of motives.*

The Doctor once more pleads for a relaxation of the rules. He argues that the Time Lords have a duty to interfere to prevent evil, but the Council remains deaf to his eloquence and he is found guilty. However, in consideration of his past good services he is merely condemned to be grounded on Gallifrey, denied permission to travel in time, and required to help teach Gallifreyan Law to Time Lords in training.

On Centros Neglos and his men and their pack of hunting animals, the size of lions with several eyes, are hot on Onyx's trail. The rebel leader reaches a cavern where he is met by LOIS and other insurgents. Onyx uses the transmitter to broadcast an SOS to Gallifrey, unaware that this is precisely what Varnax wants him to do.

As soon as he has finished, Neglos and his men burst into the cavern. The rebels escape but Onyx chooses to remain behind. POG, a furry little creature, 'something like a raccoon with a prehensile tail and a hairless face', stays with him. Onyx is taken prisoner, realising at last that Varnax wanted him to use the transmitter, but Pog escapes. A small recording device containing Onyx's story is attached to his collar.

On Gallifrey the Doctor is reluctantly attending to his new tasks when he passes a docking bay and spots his TARDIS. The urge to check it out is too strong and he enters the ship where he meets CORA, a beautiful, strong-willed and rather humourless mechanic, who is engaged in removing the TARDIS's Time Rotor in order to decommission it. It's to be sent to the Museum of Primitive Transport! Introductions are performed:

> **Cora** *Hey, who do you think you are?*
> **Doctor** *That's right.*
> **Cora (confused)** *What?*[7]

Just as Cora is about to walk out with the Time Rotor, Onyx's distress signal comes in. In spite of the Time Lady's loud protests the Doctor seizes this opportunity first to reinstall the Rotor and then to take off for Centros.

> **Doctor** *You look like you could do with a vacation. Loosen up a bit. What's your name?*
> **Cora (panicked)** *What kind of vacation? I've never left Gallifrey before!*
> **Doctor** *Oh dear, a typical Gallifreyan. You ought to get out more. See the universe.* (**He checks Centros in the TARDIS's memory banks.**) *We once used Centros as a place of exile . . . For one of our most evil villains . . . But it's been abandoned for a very long time.*[8]

The TARDIS rematerialises on a bleak, sulphurous plain on Centros. After a scary encounter with a WOOG, a seemingly cute and harmless creature which suddenly turns into a fanged monster, the Doctor and Cora are captured by Varnax's men. They are taken to the Citadel foundry, underground, where the renegade Time Lord is supervising the final repairs to his own black menacing TARDIS.[9] The Doctor recognises Varnax, which pleases the villain:

Varnax *So I have not been entirely forgotten on Gallifrey. That is good, for the High Council will soon have reason to tremble at my name again.*

We learn that Varnax has used all his regenerations and is on his final, thirteenth life.[10] Varnax lured a Time Lord – the Doctor – to Centros because he wants a Time Rotor to power his own TARDIS in order to escape from doomed Centros. The Doctor points out that even Varnax's TARDIS is not enough to transport his entire army. Varnax replies that he has a plan, but won't divulge what it is. He orders that the rebel leader, Onyx, be brought to him.

As Neglos comes into the scene, dragging Onyx bound in chains, he is briefly attacked by another Doctor (the same Doctor, from the future – see below), who takes Onyx away. But, just as suddenly, Onyx reappears and surrenders himself. Looking confusedly at the present-Doctor, who is still Varnax's captive, Neglos places the rebel leader in a space capsule. At Varnax's command the rebel leader's body is frozen, then launched into space to fall into Centros' doomed sun.

The Doctor and Cora are then chained to a spot where they will soon perish under a flow of molten metal. Varnax and Morgana leave in their TARDIS.

The situation seems desperate when, suddenly, Pog appears and succeeds in diverting the flow of molten metal into another channel. The foundry collapses, enabling the Doctor and Cora to get free. Cora tells the Doctor that all is not lost, because she can jury-rig another Time Rotor. She collects various pieces of machinery while the Doctor keeps Neglos at bay. Finally, the two Time Lords, still followed by Pog, manage to get into the TARDIS. Cora puts together a new Time Rotor just in the nick of time, before Neglos and his men can batter their way in. They dematerialise.

The Doctor has noticed the recording device attached to Pog's collar and plays Onyx's pre-recorded message:

Onyx *I am Onyx, leader of the people of Centros, enslaved for many centuries by the renegade Time Lord Varnax. We would still be a happy, peaceful race, if the High Council of Gallifrey had not chosen our planet as his place of exile. My people, the rightful inhabitants of Centros, are in mortal conflict with Varnax. Now they are in hiding, but time is running out fast. Our planet is burning up, our Sun dying. Varnax intends to colonise Earth, and placed three powerful transporter crystals on that planet to carry his armies there. But when he was banished to Centros the pathway to Earth was lost and the crystals scattered in time. Now he has rediscovered the co-ordinates. It is imperative that the crystals are found and destroyed or planet Earth and its people will suffer the same fate as our own.* [11]

But the message is interrupted before Onyx can reveal the three crystals' space-time location. The Doctor decides to go after Onyx to get the information. The TARDIS rushes after the space capsule which is plummetting towards the ready-to-explode sun. Matter, light and time are being sucked into it. The TARDIS is shaking wildly and its passengers ageing rapidly, but thanks to a series of perilous manoeuvres the Doctor manages to retrieve the capsule. However, upon opening it, the two Time Lords discover that they are too late. Onyx is already dead.

The Doctor decides to break the rules and travel back in time to just before Onyx was placed in the capsule. The TARDIS rematerialises in the foundry cavern. There, he attacks Neglos and spirits Onyx away (as shown in the previous scene above). [12]

The Doctor knows that they only have a few minutes. Onyx tells the Time Lord the location of the transporter site on Earth (Stonehenge), and gives him a fragment of a map giving the co-ordinates of the crystals. The rebel leader then asks if he lives or dies, and the Doctor reluctantly tells him that he dies. But Onyx finds strength in knowing that he sacrificed himself to give his people a chance to live. He then heroically returns to his pre-ordained fate.

The Doctor and Cora, still accompanied by Pog, return to the TARDIS and, using Onyx's map, travel to the Smithsonian Museum in present-day Washington DC.

There, we meet MIKE BRADLEY, a sixteen-year-old intern whose life is being made miserable by GILBERT CHUBLEY, a snide young man in his twenties. Chubley confiscates and destroys one of Mike's comics, *Titan, Terror of Tremidor*. MISS CRABTREE, a spinsterish supervisor, reassigns Mike to filing. But suddenly they encounter Varnax's men. Mike runs away and bumps into the Doctor, who pulls him to safety:

Mike *Say, who are you?*
Cora *Just call him the Doctor.*
Mike *Doctor who?*
Doctor *That's right.* [7]
Mike *Eh?*

The Centrosian warriors are looking for the other missing fragment of the map. Using his own fragment and a scanner the Doctor determines that it is being kept in the Museum's vaults, and persuades Mike to take him and Cora down into the Archives. There they run into Chubley, who loudly objects to their presence. The Doctor recovers the missing fragment, but a snotty Chubley tears a piece off while trying to stop them.

Varnax's men burst into the room. Chubley faints at the sight. They snatch the fragment from his hands. But when they look for the Doctor, Cora and Mike, they have already escaped. They return to the TARDIS, which stood as part of a Victorian exhibition, and dematerialise.

Mike is properly amazed by the sight and concept of the TARDIS. Using the map fragment, they travel to London in Victorian England. After the Doctor, Cora and Mike, all correctly dressed in period attire, have left, Pog is alone in the TARDIS. The little creature starts exploring and unwittingly finds and releases K-9. [13]

19

K-9 *Greetings master. It has been a long time since you last let me out of my kennel. I regret to say this is not your most attractive incarnation.*

K-9 eventually figures out that Pog is not a regenerated Doctor. Meanwhile Pog, in a monkey-like fashion, has begun to 'play' with the TARDIS console, damaging the Time Rotor and even creating zero gravity. Eventually K-9 restores order while a contrite Pog slinks back into a corner.

The Doctor, Cora and Mike have arrived at the Tower of London. The Doctor tries warning the CAPTAIN OF THE GUARD that someone is going to steal the Crown Jewels, but is not believed at first, until he is mistaken for Sherlock Holmes.[14] Unfortunately by then it is too late. Neglos and his warriors have made off with the Crown and the Sceptre. A hair-raising pursuit ensues along the ramparts and the roof-tops. Eventually, Neglos escapes with the Crown while, thanks to Mike, the Doctor has retaken the Sceptre.

They take off in the TARDIS, but Pog's previous tampering causes them to 'crash-land' in 1492, aboard the *Santa Maria*, during CHRISTOPHER COLUMBUS's fateful journey. After Cora has fixed the Time Rotor they leave, this time rematerialising in the Peruvian jungle in 1572. They are soon captured by Spanish Conquistadors, led by CAPTAIN MENDOZA, engaged in the looting of the great Sun Temple of Machu Picchu. The Inca Leader, XANTOTAN, is tied to an altar. Inside a temple they discover a large golden idol whose head is a life-size crystal skull – the crystal they are seeking.

The Doctor and Mike are separated from Cora, who is taken away by the lustful Conquistadors. The cunning Time Lady provokes the Spaniards into fighting over her. Then she disables three more Spaniards and frees the Incas. Inside the temple the Doctor and Mike succeed in snatching the crystal skull. Unfortunately the statue breaks up, and they are caught by Mendoza and his Inca puppet, PETAQUETL. They are tied next to Xantotan and about to be burned alive – the skull being used to magnify the sun's rays and set fire to their pyre – when they are saved by a lunar eclipse of the sun.

The Inca High Priest kills Petaquetl and frees Xantotan. The other Incas previously released by Cora attack the Spaniards. During the battle, Varnax's black TARDIS appears. Varnax and the Doctor vie for possession of the skull.

At one point a stray blow from an Inca spear knocks the crystal from the Doctor's hand and sends it crashing towards the ground. Varnax uses his Time Rotor to slow down time – he and the Doctor are not affected – which enables the Doctor to catch the crystal before it smashes.

The Doctor and his two companions then manage to escape from the Incas and regain the safety of the TARDIS with the skull. Pog is thrilled to see them back, but is afraid of the skull. The Doctor tells Cora and Mike that Varnax was able to find them by following their timestream. Now they are going to do the same to him in order to get the third crystal.

The TARDIS rematerialises in a very far future when Earth has become a desert-like planet. They locate Varnax's TARDIS, but it looks empty. During their exploration Cora falls through a trapdoor but is eventually released.

They then set out across the desert and, led by the seemingly tireless Cora, eventually reach a City. There they are captured by human-size silver praying mantis-like robots, the SANDROIDS. The robots take them to three hooded characters led by a woman, AXIS, who welcomes them to the City of Aquatia.

Aquatia is an oasis in the desert. Axis's and the other two men's heads are enlarged, with small mouths and ears. They explain that since Earth lost its ozone layer the planet has become a desert. Water is their most precious commodity. They offer it to the travellers, but Cora refuses.

The Doctor mentions that they have come for a crystal. Axis takes them to an Ice Chamber which houses the City's frozen population.

Axis *Each of our great Cities has the responsibility of preserving certain species of wildlife and plants ready for the day when we shall colonise the planet again. It is only necessary for three of us to remain awake at any one time.* [15]

21

Axis takes the Doctor to the frozen body of their founder, who was once her husband. In his hands is the crystal they seek. She explains that it keeps life in his body until the time has come to resettle the planet.

Suddenly Cora lunges, smashes the glass coffin and grabs the crystal. In the ensuing fight the Doctor tears her face away revealing her to be, in reality, a robotic duplicate (thus explaining her endurance and strange behaviour). The Sandroids attempt to capture the robotic Cora, but she is rescued by Varnax's TARDIS, which rematerialises. Morgana and Neglos hold the real Cora hostage. Thanks to her the villains have seized the Sceptre and crystal skull held in the Doctor's TARDIS.

After Varnax leaves, the Doctor and Mike manage to escape from the Sandroids, who it turns out, are afraid of water. They make their way back to the TARDIS, and set course for the twentieth century, on Varnax's tail. But the villain has sabotaged their Time Rotor and the ship spins out of control, until the Doctor switches to manual drive. The Time Lord then tells Mike they are going to pay a visit to an old friend of his.

We cut to an English golf course, where BRIGADIER LETHBRIDGE-STEWART and his wife DOROTHY are playing golf with friends BASIL and SYBIL.[16] The Doctor appears and takes the Brigadier away.

We then cut to Stonehenge. Morgana and Neglos tie Cora to the altar stone. Varnax positions the three crystals. Suddenly, six UNIT tanks led by the Brigadier take up position surrounding the stone circle.

The sun appears. Its beams channelled through Stonehenge hit the crystals and create a force field around the circle. Inside, the rocks glow and reform into their original state.

> **Brigadier (wearily)** *Don't you know any alien creatures who aren't immune to shell fire?*

The Doctor and Mike move towards the circle. They manage to crawl under the force field. The Doctor rushes to free Cora, while Mike bravely uses the service revolver entrusted to him by the Brigadier to keep the Centrosian warriors at bay.

The Doctor then uses reflective plates from Cora's belt to divert the light beams from the crystals, thereby causing the energy field to break down. The Brigadier is then able to order his troops to attack.

But Varnax seizes the crystal skull and points its light beam straight at the Doctor. The Doctor, still holding a reflective shield, fights back. The skull shatters. Varnax screams in pain and flees into his TARDIS with Morgana.

Meanwhile, Neglos is using Cora as a shield. The Doctor and Mike throw themselves to the ground as all the energy released by Varnax is sucked back into the sky. Cora holds tight to a stone pillar. Neglos is drawn, screaming and flailing, into the air. Even Varnax's TARDIS is sucked away as it begins to dematerialise.

The Doctor and Mike rush to Cora's side. The Time Lady appears to be dead, but a tear from Pog brings her back to life. The Doctor then tells them they have to return to Centros to keep the promise he made to Onyx. They shake hands with the Brigadier and leave.

When Mike asks the Time Lord what happened to the three crystals the Doctor winks. A series of cuts shows them being restored to their original locations in space and time, making the Captain of the Guard, Xantotan and Axis very happy.

On Centros the Doctor manages to herd all of Onyx's freedom fighters inside the TARDIS and leave before the sun explodes, annihilating the planet. [17]

They then return to Gallifrey, in time to discover that Varnax (who is still alive) is now threatening to destroy the planet. The three High Council Time Lords blame the Doctor for this crisis, but the Doctor is able to turn the tables by revealing that Varnax was unlawfully exiled to Centros. It turns out that this was a decision made secretly by two of the members of the Council, who did not inform the first:

Time Lord 3 *It had to be done. Varnax had to be disposed of quickly.*
Doctor *And so you sacrificed an innocent population.*

Time Lord 1 *That is not the way of the Time Lords. Why was I not informed?*

Time Lord 2 *You would have objected. Varnax was too dangerous to keep on Gallifrey.*

Time Lord 1 *Brother Time Lords, you make me ashamed to be a member of the High Council. We have done a great wrong to the people of Centros. Amends must be made. But first, we must give an answer to Varnax. He will destroy Gallifrey unless we cede all power to him.*

Varnax now also requests that the Doctor be delivered to him. The Doctor agrees, but begs Varnax not to open the Time Warp, which would give him absolute power. Varnax's curiosity is tickled. The Time Lords are horrified.

While the Time Lords argue, Mike performs a secret operation at the Doctor's behest.

Soon after, the Doctor's TARDIS rematerialises aboard Varnax's ship. The Doctor steps out. His TARDIS automatically returns to Gallifrey. Varnax still intends to break his word and destroy the Time Lords' planet, but first he wants the Doctor to reveal the secrets of the Time Warp. The Doctor refuses. Morgana tortures him, but in vain. Finally Varnax uses a mind probe to wrest the information from the Doctor's mind:

Doctor (monotone) *The Time Warp is a highly sophisticated method of Time Travel. Vast objects, even whole armies, can be transported through time and space with the maximum of speed and the minimum of power.* [18]

Varnax (excited) *How is it reached?*

Doctor *Very simply. A small adjustment of the Time Rotor will do it.*

An eager Varnax proceeds to modify his Time Rotor just as the Doctor instructed. Then, as the pitch-black Time Warp opens, he and Morgana watch in horror as Zargon's deadly missile, stored by the Doctor inside the Time Warp, hurtles out of the blackness straight at them.

The Doctor, who had secretly kept a transporter crystal

earlier stolen by Mike from the High Council chamber, dematerialises. Varnax's TARDIS is blown to pieces, while the Doctor reappears safely on Gallifrey.

Having saved Gallifrey, the Doctor is allowed to continue his travels with the blessing of Time Lord 1. They wave at the Time Lords and leave in the TARDIS:

> **Mike** *Doc, I'll be going home soon. Just tell me one thing. Will we ever meet again?*
>
> **Doctor** *Oh yes, Michael. We already have.* [19]

The TARDIS is seen spinning through the Time Vortex, when its Time Rotor breaks again:

> **Doctor** *Cora? I thought you checked the Time Rotor?*
>
> **Cora** *Me? I thought you did it?*
>
> **Mike** *So where are we going?*
>
> **Doctor** *Heaven knows!* [20]
>
> **Pog** *Squeek!*

As end credits roll.

Notes

1 This adventure clearly takes place in the Doctor's future. Unlike future scripts, which will re-establish the origins of the TARDIS as a London police box, this script assumes the viewer's familiarity with the basic tenets of *Doctor Who*. Because, at the time, the BBC intended to continue production of the original television series (and did indeed make the 25th and 26th seasons after this script was written), the Daltenreys producers were precluded from using any of the Doctor's regular villains, e.g. the Master, the Daleks, etc. Since the television series was ongoing at the time, the producers and writer of the movie may also have felt that the concept of the police box exterior would be fresh in the audience's mind.

2 The concept of the 'Time Rotor' not as the console's centrepiece but as a small, portable gadget controlling the entire TARDIS is introduced for the first time here. Interestingly, although most *Doctor Who* fans refer to the

column in the centre of the TARDIS console as the 'Time Rotor', it is never actually called that on screen, the closest being in *Terminus* (6G) when the Doctor calls it the 'Rotor'.

3 Clearly Ezra expected the producers to cast a famous actor in the part.

4 This 'Time Warp' concept is somewhat analogous, in effect if not in description, to the Time Loops used by the Time Lords in *Image of the Fendahl* (4X), *Invasion of Time* (4Z), etc.

5 The renegade Time Lord Varnax, whose villainy is one of the few constants throughout the Daltenreys scripts, is introduced here as a character reminiscent of Morbius from *The Brain of Morbius* (4K). In this version, he too raised an army against the Time Lords, but was merely exiled instead of being executed (as in later versions – see *The Time Lord*). Varnax's crippled cyborg body is another concept that is carried through the succession of stories.

6 This trial of the Doctor is clearly inspired by his previous trial in *The War Games* (ZZ), and the Doctor uses the same defence. However, the fact that the original BBC television series later revealed the existence of a 'Time of Darkness' in Gallifreyan history (cf. *The Five Doctors* (6K)) is also incorporated here, which makes the High Council's charges even more hypocritical. This presents an interesting parallel with *The Trial of a Time Lord* (7A–7C), where the Time Lords were ultimately demonstrated to be just as hypocritical.

7 Most of the scripts reviewed in this book attempt to incorporate a humorous reference to the Doctor's unusual identity.

8 The concept of the Time Lords having their own 'planet of exile' may well be derived from *Shada* (5M). It reappears in a more sophisticated fashion in Johnny Byrne's *The Time Lord*, Version 2 (*The Crystals of Power*).

9 Varnax's 'Dark TARDIS' is described as 'black and menacing', and having huge metal plates riveted to its shell.

10 Renegade Time Lords like Varnax or the Master appear to run out of lives more quickly than others.

11 In Ezra's script Varnax needs to gather three crystals scattered through space and time to transport his troops to Earth and take over our planet. This argument is considerably modified in later versions of the story (see Chapters 2 and 3). It is somewhat similar in concept to the quest for the Key to Time which occupied the Fourth Doctor during the 16th season – an idea finally re-used in *The Jewels of Time* (see Chapter 4). The notion of 'transporter crystals' is not dissimilar to that of the Time Rings used in *Genesis of the Daleks* (4E).

12 The simultaneous appearance of two Doctors from two different moments in time is a clever idea which only appeared in this script. On the face of it, though, it would appear to conflict with the famous Blinovitch Limitation Effect, as mentioned in *Day of the Daleks* (KKK) and *Mawdryn Undead* (6F), by having the same physical person meet (or nearly meet) himself.

13 This rare guest appearance by K-9 (who returned in *The Jewels of Time*) confirms that this story takes place in the future.

14 As hinted in *The Talons of Weng-Chiang* (4S) and confirmed in the New Adventures *All-Consuming Fire* and *Happy Endings*, Sherlock Holmes is not a fictional character in the *Doctor Who* universe.

15 This future, desert-like Earth is reminiscent of the planet Aridius (R). The script does not provide any specific dates as to its location in time, other than that it is very far in the future.

16 Sadly, this welcome guest appearance by the Brigadier was one of the first things to be written out during the revisions. Note the cameo by Basil and Sybil from *Fawlty Towers*. Also note that the Brigadier's wife's name given here is Dorothy, not Doris.

17 The Fourth Doctor similarly rescued the Minyans in *Underworld* (4Y).

18 The Doctor seems to be describing the notion of a Time Corridor (cf. *Resurrection of the Daleks* (6P)), using Br'er Rabbit's 'don't throw me in the briar patch' method to defeat Varnax.

19 This cryptic bit of foreknowledge is not elucidated further,
   providing food for a future plot.
20 This sets up a situation very much like that of the original
   BBC television series, with the characters basically lost in
   space and time.

Review

The Return of Varnax is very faithful to the spirit of the
original BBC television series, and – barring any fine tuning
required to take into account a specific Doctor's personality –
reads just like another episode of the show, especially during
the Fourth Doctor's tenure. Indeed, with its segmented structure it is very reminiscent of a BBC five- or six-parter.

Litten and Dugdale's story provides a comfortable excuse
to send the Doctor careening through space and time to
thwart the evil plans of yet another megalomaniac Time
Lord. With a proper budget, the sequences on Centros, the
future desert Earth and the attack on Stonehenge could have
been most effective. The final climax on Gallifrey, however,
seems a little like a coda after the main battle has been won.

The character of Cora, possibly inspired by Romana, is
very successful and, while hints of romance between her and
Mike are dropped, the script, unlike its successors, never
takes the plunge into adulthood.

2

THE TIME LORD

by

Johnny Byrne

from a story by
Peter Litten & George Dugdale

Background

Although pleased with Mark Ezra's script, Daltenreys soon realised that to secure the multi-million-dollar financing and distribution required they needed a rewrite by someone with a bigger name in the industry.

In early 1988 Daltenreys called in Johnny Byrne, former executive story editor of *Space: 1999* (first season), script consultant on *All Creatures Great and Small*, writer of *Doctor Who* stories *The Keeper of Traken* (5T), *Arc of Infinity* (6E) and *Warriors of the Deep* (6L), and now creator of the successful ITV series *Heartbeat*.

Meanwhile, Daltenreys was working hard at trying to get the production off the ground. Now that they had a script, entitled *Doctor Who – The Time Lord*, they were able to prepare a budget for their intended film.

Because of the state-of-the-art special effects needed and the necessity of hiring at least one major star and/or director, the cost for a science-fiction picture of that kind would have easily ballooned to $30 million, a large sum in the late 1980s. (Over $60 million would not be unusual today.) That much money can only be found in two ways.

The first possibility is that a major Hollywood studio finances the entire budget. However, in return, they will take over the picture, owning all the rights and making all creative decisions. While this can be financially lucrative for the original producers, writers, etc., it can also be creatively frustrating, as often the fruits of their efforts are discarded in favour of a new team hand-picked by the studio.

As anyone who has seen Robert Altman's brilliant Hollywood satire *The Player* knows, studios are offered hundreds of projects every year and realistically cannot produce all of them. With such large sums of money at stake, simply to produce a film (without counting the costs of marketing it, such as prints and advertising, that often double the budget), studios generally prefer to have the movies they choose to finance produced by teams with whom they have already worked. The larger the budget, the more likely it is that the studio will not want to trust strangers. In that respect, from the viewpoint of a major Hollywood studio, the Daltenreys team didn't have the credentials necessary to do the job.

Alternatively, the budget can be raised independently, from non-studio sources. This is achieved through the selling of foreign distribution and ancillary rights to the movie before it is actually made, although it is naturally easier to accomplish this with a low-budget film than an expensive one. In this respect the deal negotiated by Daltenreys with BBC Enterprises proved to be a handicap to the producers, since it did not include all the usual ancillary and merchandising rights. These had been retained by BBC Enterprises, therefore depriving Daltenreys of potential future revenues that could have been pre-sold to help finance the film.

Naturally the person or persons who put up their own money to produce a film want to have a fair guarantee of someday getting it back, hopefully with a tidy return on their investment. For this to happen, the intended movie must secure distribution guarantees, in particular from the largest territory in the world, the United States. Most films make about 40 to 50 per cent of their revenues in the US market and the balance in the rest of the world lumped together. Without a US distribution deal, the possibility of raising a $30 million budget would be virtually nil.

In order to secure such a deal the producers have to convince a US distributor – probably a major Hollywood studio, which would be expected to pay approximately half of the budget for the finished film, plus nearly as much money in prints and advertising – that the film will attract audiences. To try to ensure that possibility the producers would want to attach at least one major film star and/or a prominent film director to their script.

This was the challenge faced by Daltenreys, a daunting one in view of the nature of their deal with BBC Enterprises, the large size of their budget, and the difficulties of convincing American studio executives that the *Doctor Who* science-fiction franchise could generate big business (like *Star Trek* or *Star Wars*) in America. Unless they thought the movie could make over $100 million at the box office, it is likely that the studio executives would merely pass on it.

It is common wisdom among those labouring in the Hollywood vineyard that Hollywood 'gives great meetings'. First, there are few executives who can truly say 'yes' ('greenlight') to a film project, and getting access to them is difficult for outsiders. Second, nobody ever lost their job by saying 'no'. At the same time, saying 'no' to someone can alienate that person, who may be important one day. And if the project gets made elsewhere and becomes a success, one could look like a fool ... Therefore it is often the safest path for an executive who cannot say 'yes' not to say 'no' either, but offer an often genuinely happy and exciting meeting, after which things discussed will not happen and calls won't be returned. People working in the town understand the unspoken message and a pleasant pretence can be maintained.

Bearing these facts in mind, one can easily imagine the Daltenreys team making the rounds in Hollywood, experiencing a series of highs (exciting meetings), followed by a series of lows (no follow-up). Various stars' names, for the Doctor as well as the Main Villain/Companion, were discussed, including Denholm Elliot, Donald Sutherland, Alan Rickman, Caroline Munro, etc.

At each step, another rewrite was requested, and *The Time Lord* script underwent numerous revisions and changes. While some of the main concepts remained the same, e.g. Varnax as the main villain, several of these rewrites were substantially different, taking the story along divergent paths. One low-budget rewrite, for example, was located entirely in the United Kingdom.

For the sake of comprehension and easy reading, we have combined the versions which contained only minor conceptual differences, and narrowed the field to only four separate versions, to which we have given made-up titles for convenience purposes. The synopses presented here are Johnny Byrne's own words, except for some editing to avoid expository material or too many repetitions.

Version 2, *The Crystals of Power*, has been outlined in greater detail to give a sense of style and dialogue. It is based on a full script written in late 1988 and sub-titled '7th Draft'.

We have chosen to focus on it because it seemed the most representative sample of this long, creative process, and because it was also one of the most widely circulated scripts at the time.

VERSION ONE: *Varnax the Creator*

Story (Synopsis by Johnny Byrne)

VARNAX aspired to emulate the gods.[1] He believed creation could be refashioned, made perfect in every way. Time, space, season, environment and the life they supported could co-exist in perfect harmony. To achieve this he designed and built a TARDIS like no other ever built by the Time Lords. In comparison to theirs, its relative dimensions were enormous.[2] His ship incorporated a crucible of infinite size and dimension. When his grand design was complete it would bear not only the name but the power of a CREATOR.

Vast, complex mechanical plants were installed. Raw materials of all kinds were gathered and made ready for the transformation, or fusion, into the perfect physical universe over which he would reign eternally. But to achieve all this, Varnax would need the co-operation of the other Time Lords. More specifically, he would need their agreement to duplicate the two MATRIX CRYSTALS if fusion of the raw materials into his idealised physical universe was to succeed.[3]

But the Time Lords opposed Varnax's scheme. It went against several of their most cherished laws which governed their successful control of Time. It would confer immortality on Varnax, and could threaten the stability of the Matrix itself by creating, in effect, a rival parallel universe.[4]

Long ago Varnax had been the DOCTOR's friend and mentor, a Gallifreyan Leonardo of shining genius. Feeling betrayed by the Time Lords, and particularly by the Doctor, that Varnax was no more. In his place was a vile travesty of the handsome man that once was. The brilliant Varnax was now a suffering, vengeful psychopath intent on revenge, a

33

one-time Prince of Light transformed by adversity into the very embodiment of dark evil.[1]

Varnax decided to duplicate the Matrix Crystals in secret. With the help of MORGANA, the woman the Young Doctor once loved, and NEGLOS, the ex-commander of the Gallifreyan armed forces, a ruthless killer, the exterminating principle made flesh, he succeeded.[5] All being ready, they set out for the temporally-sensitive world of Demos to carry out the last stage of the transformation: using the sun of Demos to effect fusion and thus convert the Creator into a self-contained, perfect physical universe.

Demos lay like a valve on the arteries of time. The universal ley lines cut through its heart, and the once-in-a-million-year alignment was perfect for fusion to take place. The ley lines would provide the conduits through which the raw, focused energy of the sun of Demos would flow and charge up the two crystals. Varnax knew that Demos and its civilisation would be left a dying husk as a result of what he was doing, but that was a price of conscience he was willing to accept for the greater good his brilliant scheme would bring about.

The Doctor discovered the plan and attacked the Creator during the process of fusion.[6] All the predictions made about the effects of the experiment proved correct. Demos was gutted physically and temporally, its sun dying, sucked dry of its vital forces. Fusion also ripped apart the barriers of extra-dimensional time and drew in helpless WINGED BEINGS from another dimension. These were left to roam for ever without any real existence in a time and place wholly alien to them. And Varnax, Morgana and Neglos were left for dead in the smoking ruin of their once-magnificent Creator.

Now, over a thousand years later, Varnax has appeared on the scene again. Kept alive artificially by the medical genius of Morgana, he and his two companions have survived beyond their natural time span by grotesquely artificial means. They have ruthlessly reconstructed the Creator, using only the crudest of available materials and technology.

Now they have to find the two crystals, which Varnax hid in the timestreams, and when both are in place they will seek out the world where the right planetary alignment is next due to take place. This happens to be Earth.

There, once again, Varnax intends to complete what he first attempted over a thousand years ago: to effect fusion and transform his miraculous Creator into the perfect physical universe. Like Lucifer, the Fallen Angel, he will emerge in his gleaming transformed TARDIS, a Creator in name and power. Varnax, with his total mastery of time, will be physically restored to the powerful, handsome Time Lord he once was. Those who have faithfully served him will also have immortality bestowed upon them.[7]

No matter that in the recreation of his perfect universe the one which the Time Lords controlled will fall apart into temporal chaos and literally cease to exist, nor that planet Earth will suffer the same fate as Demos. To Varnax these are things of the past, of no interest: all that matters is that he has been vindicated.

The Doctor chases the lumbering hulk of the once-mighty Creator through the timestreams. Varnax, with an army of savage, mercenary MORDREAD warriors in support, must be prevented from finding the twin Matrix Crystals.

In the quest for the crystals the action ranges through space and time: Raqetz, a medieval wheeler-dealer world teeming with exotic alien life forms; elegant Gallifrey, home planet of the Time Lords; Centros, a world inhabited by ferocious, hallucinating warrior monks; present-day Washington, DC; and finally the ruined world of Demos, where the epic final confrontation is played out.[8]

Alongside the Doctor are three very special people: GONJII, a life-long friend and an ex-soldier of fortune, who originates from the ruined world of Demos and has sworn to destroy Varnax for the holocaust inflicted upon his world and people; CORA, a beautiful young Gallifreyan communications expert, a gutsy, wide-eyed innocent abroad; and finally SPANISH, a street-wise young American kid who gets caught up in the titanic struggle between the Doctor and Varnax.[9]

When Varnax almost achieves fusion at the end, all that he has imagined brilliantly comes to pass. We see landscapes of utterly enchanting beauty materialise just before the Creator self-destructs, releasing the Winged Beings from their captivity and taking with them the near-formless Varnax and Morgana, who will now experience the fate they had earlier inflicted on these creatures.

Notes

1 While retaining Litten and Dugdale's basic story structure, Byrne created additional background for Varnax, turning him into a Gallifreyan Leonardo, and making his motivation even more grandiose. The villain is no longer merely trying to invade Earth or annihilate Gallifrey, but seeks no less than the creation of an entirely new universe which will replace – and destroy – ours. We also learn new information about the Doctor's past, and more specifically his younger years on Gallifrey.

2 Varnax's 'Dark TARDIS' also gains in importance, becoming a miniature world (first a beautiful paradise, then a wretched patched-up husk), dubbed the 'Creator'.

3 The 'transporter crystals' have become the Matrix Crystals, and their numbers have been reduced to two, making the 'quest' aspect of the plot more manageable.

4 In one version an anti-matter universe.

5 The other characters also gained in depth. Morgana is now the Young Doctor's former flame. They were both students of Varnax, but she chose Varnax over the Doctor. This is the first time that the concept of a romance for the Doctor, even one that clearly took place a long time before, is introduced in *Doctor Who* (other than the rather chaste hints offered in *The Aztecs* (F)). Neglos is basically as he was in Mark Ezra's *The Return of Varnax*, but with added background.

6 In one version under orders from the Time Lords.

7 This is the first mention of the search for immortality as an alternative motivation for Varnax.

8 First appearances of Demos and Raqetz, as two separate worlds. Centros has now become a world of warrior monks, although the action taking place there is virtually similar to the Ancient Peru/Inca scenes from Mark Ezra's *The Return*

of Varnax. In one version, before the story climax, the heroes trek through a devastated Demos and are captured by the Winged Beings.

9 Cora is still present. Mike Bradley has become 'Spanish', a street-wise Latino kid the Doctor meets in the Smithsonian, in Washington. Gonjii is introduced as a Samurai-like Demosian warrior. Pog has completely disappeared from this version (but will return).

VERSION TWO: *The Crystals of Power*

Story

We open on the planet Demos, home of an ancient advanced civilisation. We first hear then see the consequences of a tremendous earthquake. We then discover its source: the CREATOR, a huge timeship of the type used by the Time Lords of Gallifrey.[1] It is drawing its power from the planet's very core, causing it to shake and fissure.

Inside the Creator, NEGLOS, a ruthless, powerful man dressed in a military uniform, sits at the controls, monitoring a shimmering, web-like screen, the Matrix Terminal. Next to him are VARNAX, a Gallifreyan Time Lord, cool, composed and aristocratic-looking, and ZILLA, a very beautiful woman. A hideous, artificial plasmoid creature, the WEAZLL, sits in Varnax's lap. Fierce, futuristic mercenary soldiers, dubbed the MORDREAD, protect the area. The atmosphere grows more tense as the experiment progresses.[2]

Meanwhile, in another section of the Creator, we hear the characteristic wheezing sound of a TARDIS materialising. A pyramid-shaped ship appears, and the DOCTOR – 'a fit, keen-eyed man with a deceptively subtle mind' – steps out, or rather walks through one of its seemingly-solid sides.[3]

Back in the control room Varnax orders Neglos to charge the fusion crystals, but the latter is worried about the stress. Still, he does as the Time Lord requested. In a crucible-like control model we see two glowing crystals, one dark, the other white, both set in a DNA-like helix contraption.[4]

The Doctor bursts into the scene, hailing Varnax, who immediately recognises him. He has come to 'plead' – the word greatly amuses Varnax – with the renegade Time Lord to stop the experiment. The Doctor claims that he is not concerned with breaking Time Lord laws, but with Demos's very survival, threatened by the forces to be released.

Varnax *You were always my most brilliant student. You were once even my . . .* (**a look at Zilla**) *friend. But you chose your path as I chose mine. And look at what I achieved, Doctor . . .* (**points to the crystals**) *The crystals are charging . . . Fusion is imminent. Mastery over the forces of life and death in the making . . . And you ask, no, plead with me to stop now?*[5]

Doctor *No one denies your genius, Varnax. But as a former pupil, one-time friend and fellow Time Lord, I beg you to reconsider . . .*

Varnax (**suddenly savage**) *Reconsider in the name of the Time Lords! They who ordered the destruction of my fusion crystals – my greatest achievement! You fools! You all chose to remain Time Lords when I could have made you Lords of Creation!*

Doctor *The power you offer takes us into the unknown, Varnax. Give us – give yourself time and you will succeed! But now – the price is too high.*

Having failed to cause Varnax to reconsider his bold decision, the Doctor tries to appeal to Neglos, Zilla and even the Mordread.

Doctor *Listen to me! All of you! This experiment is forbidden by the High Council of the Time Lords! What Varnax does here betrays his oath as a Time Lord – forfeits his right to command this TARDIS. Obey him, and you too become outlaw! You Mordread mercenaries . . . Side with Varnax and you declare war on Gallifrey. The Gallifreyan Time Battalions will hunt you down to extinction!*[6]

> (to Zilla)
>
> *Varnax I understand – a mind corrupted by an insane
> lust for power. But you, Zilla ... You not only betray
> your people, you betray yourself!*
>
> **Zilla (stung)** *You say that because I chose Varnax and
> not you!*

But the Doctor's appeals are in vain. As a last resort, the
Time Lord pulls out a gun and attempts to fire at the crystals.
However, Varnax's Weazll leaps, morphs into a humanoid
shape and savagely attacks the Doctor, preventing him from
destroying the crystals. Just as the Mordread leap into the
fray, various alarms start ringing. The power released by the
Creator is out of control.

Outside, the planetary surface explodes and begins to
disintegrate. Inside the massive ship chaos reigns. The Doctor attempts to pull the two crystals out of the crucible, but
Varnax activates a safety switch and they vanish, dispersed
through the timestream. However, the renegade Time Lord is
suddenly caught in a violent explosion which chars and
disfigures his once patrician-looking body. He howls in rage
and despair before being engulfed in further destruction.

As the Creator is literally being torn apart, the Doctor
hastily retreats to his TARDIS and dematerialises. Behind it,
Demos lies in flames.

We cut to the Palace of the Time Lords on Gallifrey. A title
card identifies the year as '9889999E78.03 A.R.'. The Doctor,
dressed in full Time Lord regalia, including a small, torch-like
object (a 'Sonix')[7] on his belt, is being publicly tried by
the LORD PRESIDENT and four other high-ranking TIME
LORDS. A female CASTELLAN is acting as prosecutor. This
is all taking place under the shimmering web of the Master
Matrix.

A great number of people have come to watch the trial.
Some are shouting curses at the Doctor. Others, like GON-
JII IBORITRIX, a professional soldier from Demos, and
LYRIA, a nine-year-old girl, observe in quiet, silent hurt.[8]

The Doctor naturally claims that the Time Lords did nothing
to stop Varnax, and are therefore ultimately responsible for

the destruction of Demos. Furthermore, he believes that Varnax somehow escaped the inferno, and is still out there, planning more havoc. The Castellan, on the other hand, is satisfied that Varnax perished in the conflagration, and accuses the Doctor of having broken their code of non-interference.

At that moment Gonjii stands up and calls the entire procedure a 'sham', a show trial meant to absolve Gallifrey of blame. The Doctor is not a criminal, he proclaims; he was a friend of Demos, and tried to save his planet. It is Varnax, a Time Lord, who should be judged, and those who failed to stop him in the name of 'non-interference'.

> **Gonjii (passionately)** *I served you people because I believed in what you stood for. A world beyond the need to advance itself at the expense of others . . . You Gallifreyans, a people who genuinely did not interfere – who sought only peace and harmony in the time-streams . . .*

Gonjii then dramatically offers his resignation from the Time Battalions. But this fails to move the Lord President, who passes sentence upon the Doctor. First, he is barred from time travel, and his Sonix – a device through which he can control his TARDIS – is taken away from him. Its distinctive imprint is then removed from the Matrix. Finally, the Doctor is condemned to solitary incarceration on one of the Time Lords' penal satellites until his last regeneration.[9]

Time passes. When we return, Lyria is now a beautiful young cadet at the Time Lord Academy. She is listening to a lecture being given by an elderly Time Lord called MENTOR. He is trying to teach about the dangers of interference by showing them films of a ravaged Demos:

> **Mentor** *Does anyone recall the name of the criminal who caused its destruction?*
> **1st Cadet** *The Master . . . ?*
> **Mentor (smiles tolerantly)** *A name* never *mentioned in polite society, Cadet.*[10]

Mentor naturally identifies the culprit as the Doctor, but Lyria rises in protest and vigorously defends him. While Mentor praises her loyalty to a 'blood relation', he asks her to apologise. She refuses and, as a result, is expelled and confined to her quarters. In her room, she starts reading Davros's treatise on 'Paranoia and Machine Intelligence'[10] when she receives a communication which pleases her greatly.

We cut to the Time Lords' penal colony, a small, mountainous island. The Doctor now wears a beard; he looks unkempt and considerably older. He is being supervised by two robotic Ovoid guardians, which he has nicknamed 'Harold' and 'Frieda'.[11] They are subjecting the Doctor to an array of petty regulations, but it is clear that he has a plan. Inside his quarters he has managed to build a miniature robotic garden with birds, etc. He is obviously working on some kind of secret project.

The Ovoids return to tell him he has a visitor – Cadet Lyria.

Doctor (distracted) *Lyria! Yes. One forgets that some-where back along the family line we are an Uncle.*[8]

In spite of the Ovoids' security measures, the Doctor manages to save the device he was working on from destruction. He then welcomes Lyria, who has come to tell him that, in her endless scans of the timestreams, she has finally come across a clue about Varnax's possible present location. More precisely, she has detected the Weazll's bio-plasmoid life form in London, 1888. The Doctor's TARDIS having been 'mothballed', the only thing they need is a Sonix – and of course this is precisely what the Doctor has been able to recreate patiently from scratch during his long years of incarceration.

The Doctor completes the reassembly of the Sonix, which then enables him to summon his pyramid-shaped TARDIS. As he and Lyria are about to step through its sides the two Ovoids rush in, primed to kill, but the Doctor uses the Sonix to vaporise them. Inside, the TARDIS is covered with a thick layer of dust. Lyria realises that the ship has become her new

41

home because from now on she too is an outlaw from Time Lord justice.

Lyria *We can't ever go back to Gallifrey, can we?*
Doctor *Time will tell.* [12]

The TARDIS rematerialises in Whitechapel, London, 1888,[13] at the time of the 'Jack the Ripper' murders. Jack – in reality the shape-shifting Weazll – is about to strike at another prostitute when she turns out to be the Doctor in disguise. A symbol stamped on the creature's wrist tells the Doctor that his foe gained illegal access to time travel through MOTHER CAJAGE, a notorious galactic wheeler-dealer from the planet Raqetz.

The Doctor uses his Sonix to destroy the Weazll, then returns to the TARDIS, which has assumed the outside appearance of a London police box. However, a power malfunction causes the chameleon circuit to explode and the ship becomes stuck in that shape.

Lyria (pained) *Great. Chameleon circuit's bust again.*
Doctor *Oh, I think it has a certain naïve charm. We'll live with it . . .* [14]

As the TARDIS dematerialises and is travelling through the vortex, Lyria helps the Doctor clear his face from the disguise he used in London and pick a new set of clothes.

Lyria *Have you any idea how ridiculous you look in make-up?*
Doctor *Thanks. Ever consider a course in confidence building?*
Lyria *When I first saw you, for a horrible moment I thought you'd regenerated as a female!*
Doctor *Could we discuss my nightmares another time?* [15]

They arrange to rendezvous with Gonjii on Raqetz, a lawless, medieval-like slum of a city, located in the Regulus star system. A title card informs us that the local time is 'Year 98349 K.X.'.[16]

While exploring the bizarre, colourful city the Doctor and Lyria are spotted by Mother Cajage, an obese alien female travelling on a sedan chair carried by eight porters. They eventually find their way to the Palace of Profit, an ill-famed bar and casino. The Doctor manages to talk his way out of a bar fight, and eventually locates Gonjii at a gambling table. The Time Lord helps his alien friend out of a tight spot, then the three of them walk outside.

They visit Mother Cajage's auction ring, which is selling illegal Time Rotors. The Doctor and his two companions follow the latest buyer, who turns out to be Neglos, now a cyborg. He takes the Time Rotor to Varnax's ship, the Creator, which now looks like an old, worn-down vessel. Aboard are Varnax, Zilla and the Mordread, all disfigured versions of their former selves. (Zilla's beauty is still intact, but she is now connected to the ship through a network of tubes attached to her back.)

The Doctor attempts to stop Neglos. The cyborg and Gonjii fight, but the villain still manages to escape and take the Time Rotor with him into the Creator. The Doctor is furious because he knows that with a Time Rotor Varnax can again gather his fusion crystals, and eventually cause another planet to suffer the same fate as Demos. Gonjii swears to avenge his world.

Aboard the Creator Varnax has now 'bonded' with the Time Rotor.[17] He too is now aware of the Doctor's presence. He decides to hurry and go after the white crystal first. But the Doctor is able to trace the villain's movements from his TARDIS. Their intended destination appears to be Washington, DC, in the later part of the twentieth century.

Aware that he is being followed through the Vortex, Varnax orders Neglos to his battle pack. This is a suit of armour packed with all sorts of offensive devices which grafts over Neglos's cyborg body.

The TARDIS rematerialises outside the Smithsonian. The Doctor and his two companions step out. The Doctor uses his Sonix to track down the white crystal, which he locates inside an exhibit case in the mineralogy area. But before they can leave they are attacked by Neglos and his Mordread. As the Doctor is about to surrender the crystal Neglos is thrown off-balance by the irruption of SCOTT MORGAN, a twenty-

43

year-old, street-wise kid from the Bronx who made it to college and who was trying to escape from a trio of street punks with whom he had had an argument.[18]

The Doctor, Gonjii, Lyria and Scott manage to leave the museum using its emergency stairs, but Varnax's ship is waiting outside, firing energy bolts at them as they run across the parking lot towards the TARDIS. They make it inside just in the nick of time, but the TARDIS is hit by a missile as it dematerialises. They spin out of control into the Vortex.

Inside the TARDIS's sick bay the Doctor makes the introductions, then asks Scott for the crystal which he picked up during the battle. Unfortunately the kid dropped it in the parking lot, where it is recovered by Neglos.

Lyria explains the TARDIS to Scott, developing a certain attraction for the brash young man.[19] Later Scott thanks Gonjii for saving his life during the parking lot attack.

Inside the Creator, having recovered the white crystal, Varnax is now intent on finding its dark 'twin'.

> **Varnax** *The white crystal. The bright power at the heart of immortality. Once we've found its dark twin . . . (. . .)* (**enraptured whisper**) *Sweet force of life eternal. Help me accomplish all I have laboured to achieve. Grant me power to exercise your sublime, undying will!*[5]

Meanwhile, the TARDIS rematerialises aboard CHRISTOPHER COLUMBUS's *Santa Maria* on its way to the New World in 1492.[20] Columbus mistakes Lyria for the Madonna, and the time travellers leave, having taken the space-time measurements they needed to repair the TARDIS.

They then track Varnax's ship to planet Kernos, Epoch 77,[21] where the dark crystal is located. They step out into an insect-infested jungle. The Kerne are cannibal warriors who worship a solar-activated beacon held in the hands of their idol, the 'Singing God'. They are ruled by PIXOLOTE, a fierce-looking warlord.

The Kerne capture the Doctor and his companions and are about to cook them in a giant pot of boiling soup when the Doctor uses his Sonix to activate the beacon remotely (a 'Varlien radioprobe'). This gives pause to the Kerne. The

Doctor then succeeds in passing some barbaric test; they would emerge as 'demon-free' brothers if not for the unfortunate activation of an automatic device reminding Lyria that the return of her library book is overdue. The holovid of the librarian throws the Kerne into a fit, and the time travellers are back where they started. Under a beam of sunlight the radioprobe starts playing the music of Fats Waller. The slow broil of the demons has started.

Later Neglos and the Mordread appear, intent on stealing the dark crystal, which is part of the radioprobe attached to the statue of the 'Singing God'. Neglos would gleefully abandon the Doctor to his fate, but by trying to remove the probe he causes the giant idol to collapse, inadvertently freeing the Doctor and his companions.

A fierce battle ensues, at the end of which the Kerne burst into the temple. Neglos escapes with the probe. The Doctor uses the Sonix to summon the TARDIS, and he and his companions manage to get back to its safety before the blood-crazed Kerne can hack them to pieces.

Inside the Creator, Varnax discovers that the Doctor tricked Neglos. During the battle, he managed to steal the dark crystal from the probe. A raving mad Varnax punishes Neglos for his failure, then instructs him to find the Doctor or else.

Meanwhile, inside the TARDIS, Lyria and Scott float peacefully in the Gravity Filter, a huge glass dome charged with electrostatic energy. By placing Scott's hand over her heart, Lyria discovers that they are 'dynamically compatible', a discovery which she does not hesitate to share with the Doctor.

> **Lyria (dreamily)** *And guess what? We're ... super dynamically compatible!*
> **Doctor (intrigued)** *Really? But you're ... And he's ...* **(stronger)** *Now listen, Lyria! Think very carefully ... If this ... Have you any idea of the chaos ...*

The holovid dies; the Doctor is about to switch it back on when Gonjii gently but firmly restrains him.

Doctor (grinning) . . . *Super compatible?*

Gonjii (smiling) *Bet that throws a curve at the gene banks on Gallifrey!* [19]

In the vortex, Varnax's Creator has caught up with the Doctor's TARDIS and achieved the same 'time velocity'. The villain attempts a 'vortex jump' – trying to occupy the same location in space-time. [22] Because each Time Lord is 'bonded' to their respective Time Rotors, this is potentially deadly, but Varnax ignores the danger.

Varnax (fanatical) *I have sworn to seek the supreme prize . . . Prime state physical regeneration . . . and with it – mastery of life and death!* [5]

The vortex jump takes place. Somehow, the Doctor is thrown into the Vortex. He ages rapidly. His very identity is being dissolved in the Vortex.

The Doctor shrieks in mindless terror. And from his disintegrating mind a name is dredged up, a name that personifies the genetic, biological and spiritual elements that collectively constitute the being known as The Doctor.

Doctor (primal scream) . . . *THEEEOOOOO!!!* [23]

The form of the Young Doctor (THEO) helps the Doctor literally pull himself together, and he is instantly transported back into the TARDIS, except that his ship is now inside the Creator.

Neglos and the Mordread invade the TARDIS and take the Doctor and his three companions prisoner. The villains seize not only the dark crystal, but the Doctor's Sonix as well. The Doctor is taken to a stateroom and is strapped to a chair. Gonjii, Lyria and Scott are thrown into a cell.

In the stateroom, Zilla taunts the Doctor:

Zilla *There was a time before Varnax when I loved you above all. You had greatness in you, Doctor. Brilliance and courage that dared dream the impossible . . . What happened to that man . . . those great dreams?* [2]

Doctor *They're still around – the ones that matter. The rest, the ones you achieve at the expense of others, I traded off in a moment of humanity.*

The Doctor tries to show her what she has become by following Varnax blindly, but cannot get through to her. Then Varnax enters and tells the Doctor he is going to get his revenge by setting up his new experiment on the world the Doctor 'favours above all others' – Earth. [24] Varnax cackles insanely and leaves.

Meanwhile, using a key Scott managed to steal from Neglos, Gonjii, Lyria and the young Earthman escape from their cell. After dispatching several Mordread they burst into the stateroom. Gonjii is ready to kill Zilla, but the Doctor orders him not to. The Time Lord tries to get her to tell them where and when Varnax plans to recreate his mad experiment, but she manages to escape.

The Doctor and Lyria rush to the Creator's bridge to steal the data from its computers, while Gonjii and Scott remain behind to keep the Mordread at bay. Neglos bursts onto the bridge. The Doctor and Neglos fight while Lyria continues the computer search. The Doctor eventually tricks the cyborg into crashing into an electric console. He reclaims his Sonix, summons the TARDIS, then he, Lyria, Gonjii and Scott leave in the time capsule. They have found out the time and place – twentieth-century United States again – but not the exact location. [25] However, the TARDIS experiences another malfunction, this time due to its 'variant catalyser'.

Varnax's Creator ship rematerialises above a nuclear waste storage silo. Neglos and the Mordread take over the security bunker controlling the site.

Having managed to fix the TARDIS, or so he thinks, the Doctor rematerialises in New York, but the year is 1626. The Doctor helps the Dutch settlers conclude their famous land deal for Manhattan (then New Amsterdam) with the chief of the Canarsee Indians. [26] Then it's a quick hop to modern Manhattan.

Meanwhile, Varnax has begun to set up his monstrous experiment. A giant crucible containing Varnax and Zilla descends from the Creator into the silo shaft. Glittering gallium ore rods are lowered through the radioactive waste, triggering a nuclear fusion reaction. If it is not stopped Earth, like Demos, will be destroyed.

In New York the Doctor telephones the PRESIDENT of the United States and obtains the information he needs. The TARDIS then vanishes and rematerialises next to the nuclear waste storage silo. The Doctor and his companions immediately become aware that Varnax has preceded them, and that a countdown to destruction has begun.

They infiltrate the bunker, either avoiding or dispatching various Mordread, before reaching the silo shaft. While Gonjii and Scott once again remain on guard, fighting Neglos and the Mordread to gain time for the Doctor, Lyria uses a gantry to carefully lower the Time Lord down to the crucible. The Doctor then manages to gain entrance into it while his friends continue their desperate battle above.

The inside of the crucible is like a forced perspective miniature Eden-like garden. The hideous, shrivelled bodies of Varnax and Zilla are encased in glass coffins, bathed in the pulsing light of the two fusion crystals. The process is restoring their bodies to their once beautiful forms and making them eternal. The Doctor starts interfering with the formidable regenerative energies being spent, and suddenly is forcibly transformed into Theo, his younger self.

Meanwhile, in the silo above, it's Gonjii against Neglos, while Lyria and Scott deal with the remaining Mordread. Gonjii is winning his fight when he sees Scott losing his. The Demosian warrior turns away from his opponent in order to save Scott's life. But by so doing, he enables Neglos to run him through with his blade. An enraged Scott comes to Gonjii's rescue and shoots Neglos, almost sending him falling to his death in the radioactive shaft. But the fatal blow is delivered by a mortally wounded Gonjii avenging his homeworld.

In the regeneration crucible, the Young Doctor faces a regenerated Varnax and Zilla. Varnax offers to share their destiny with him, but the Young Doctor turns him down, knowing full well that they are only minutes away from causing Earth's annihilation. He begs Varnax to abort the fusion process. Varnax cannot believe that the Doctor would refuse instantaneous regeneration and eternal life to save the life of one primitive planet. Finally the Young Doctor has no choice but to shoot at the twin crystals, causing the white crystal to shatter.

In the ensuing energy vortex the Young Doctor reverts to his natural form, while Zilla disintegrates. Varnax's body remains restored, but not in its handsome form. He now looks 'lumpish'. 'His flesh appears to be crawling, shifting about in the spookiest way imaginable.' The dark crystal continues to bathe them in ominous-looking rays.

> **Varnax (anguished)** *Look at me! You have made me one with the dark crystal! Its power has corrupted my immortal being!*

While above, Scott and Lyria attend the dying Gonjii, the fusion reaction continues, still threatening Earth. Inside the crucible the Doctor outsmarts Varnax and succeeds in restoring the fail-safe systems which the villain had previously disconnected. However, Varnax now turns into 'Dark Varnax'.

His bones stretch and twist. Muscles ripple as they swell with size and strength. His face, agonised by the process, deforms almost beyond recognition. Thick hairs sprout through the shifting skin and wings form on his back. He rises up, wings unfurl and he roars in bestial rage. It's recognisably Varnax, but a Dark Varnax, a terrifying being from the realms of vengeful darkness.[27]

While the computers are broadcasting warnings to evacuate the facility, the Doctor runs for his life, chased by this new abomination. Automatic entombment procedures are starting, in order to prevent a meltdown. Thanks to last-minute help from Scott, the Doctor manages to escape Varnax barely in the nick of time. As they rise out of the shaft they see the immortal villain being entombed alive behind massive steel shields in a radioactive hell of his own making.

Outside, with the crucible torn from its hulking mass, Varnax's Creator ship explodes. The Doctor, Scott and Lyria look down at the now sealed silo. The Time Lord then turns to the dying Gonjii, pleased that Demos has been avenged. The Doctor wants to take Gonjii back to Gallifrey for treatment, but the old warrior refuses. He exhorts Lyria to stay true to her course, and passes his sword to Scott. He then offers his hand to the Doctor and dies.

The three of them walk back to the TARDIS, looking with fresh eyes at the planet they have just saved. While the Doctor asks Scott if he wants to join him and Lyria in their travels, the young woman enters the TARDIS then comes out again to tell the Time Lord about a 'Delta Alarm'. At first reluctant, Scott finally makes up his mind and joins them in the TARDIS, which powers up and dematerialises.

Notes

1 While, dramatically, the opening scenes are somewhat similar to those of Mark Ezra's *The Return of Varnax*, we now open directly on Demos (which is central to the plot). The Creator remains Varnax's TARDIS-cum-worldship.

2 Neglos is still here, but Morgana has now been renamed Zilla, possibly to avoid confusion with the Arthurian 'Morgana', who, coincidentally, appeared in *Battlefield* (7N). Her background remains the same as in Version 1, in particular her previous romantic entanglement with the Young Doctor. The Weazll is an interesting addition to the villain's team. The soldiers are no longer Centrosian or Demosian but 'Mordread'.

3 In this version the TARDIS has not yet acquired its London police box shape. The script goes on to show how it does, in an attempt to co-opt spectators unfamiliar with *Doctor Who*. While justified, this nevertheless creates a potential continuity conflict in terms of the basic assumption that this is a future Doctor story. It is worth noting that the pyramid shape was independently assumed by various writers (cf. Robert DeLaurentis's *The Time of My Life*) to be the TARDIS's natural shape. Perhaps they were all separately inspired by the Doctor's demonstration in *Logopolis* (5V), where he shows how the

TARDIS would be reconfigured into a pyramid if its chameleon circuit were working properly.

4 Byrne is still using two crystals as the focus of his plot, but they are now fusion crystals, a white crystal and a dark crystal, no longer connected to the Gallifreyan Matrix.

5 More importantly, in this version Varnax's motivations have changed again: he is now searching for true immortality, like Borusa in *The Five Doctors* (6K). It is implied that the Time Lords are not opposed to his ultimate goal, just his reckless methods. And it is their opposition that has sent Varnax over the edge. However, his past relationship with the Young Doctor and Zilla remains the same.

6 The concept of Gallifreyan military forces, staffed by non-Gallifreyans and used by the Time Lords to maintain order or protect their monopoly, is developed here. It contributes to making the Time Lords' later condemnation of the Doctor for interference more hypocritical.

7 The concept of the 'Sonix' appears to replace (temporarily) that of the Time Rotor, as defined in Mark Ezra's *The Return of Varnax*.

8 Gonjii is now both a Demosian and a warrior from the Gallifreyan Time Battalions. But the greater change is the replacement of Cora by Lyria who is actually related to the Doctor – she is said to be his niece.

9 Byrne kept the concept of the Doctor being tried and unjustly condemned for interference, but had him actually exiled to a Gallifreyan penal colony, like Varnax himself in *The Return of Varnax*.

10 There are a few, cleverly inserted references to the original BBC television series. When this script was written (late 1988), *Doctor Who* was still on the air.

11 The description of the Gallifreyan penal colony is ingenious and owes nothing to *Shada* (5M), although its two robotic guards are somewhat reminiscent of the Mogara from *The Stones of Blood* (5C). The concept of ten years elapsing between the sentence and the Doctor's return to action, giving time for the character of Lyria to age accordingly, is also effective.

12 An interesting parallel with the First Doctor's and Susan's situation.

13 Byrne kept the trip to Victorian London, but instead of Sherlock Holmes and the Tower of London he plugs into the Jack the Ripper murders.

14 This is also used to justify the TARDIS assuming the appearance of a police box (see note 3 above).

15 An interesting comment on the ever-popular fan debate of the Doctor regenerating into a woman. Byrne defuses what could have been an unintentionally funny scene with true humour.

16 In this version Raqetz and Demos are definitely two different worlds.

17 This appears somewhat similar to the Rassilon Imprimature concept featured in *The Two Doctors* (6W).

18 'Spanish' has now become Scott Morgan, but he remains a street-wise American youth and the Doctor still meets him at the Smithsonian. In a later version Scott acquired Irish, i.e. Celtic, origins.

19 The romance between Lyria and Scott is emphasised, and for the first time in *Doctor Who* history develops the theme of genetic compatibility between Gallifreyans and humans.

20 The Christopher Columbus scene from *The Return of Varnax* survived the various rewrites to this point.

21 While the scene remains dramatically similar to Ezra's Ancient Peru/Inca sequence (except for the 'Singing God'), Centros has now become Kernos.

22 This is a combination of a Time Ram and what the Master attempted in *Logopolis* (5V).

23 One is tempted to speculate whether the name of 'Theo' applied here to the Young Doctor is, in any way, related to his Time Lord Academy nickname of 'Theta Sigma'.

24 The existence of a 'special relationship' between the Doctor and Earth – which is at the core of *Fathers and Brothers* and *Enemy Within* – is first hinted at here.

25 The story climax now takes place on Earth rather than on Demos. The trek across Demos and the encounter with the Winged Beings have been eliminated.

26 This side trip in time proved influential in the development of the next version.

27 Most of the 'beats' used for this ending – entering the crucible, the Regeneration Chamber, 'Dark Varnax', etc. – remain identical throughout most of *The Time Lord*'s versions.

VERSION THREE:
The Immortality Bullet

Story (Synopsis by Johnny Byrne)

It began because they were friends. VARNAX and the DOCTOR were younger then, gifted, radical-minded Time Lords who dared dream the impossible.

One dream in particular obsessed Varnax: immortality, control over the forces of life and death, a dream common to people in all times and places, and forever elusive, until, almost by accident, the Doctor and Varnax created the one-off, impossible to duplicate IMMORTALITY BULLET.[1] Now living matter could be altered. Prime-state physical immortality was within their grasp. But their people, the Time Lords of Gallifrey, were not ready for such an evolutionary quantum leap.

The High Council of the Time Lords believed that immortality would destroy the existing order and banned the project. The unique Immortality Bullet, too precious to destroy, too dangerous to leave to the control of any one individual, was consigned indefinitely to the Time Vaults.

The Doctor agreed with their decision. He'd seen the corrupting effect that the discovery had had on Varnax. He knew Varnax would stop at nothing to realise his dream, and the terrible price others would have to pay should he even attempt to do so.

The Doctor's friendship with Varnax died. ZILLA, the woman he loved, rejected him in favour of Varnax. The Doctor became a virtual exile, a maverick Time Lord who adventured in time and space in his TARDIS.[2]

Time passes. The Doctor's talent for friendship has stayed the course. So have his feelings for Zilla. But they are long buried in a private place inside the Doctor's twin Gallifreyan hearts. Buried but not forgotten, and still responsive when word comes from Gallifrey that Zilla has returned and wants to see him again . . .

The Doctor returns to a joyous welcome from LYRIA.[3] Lyria is his blood relative. Lyria is eleven years old, an impetuous, precocious and very brainy Gallifreyan whiz-kid. She knows about the Doctor's long-ago love affair with Zilla and is very curious as to why, after all this time, Zilla should want to see the Doctor again – and secretly!

GONJII is another reason why the Doctor is glad to be home. Gonjii is from the planet Demos. He's a tough fighting man who commands the Gallifreyan Time Rangers – the elite outfit which polices the timestreams for the Time Lords.[3] He and the Doctor are long-time friends, and the pleasure they get from their abrasive, enduring friendship is mutual.

The Doctor meets Zilla as arranged. She is as beautiful as ever, and as treacherous. The Doctor has been set up. Zilla was the lure to deliver the Doctor into the hands of Varnax and his companions, the psychopathic henchman, NEGLOS, and the WEAZLL, a bio-plasmoid, the result of one of Varnax's genetic experiments. Normally the Weazll looks like a small, hideous-faced otter. But the Weazll is not normal – it can change into humanoid form and it has an unquench-able urge to kill people.

And the Weazll has Lyria. A word from Varnax and it will tear her to pieces, unless the Doctor helps Varnax to break into the sacrosanct Time Vaults.[4] Varnax wants the Immor-tality Bullet, and he wants it right now. They penetrate the defensive screen around the Time Vaults, severely harassed by automatic killing devices. But they succeed and, with essential help from the Doctor, Varnax recovers the bullet.

Pursued by Gonjii and his Rangers, Varnax makes a rendez-vous with the PHOENIX, the vast timeship he's designed and built for his own special needs.[1] Here the Doctor makes his play, but Varnax anticipates his move and the Doctor is rendered unconscious. The Phoenix enters the Time Vortex and vanishes without trace.

The Doctor revives and finds himself imprisoned among Varnax's deranged laboratory creatures. His live-and-let-live philosophy is giving way to one of kill-or-be-killed when Zilla extricates him. The Doctor is taken to the crucible, a gigantic detachable laboratory. He discovers they're on Demos, Gonjii's home planet, and Varnax is already attempting to charge up the Immortality Bullet. Impossible, the Doctor thinks. He knows that only on Gallifrey, with its advanced technology, can Varnax generate the stupendous power needed. But Varnax has devised ways and means.

The monitor shows the Phoenix in a remote area of the planet. From its underbelly a massively thick, hollow bore, incandescent with heat, is sunk into a nuclear waste pit buried deep below – the heritage of Demos's long-abandoned nuclear age. Varnax has injected the lethal nuclear waste with gallium, a highly unstable chemical agent, and it is working, or so he believes. But both know that, even if it does work, it will set up an uncontrollable chain reaction that will reduce the populated world of Demos to rubble.

Which is exactly what happens, and the Phoenix is caught up in the destructive mayhem. Flames sheet through the interior of the crucible and almost consume Varnax. It's every man for himself now. The Doctor wants the Immortality Bullet back. So does the Weazll, who gets it first. As they struggle, the onboard Time Rotor, which is powering up, is smashed by flaming debris.

This unleashes forces that pitch the Doctor and the Weazll into the Time Vortex.[5] Both are hurtled along at colossal velocity. Along the way, they are plucked off into different timestreams. As the Doctor travels he's rapidly ageing, and as his physical existence disintegrates, his identity siphons off into the elemental maelstrom of time . . .

Meanwhile, on Gallifrey, Gonjii and Lyria are in an audience of senior Time Lords. They're watching a recording of the shattered world of Demos. Gonjii weeps inward tears at the sight of the once-beautiful capital city of Raqetz. It's a tumbledown, polluted ruin. Law and order have completely broken down and already the galactic carpet-baggers, who thrive on anarchy, are swarming in to make a fast buck.

The Time Lords blame Varnax and the Doctor. They think both of them died on Demos. Lyria and Gonjii try to defend the Doctor, but no one wants to listen. The High Council pronounce the Doctor and Varnax guilty of genocide, posthumously strip them of their honours and obliterate all memory of their existence from the historical records.

Bitterly disillusioned, Gonjii resigns his commission and returns to live among his own people. Lyria, illogically convinced that the Doctor somehow survived, lives in hope of his return.

We cut to Buckhorn, Idaho, present day. It's a late Saturday evening in this town located on what was once Indian hunting land. In earlier times the northwestern Indian tribes ranged this wild, stunningly beautiful territory. That was then. Now a deep-site nuclear burial depository is located outside town. Logging and mining have been in progress for years and Buckhorn wallows in environmental sleaze. But Buckhorn has another presence, an almost invisible underclass, the descendants of the tribes whose homeland it once was. One of them is the nineteen-year-old BILLY DREAMER.[6]

Billy left his reservation home to work in Buckhorn. He's a reserved, capable, good-looking kid who rents a shack outside town. Billy has few friends. He's too proud to knuckle under, too reserved to assert himself. But his aspirations, if they exist, are confused and lacking in direction and guidance – but all that is about to change.

On this evening Buckhorn is crowded, beginning to warm up to its inevitable violent Saturday-night peak, and Billy is in trouble. TIMMONS, the racist Security Chief from the nuclear depository, and his SIDEKICK have blocked Billy's beat-up old jeep and they won't move their car. Billy appears to accept defeat. But as they head off they hear a series of tremendous crashes. Billy is ramming their car out of his way. Billy has a temper that burns on a slow fuse. Right now, it's red hot.

They grab Billy, and Timmons begins to enjoy beating him

up. But something unexpected happens. The darkened sky flashes very eerily. There is a tremendous, almost supernatural flash and the figure of a weirdly dressed man appears, literally out of nowhere, which spooks the security guys who take off. Billy is about to do the same, but he hears a whispered plea for help. He goes to the sprawled figure and what he sees now almost makes him doubt his sanity. It's the face of a man shrivelled with extreme old age. But something is happening. The face is unshrivelling, age and years rolling swiftly back until the process stops and he sees the Doctor, now physically restored.

The Doctor looks crazed, disorientated after his ordeal in the Time Vortex. He grabs Billy's wrist and again pleads for help, then he passes clean out. Rationality of a kind returns. For the Doctor, it's been a timeless, feverish period. Even now, he's in a severely amnesiac state. But he has help. He's come to depend on Billy, who's befriended him, and with Billy's help – a witness to his fevered ramblings – the Doctor's identity reintegrates and he remembers who he is.

Billy has a problem coming to terms with the Doctor. It's the first time he's met a Time Lord with two hearts. But while the Doctor may be an alien, something about him gets to Billy and a friendship develops.

The Doctor sets out to re-establish contact with Lyria – he needs his TARDIS, and only Lyria can deliver it. But to contact her he needs to build a Time Phase Communicator, easy on Gallifrey, but not in present day Buckhorn. Billy thinks the Doctor has about as much chance of finding what he needs in Buckhorn as paddling a canoe to Alpha Centauri, but the Doctor pushes hard and he does all the things you shouldn't do – not if you're Indian and living in Buckhorn. It's living dangerously, which Billy has learned not to do, but the Doctor gets away with it, even with people like the racist Timmons, who remembers he has unfinished business with Billy. He's about to pulp him, when the Doctor intervenes. He drapes a friendly arm around Timmons' shoulders and gently extols the virtues of peace and harmony. Billy is amazed at the effect it has on Timmons. His eyes bulge, his breathing labours like a man after a sprint up Everest and he collapses after they've gone. Billy doesn't know about Synaptic Block yet. All it takes is the slightest pressure with a finger – if you know where to put it.

The Doctor's interest zeroes in on the only local source of high technology: the nuclear depository. The problem is security, which is intense and round the clock. With the connivance of Billy's old Indian NEIGHBOUR, who has a menial job there, they break in and find what the Doctor needs. This is not without problems though, because Timmons surprises them in the act, and the Doctor needs more than Synaptic Block to cancel out the advantage of Timmons' firepower. He needs superior cunning, of which he has plenty, and they escape, but Timmons has them marked down for retribution. Now that he has the core elements the Doctor rigs a fantastic construction virtually out of scrap, but it works.

On Gallifrey, time has passed. Lyria is now a beautiful twenty-one-year-old and in all kinds of trouble. She's discontented, rebellious, a real pain in the neck to the authorities at the Academy – all stemming from the Gallifreyan belief that the Doctor is a genocidal criminal.

She's in the library storing up her prerecorded reminders about a book she's borrowing when the Doctor's signal finally registers. No one else knows it's the Doctor calling, but she does. She steals the Sonix, the device that controls the Doctor's TARDIS, and makes off to rendezvous with him. Lyria, like the Doctor, has burned her boats on Gallifrey. She arrives in Buckhorn and suffers immediate culture shock – and sexual harassment, but she has her own unique way of dealing with that.

She meets up with the Doctor and Billy. The Doctor now sees a young woman instead of a child and realises the shocking truth that he has lost ten years in the journey through the Time Vortex. Her arrival, however, is timely because Timmons and his security gorillas are closing in, with the full sanction of the law to back them up. But they're stymied when the Doctor, Lyria and Billy, who now has nowhere left to hide in Buckhorn, make off in the TARDIS.[7]

The Doctor has unfinished business with the Weazll, who

has the Immortality Bullet. The Doctor wants it back. Without it Varnax – if he is alive – can never repeat what he did to Demos. With Lyria's help he pinpoints the location of the Weazll's exit from the Time Vortex to London, AD 1888 – a city gripped in terror by Jack the Ripper, but the Doctor knows he's really the Weazll. The Doctor destroys the Weazll when it insanely attacks him, but the plasmoid hasn't got the bullet – he was separated from it in the Time Vortex.

The TARDIS then travels to Raqetz, on ruined Demos, in response to a message from Gonjii. He's discovered that MOTHER CAJAJE has an illegal Time Rotor for sale. The Doctor knows that Varnax's own Time Rotor was destroyed. If he is alive, he'll need a replacement to search time for the Immortality Bullet.

They find Gonjii gambling in the Palace of Profit. He's changed since they last saw him. The ex-Commander of the elite Gallifreyan Time Rangers is now a down-on-his-luck soldier of fortune. Gonjii wins the game, with a little help from the Doctor. Later, at Mother Cajaje's auction, the rotor goes to an unidentified buyer who is revealed to be Neglos, but it's a very different-looking Neglos. He retains some of his classically handsome good looks, but the rest of his reconstructed face and body is pure bio-metallic nightmare. A furious battle ensues, but a scorched lumbering hulk of a ship appears out of the night sky and rescues Neglos. It's Varnax's timeship, the Phoenix. The once scientific marvel is now a patched-up hulk, restored for use by means of the most primitive materials.

Inside we see Zilla. Her beauty seems intact, but it now has a curiously harsh, ageless aspect. Even more disturbing is the nutrient plug socketed into her back. Even the Mordread, Varnax's mercenaries, are now hideous bio-metallic versions of their former selves. As for Varnax, the once handsome, aristocratic Time Lord is a vile travesty of the man he once was. His shrunken body is supported by a variety of pistons, rods, calipers and nutrient clusters, his face a shrivelled nightmare. He's now a tortured, vengeful megalomaniac, consumed with hatred for the Doctor. He needs the Immortality Bullet more than ever. Without it, all of them are

59

doomed to eke out the bio-mechanical nightmare of their present existence.

Inside the TARDIS the Doctor and Lyria are trying to get to the missing Immortality Bullet before Varnax. The Doctor sets course for Kernos, at a period when it was peopled with ferocious warrior monks. Gonjii confirms that they're on the right track. He once led the Time Rangers on a mission to Kernos – the Rangers enforce the Time Lords' strict non-interference code, and a piece of high technology had to be fetched back from Kernos.

Gonjii has made a profound impression on Billy. In the battle with Neglos Gonjii saved his life, and his near miraculous skill with his favoured weapon, a kind of powered sabre, has evoked a response in Billy, an unconscious bonding stemming from his own dormant warrior genes.

And then there's Lyria. Billy is the first Earthman she's known. She's often wondered what the Doctor has found so fascinating about Earth people. It can't be their knowledge which she finds frankly pathetic, though she is impressed by Billy's natural intelligence. But Lyria is even more impressed by Billy's muscular body. Lyria has a hankering to share a Gravity Filter with him – she thinks they might just turn out to be dynamically compatible.

On Kernos the TARDIS travellers are captured by the Kerne and end up in a suspended cage above a giant cooking pot set into the lap of a huge metal idol, the Kerne's Singing God. The Singing God has a revered artifact in his hand. It's a radio, but the Kerne have totemised it as the mouthpiece of their god. The Doctor succeeds in proving to the Kerne that the travellers are not 'demons' when Lyria's prerecorded library reminder pipes out an aggrieved spiel, undoing his efforts.

Suddenly, the walls of the Kerne temple explode inwards. Neglos and his Mordread leap off a battering ram attached to the Phoenix and enter the temple. Varnax has tracked down the location of the Immortality Bullet. A furious battle see-saws about the confines of the temple. The Doctor and Neglos grapple for the Immortality Bullet, which is encased in part of the radio. Neglos wins, or thinks he does. He races off and leaps onto the powered ram attached to the Phoenix, leaving the Doctor and the others to get to the TARDIS before the Kerne finish them off.

Inside the Phoenix, Varnax realises that the Doctor has conned Neglos and explodes with rage. The Doctor's sleight of hand has recovered the bullet. His dilemma now is what to do with it. He decides to return it to the Gallifreyan Time Vaults. Future generations will have to decide its ultimate fate. To make sure that Varnax can't get his hands on it again, he prepares to enter the Time Vortex ahead of the Phoenix. Once he does, the Phoenix can never catch up with them, and they'll lose Varnax for good.

But Gonjii doesn't want the Doctor to enter the Vortex. He wants Varnax to find them. He and Neglos owe him for Demos. Gonjii is so strongly opposed that he pulls a weapon on the Doctor. The stand-off that follows severely tests their friendship, but the Doctor holds his ground. If Varnax got his hands on the Immortality Bullet again, the result could be another Demos – could Gonjii live with that?[8]

Gonjii cools off, but the delay has been fatal. It has given time to Varnax to second guess their intentions and he's ready for them. When the Doctor activates the Time Rotor, the TARDIS ends up not in the Vortex, but trapped, imprisoned deep inside the Phoenix.

Billy manages to pick the crude lock of their cell and they escape. Led by Gonjii, they set out to free the Doctor. Along the way they run into patrolling Mordread and destroy them – Billy and Gonjii are shaping up into a formidable fighting team. They find the Doctor and release him. They then proceed to the bridge. But Neglos and the Mordread are close behind. Gonjii and Billy hold them off while the Doctor and Lyria look for the Bullet. The Doctor sets Lyria to trace the time and location on Earth where Varnax intends to charge the Bullet. The moment she has what she needs, they rush into the TARDIS. As the Doctor powers up, Lyria feeds in the co-ordinates she's filched from the Phoenix. But as the TARDIS is about to disappear into the Time Vortex, a colossal explosion warps its Time

Rotor, sending the ship whirling uncontrollably through time.

Cut to northwestern USA, AD 1800. The TARDIS appears out of the Time Vortex and settles down in a spectacular wilderness area. They don't know where they are. The TARDIS instruments were hopelessly scrambled in the explosion. They need time to repair the equipment, which will also have to be reprogrammed. To do that they will need a precise fix on their present time and location – a task for Lyria and Billy while the Doctor fixes the Rotor.

It isn't long before Billy becomes aware of something very strange about the country that he and Lyria are moving through. He tries to dismiss the feeling. Then he sees Eyrie Rock and he knows he's not going loopy. Eyrie Rock is situated right outside Buckhorn – only this isn't Buckhorn, it's a primitive wilderness. They hear sounds and a band of Indians ride into view. They gallop up and surround Billy and Lyria. They're fierce, magnificent-looking warriors, all armed.[6]

Their LEADER speaks, and Billy understands. It's the language of his own tribe which he'd learned as a child on the reservation. When Billy responds haltingly, the Indians are equally astonished. These free-ranging, fierce warriors are Billy's ancestors.

Meanwhile, the Doctor has fixed the kinks in the Rotor and, after unscrambling the coded data that Lyria took from the Phoenix, he discovers where Varnax intends to charge up the Immortality Bullet – the deep-site, nuclear burial depository outside Buckhorn. Bad news for Earth, but doubly bad news for Billy, whose home patch it is. The news upsets Gonjii. He's grown close to Billy. The kid's courage and natural warrior skills have forged a bond between them. Gonjii blames himself for losing the Immortality Bullet to Varnax. He'd put personal revenge above all other considerations. Now Billy and everyone else on Earth are about to pick up the tab.

The door of the TARDIS suddenly opens and a very flustered, breathless Lyria rushes in. She tells them that some people want to see them outside. Gonjii and the Doctor leave the TARDIS and find it surrounded by a mounted band of barbarically accoutred Indians. One of them rides forward. It's Billy, in full warrior regalia. A little self-consciously, he tells them that they are the guests of his people.

Meanwhile, in present-day Buckhorn, the menacing silence above the nuclear depository is shattered when the Phoenix suddenly appears out of the Time Vortex. Neglos and the Mordread attack and kill everyone they meet, including Timmons and the Indian labourers. Neglos opens the massive overhead steel shutters that seal off the silo pit from the outside world. Deep down at the bottom of the shaft is an emergency radiation shutter – now open – and deeper still is the nuclear waste burial pit itself. Next, Varnax lowers the vast crucible from the belly of the Phoenix. It descends into the silo shaft and finally comes to rest above the waste pit. The gallium rod is inserted and the charging of the Immortality Bullet begins.

Back in 1800, the Doctor, Gonjii, Lyria and Billy are the centre of attention in the Indian village, situated in an idyllic location. These Indians have not yet learned to fear the white man and it shows in their proud, independent and very hospitable ways. The strangers fascinate them, especially Billy whom they know in some strange way is one of their own. One in particular is very much taken with Billy: the Chief's beautiful DAUGHTER, and Lyria is not nearly so impressed by her charms as Billy appears to be. Gonjii lets some of the braves handle his weapons. The powered sabre especially fascinates them. He shows them how to use it, along with some other tricks he's picked up along the way. Their aptitude and warrior skills don't surprise him – he's seen it all before in Billy.

The Doctor, with the help of the MEDICINE MAN, translates the recorded history of the tribe, woven in pictures on cloth, and gets the information he needs: a fix on when and where they are. He realises the TARDIS has come to the right place, only two hundred years too early. Their hospitable pause among the Indians is a memorable and happy event, especially for Billy. Never again will he doubt who he is and where he comes from. The Native Americans provide a chanting escort back to the TARDIS and, after a dignified leave-taking, they set off for their final confrontation with Varnax.

They travel forward in time to present-day Buckhorn. The natural beauty of the place as it once was contrasts glaringly with what it has become, environmentally, two hundred years on. Billy feels the keenest regret for what has been lost. But, as the Doctor points out, what was beautiful once could be beautiful again, if people have a mind to make it so. It fortifies Billy for the trial ahead. He now knows why they've come back to his home town. He remembers Demos and what Varnax had done to it. He's fiercely determined not to let it happen here.

They reach the nuclear depository and see the Phoenix suspended above the open silo shaft. A massive steel cable supports the crucible, which is in the shaft below. A pall of death hangs over the complex. They beat a stealthy path into the area and stumble across the body of Billy's friend, the elderly Indian who had earlier helped the Doctor. It has a transforming effect on Billy. It's the final straw, the catalyst that brings to the fore all his buried resentments and anger. His fierce warrior instincts, which found expression in his relationship with Gonjii, spring to life. He screams out a war cry and runs off, drawing his weapons as he does so. They see Billy dash into the above-ground security bunker, hear the thunder of weapons, and by the time they catch up with him Billy has already destroyed the Mordread on guard there.

By guile and force they battle their way into the heart of the high-tech complex and hole up deep underground in the control bunker. Varnax has rigged the control systems. Gonjii and Billy hold off the outflanked Neglos, leaving the way clear for the Doctor to force his way into the crucible.

Once inside, the Doctor threads warily through the enormous laboratory space. The experimental area is the worst. Here mutant bio-plasmoid horrors lurk in shadowy retraining pens. Some wander freely about – mindless, featureless living things that crawl and slither purposelessly. Then the Doctor finds the Regeneration Chamber. It's an area enclosed by transparent columns, all coursing with superheated liquid. This converges on a central column, into the top of which is set the Immortality Bullet. It's now active, spewing out timed bursts of charged particles, one burst black, the next white. These are calibrated to hit the two figures sitting below – Varnax and Zilla. Both are changed out of all recognition, almost regenerated to the peak of their physical prime.

Gonjii, Billy and Lyria have meanwhile managed to hold off the Mordread. All Gonjii's pent-up hatred for Neglos surfaces. He soon has him reeling, fated to fall to his doom. But Lyria's desperate cry rings out. Billy has gone down. A Mordread stands over him, poised to deliver a death blow. Gonjii unhesitatingly destroys the Mordread. But the diversion is fatal. Neglos's blade buries itself mortally deep in his back. However, Billy makes a despairing grab for a weapon and fires. Neglos is sent reeling onto the weakened rail which gives way. He screams as he teeters on the brink. Billy looks at Gonjii who's somehow still erect and watching him with terrible intensity. He hands the weapon to the Demosian warrior. Drawing on his last reserves, Gonjii raises the weapon and fires. His hated enemy, Neglos, is knocked clean away and hurtles down into the void. And Gonjii, hearing his death scream, smiles as he collapses onto the gantry.

Inside the crucible the Doctor has been trying to shut down the regeneration process. Varnax taunts him. In a few more minutes the regeneration process will be complete. But the Doctor succeeds in rigging the mechanism to explode. It does so when the charged particles are focused on Zilla. She's atomised in the resulting chain reaction. When the debris clears, the Doctor finds that Varnax is still alive. But he's been transformed almost beyond recognition into a terrifying being from the realms of vengeful darkness.

The Doctor does the only sensible thing – he takes to his heels and runs like hell, pursued by the thing that was once Varnax. He's chased all the way out of the crucible. Varnax erupts onto the crucible platform and traps the Doctor. But the Doctor pulls another ingenious delaying tactic and makes it out just in time before the overhead shutters close. The waste pit is now sealed for all time. The immortal thing that was Varnax has found its final resting place.

When the Doctor rejoins the others, Gonjii is close to death. He's already passed on his prized sabre to Billy. The Doctor grieves for his friend. And so Gonjii lets go, content in the knowledge that Demos is avenged. And as he dies, Billy Dreamer chants the Death Song of his people, the age-old tribute of one warrior to another.

It's a beautiful day outside as they make their way back to the TARDIS. It's a moment of choice for Billy, but one that he'll decide to postpone, because right now he still has a lot to learn from the Doctor and Lyria. Especially Lyria . . .

Notes

1 In this version, Varnax is still looking for true immortality, but the Crystals of Power have been replaced by the Immortality Bullet, which is being kept in the Time Vaults of Gallifrey. Varnax's Creator is now called the Phoenix.

2 The Doctor's past is shown here to be the result of a self-imposed exile caused by Zilla's rejection.

3 Lyria and Gonjii remain basically the same characters, except that the Gallifreyan Time Battalions are now dubbed the 'Time Rangers'.

4 This entire sequence of events – the Doctor being coerced into breaking into the Time Vaults – is new.

5 The cataclysmic scene on Demos ends with sharply different results in this version. Instead of being tried for interference by the Time Lords and sentenced to a penal colony, the Doctor is now thrown into the Time Vortex and ends up on Earth.

6 The Native American/ecological angle is the main highlight of this version. Scott Morgan now becomes Billy Dreamer. Billy's background is much more fleshed out.

7 From this point onward, Version 3 is substantially similar to Version 2, except for the story's climax, which is shifted to Idaho.

8 A slight variation on Gonjii's motivations.

VERSION FOUR: *The Genetic Duplicate*

Story (Synopsis by Johnny Byrne)

There is a theory, based on statistical probability, that some-where, sometime, someplace there exists, or has existed, the genetic duplicate of every individual. Such a theory, if true, cannot be proved or disproved. The scientific means to do so lie beyond the frontiers of knowledge. But whose knowledge? Which frontiers?

Tempers are fraying in the MELVILLE family. Seventeen-year-old BILLY[1] has fallen out with TESSA, his gawky, irritating eleven-year-old sister. DAD, sweating over the barbecue, blames MOM for allowing the family mutt to eat the prime rib, and neither of the children are around when they are needed. Situation normal in the unusually close-knit, small-town Melville family. Eventually tempers flare and BILLY bicycles off in a temper, and he doesn't even see the truck that comes from nowhere to smash him into near brain death.

In the hospital the Melvilles almost break down under the crushing shock and grief and heartbreak for a deeply loved son and brother. Billy is hooked up to life support, lost in pre-death coma. His brain damage is such that it's merely a question of time before the family have to pull the plug on his support system. But Billy Melville could never have known that his fate is inextricably bound up with dramatic events in other times and impossibly distant places.

The DOCTOR is enjoying a brief spell on his home planet of Gallifrey. He is perched on a remote mountain, inside his TARDIS. Not even the Doctor knows how big the TARDIS is. Someone who might know is POG, his constant com-panion, who often goes walkabout in its unexplored, secret recesses.[2] POG is an intelligent, alien creature. He has a weird whiskery face, a shape resembling something between an otter and a monkey and a voice with an endearingly grumpy edge to it. Their abrasive dispute is cut short by an

67

urgent summons to the elegant Gallifreyan Capital. The Time Lords are in a state of panic. They have received information that VARNAX and his gang – all long believed dead – are in fact alive and on the rampage again.

This is news which also disturbs the Doctor. Varnax was once the most brilliant of the Time Lords, a gifted geneticist, the Leonardo of the Gallifreyans. He was also the Doctor's close friend and partner when long ago they had both worked to unlock the secret of immortality. Somewhere along the way Varnax turned to evil. He became a megalomaniac obsessed by a psychopathic vision of creating a genetically pure and immortal master race, which left the Doctor no choice but to betray his destructive schemes to the High Council. But Varnax escaped justice. He fled Gallifrey in his monumental timeship, the CREATOR.[3] Later he and his accomplices, who included ZILLA and NEGLOS, were hunted down by the Gallifreyan Time Rangers and were blasted to destruction on a remote world – or so everyone believed.

Now Varnax is alive. The Doctor never doubts that he is still bent on achieving his aim – to restructure the forces of life and death in his own evil image. To succeed Varnax must first make himself immortal, and to do so he must track down a genetic duplicate – only traceable when the living carriers of the duplicate material are on the threshold of death.[3]

The Doctor discovers that Varnax's genetic duplicate exists on twentieth-century Earth. It is Billy Melville. Time is critical. Varnax must take possession of Billy before death. If he fails, the duplicate genetic material will be lost, until thrown up again by the random forces of death and rebirth, and Varnax can't wait that long.

To find Billy, Varnax's ship, the Creator, will need to travel in time. But the Creator hasn't got a Time Rotor. There are only two places in the Galaxy where a Time Rotor can be found – Gallifrey, where they are jealously guarded and only issued to Time Lords, and Racqets, a lawless, wheeler-dealer world, where everything can be had for a price.[4]

The Doctor travels to Racqets. All manner of vice and crime flourishes in its teeming alleyways. Here he renews his life-long friendship with GONJII. Gonjii is an alien of high birth, one of the last of a destroyed warrior race. He is a man of grim, mordant wit and terrifying martial skills. Once Gonjii held the most prestigious military rank in the Galaxy. Now he is a wandering, down-on-his-luck soldier of fortune. It has been a long time since the Doctor last saw him, but their friendship has stayed the course. Gonjii was also the then-Commander of the Elite Gallifreyan Rangers who destroyed Varnax and his gang. He finds it hard to believe that anything could have survived the smoking ruin he and his Rangers made of Varnax's ship.

Intrigue, suspense and sudden death stalk their heels as they try to locate Varnax. They finally confront him after the illegal Time Rotor is auctioned at the Galactic junk lot of MOTHER CAJAGE, the obese female alien who is Racqets' deadly queen of crime.

Varnax gets the Time Rotor. The Doctor's only alternative is to get to Planet Earth before him. Without his genetic duplicate, Varnax's plans will come to nothing – and the Doctor intends to put it permanently beyond his reach. If Billy isn't already dead by the time he finds him, the Doctor will have to kill him.

Gonjii has joined the Doctor and Pog. He has discovered that Neglos, Varnax's merciless henchman, is alive. Gonjii has sworn a blood oath to destroy him – Neglos is the genocidal mass killer of Gonjii's people.

The Doctor enters the Time Vortex. Varnax is behind him. He knows what the Doctor plans to do, but he can't overtake the TARDIS while travelling in time.

Meanwhile, Tessa is alone in Billy's intensive care room. She often comes here alone. She believes that if she wills it hard enough, she can pull her brother back from the brink. But even as she tries the hardest she knows how, tears are in her eyes . . .

It is at this moment that the Doctor walks into the room and into the life of the Melville family. [5]

The medical opinion is that Billy is brain dead. Even Billy's grieving parents have given up hope and are steeling themselves to make the irrevocable decision to have his life-support system turned off. But the Doctor, with his vastly superior knowledge, knows that the spark of life is still present, which is something Tessa also knows. She may know nothing about medicine, but she does know that her brother is still alive. Tessa intuitively senses that the odd stranger who calls himself the Doctor knows it too. A rapport develops between them. Through Tessa, he comes to know her parents. The result is, to the Doctor, Billy becomes not just Varnax's anonymous genetic duplicate, but an individual, a much-loved kid whose hopes and aspirations were shattered in a moment of accidental violence.

But there is something else about Billy that disturbs the Doctor. The duplication is not only genetic, but seemingly biological, for Billy bears an uncanny resemblance to the youthful Varnax. The Doctor knows to his cost how that Varnax turned out. Perhaps Billy is destined to go the same route. If so, the Doctor would be more than justified in completing the task for which he travelled to Earth – to arrange for Billy to die. The cranky Pog rubbishes this notion. He believes the Doctor is just trying to justify the morally repugnant task he has set himself. To Pog, evil is not innate. It is acquired along the journey through life, a journey Billy has not yet even begun.

Time is pressing. Varnax's appearance on Earth is imminent. The decision to put Billy beyond Varnax's reach cannot be delayed any longer. The Doctor is alone in Billy's hospital room. There is nothing to stop him pulling the plug. No one would be any the wiser – most would see it as a blessed release for the kid. But the Doctor can't do it. Though millions may die if Varnax succeeds, as Pog has reminded him: the end can never justify the means.

That night, the terrifying figure of Neglos appears in town. He stalks the streets like an exterminating angel, killing anyone brave or foolish enough to confront him. He finds Billy in the hospital, disconnects him from his life support and takes him to the Creator. The Doctor and Gonjii are alerted too late to prevent Varnax making off with Billy.

Varnax escapes into the Time Vortex. Just as Varnax could not overtake the TARDIS on its journey to Earth, the

TARDIS can't make up the distance between itself and Varnax's ship. Varnax now has everything he needs to transform his crazed dream into evil reality.

The small-town community is shattered by the violent events of the night, and none more so than Billy's family. But somehow the Doctor inspires their trust – especially Tessa's – and it is to him they look, if not for answers then maybe the hope that somehow he can contrive to restore Billy to them.

Tessa never doubts that the Doctor can do it. Her unstinting faith and trust in him, and at a time when the Doctor feels acute guilt at his failure to prevent the destruction Varnax has unleashed on this small community, revives his flagging spirit. He sets out after Varnax, determined to destroy the evil he represents, no matter how impossible the task now seems.

On the Creator, Varnax takes urgent steps to prevent Billy from dying. Varnax and Zilla perform an operation that completely restores him – they need Billy healthy and alive. Billy wakes up and meets Varnax, Zilla and the other frightening occupants of the ruined ship. His first reaction is that he has actually died and woken up in hell. Then he remembers that he doesn't believe in hell – at least he thought he didn't. Varnax, particularly, scares the hell out of him. At one stage he finds himself in some kind of half-ruined, very scary laboratory. It is full of cages, huge tanks and containers full of nutrient liquids. All are filled with living alien life forms. Billy doesn't know that these creatures have been collected to provide the living pool of genetic material from which Varnax will fabricate the immortality gene. He gets another shock when he sees a picture in Zilla's room. It shows a beautiful Zilla standing beside a handsome Time Lord, and Varnax and Zilla are identical to his own father and mother!

The Doctor's pursuit of Varnax in the Vortex has proved fruitless. Only one last desperate option remains, a vortex jump, a theoretical means of shrinking relative distance inside the Vortex. If it succeeds, it would place the TARDIS inside Varnax's ship – a big if. A vortex jump would mean two objects having to occupy the same space-time co-ordinates, a physical impossibility that promises instant and catastrophic oblivion for the TARDIS. The Doctor goes through a series of complex manoeuvres aimed at matching the temporal velocities and co-ordinates of both ships. Judging the time to be now or never, he presses the button that will harness all the power the TARDIS possesses.[6]

The TARDIS expands to colossal size, which shrinks the relative distance. But the bigger the TARDIS grows, the less substantial it becomes. The TARDIS is stretched to the point where it has virtually ceased to exist, when it locks onto the Creator's temporal co-ordinates. A titanic detonation occurs that warps the fabric of the Vortex. When the debris clears, the TARDIS has reverted to its normal size and shape. But there is no sign of Varnax's Creator – it appears to have utterly vanished.

Only it hasn't. The tiny TARDIS has absorbed Varnax's huge ship, which is now scattered piecemeal throughout its interior space. The result is a nightmare combination of both ships. And something else has happened. The vortex jump has fractured space and time. Time, even history, has been sliced like a salami and is now sandwiched inside the distorted dimensions of the TARDIS.[6]

The Doctor, Gonjii and Pog find themselves lost in the lethally dangerous wonderland that is now the TARDIS. They need to find the TARDIS control area. Only then can they leave the Vortex before the effects caused by the jump will right themselves. When that happens, anything left inside the Vortex will be reduced to free-floating atoms.

Pog comes into his own. He intuitively knows his way about the unknown areas of the TARDIS. And it is through Pog that they find and rescue Billy, who is trapped in a sliced-off section of the Creator. The Doctor and his group have a lot of adjustments to make as they battle their way through the TARDIS. Billy is overjoyed when they emerge into what appears to be a section of his own home town – but it proves to be a transitory time slice which rapidly fades out of existence.

Later they emerge into Kernia, a savage, primeval world.[7] The Kerne are hallucinating warrior monks who believe everyone not a Kerne is a demon. The Kerne eat demons, which is what they are about to do to the Doctor's group when Neglos ambushes their temple. Neglos fails in his task to recapture Billy.

Nothing in Billy's previous life has prepared him for what he is now experiencing. He is fascinated by Gonjii and in awe of his bravery and martial skills. There are moments when Billy himself has to display similar qualities if he is to survive, which he does and in such a way as to evoke Gonjii's respect. Billy finds the Doctor the hardest of all to understand. At times the Doctor appears to like him. But at other times he feels himself under a dark, watchful and very hostile scrutiny from this strange and unpredictable Time Lord. A moment comes when Billy actually feels intense hatred for the Doctor. It happens when the Doctor reveals why Varnax needs Billy. The knowledge that he is Varnax's genetic duplicate fills Billy with anger and revulsion – anger he turns against the Doctor.

They survive the perils that beset their path to the TARDIS's control area. But all their efforts have been in vain. Varnax has anticipated what the Doctor planned and is waiting for them. All except Pog are taken prisoner.

Varnax sets to work. Billy is prepared for the surgical removal of his duplicate genetic material. At the same time, the massive crucible, a gigantic sphere inside which Varnax will transform himself into an immortal, is lowered down into close contact with the ship's hellish fuel pits. [6]

But with Pog's help the Doctor and Gonjii escape. They battle their way down to the area where the transformation is taking place. While Gonjii holds off Neglos and his henchmen, the Doctor tries to get inside the crucible – a hazardous death-defying feat that only just succeeds. Once inside, he manages to free Billy and substitute new genetic material. Billy goes off to help the hard-pressed Gonjii, leaving the Doctor to have his final reckoning with Varnax. [8]

He locates Varnax in a regeneration chamber. Varnax has transformed. The human travesty appears to have been restored to full physical vigour. Varnax believes himself to have finally achieved his dream of immortality. But the Doctor knows different. The genetic material he substituted in place of Billy's is a compound derived from the captive alien creatures. The Doctor has also added a refinement of his own – the entropy factor. This means that, while Varnax may have regenerated into perfect physical state, his condition will rapidly decay.

What this means for Varnax is all too apparent. His perfect physique begins to stretch and distort. Soon he has transformed into a giant, deformed alien being – a nightmare beast from the realms of vengeful darkness. The thing that is now Varnax has but one purpose, to destroy the hated Doctor once and for all. The Doctor does the only sensible thing – he takes to his heels and runs like hell.

After a heroic defence Gonjii is outflanked by Neglos, who creeps up on him unaware and mortally stabs him in the back. With Gonjii now dying and helpless, Neglos takes his time in finishing him off. In doing so he gives Billy the chance to destroy him and so avenge Gonjii, a man he has come to revere.

The Doctor is chased out onto the narrow crucible platform, where his final confrontation with Varnax takes place. Below them are the superheated fuel casings. The Doctor seems doomed. It is impossible for anything merely human to withstand the giant, demoniac beast that Varnax has now become. But at the last moment the Doctor activates Varnax's discarded mechanical exoskeleton and hurls it at him, pitching him off the ledge. Varnax sails down into the void, hits the superheated fuel casings, and everything that is Varnax melts away in micro-seconds.

But the price paid is a high one, because Gonjii is dead. The Doctor grieves for the man, and the loss of their enduring friendship.

Billy, Pog and the Doctor return to the TARDIS and jump out of the Vortex just before the effect of the vortex jump rights itself. The manoeuvre separates them from the Creator, which is atomised moments later, its debris scattered throughout the timestreams of the Vortex.

Billy now faces a fateful decision.[9] He wants to return to his own time and place on Earth. He can do so, but re-entry can only take place at the same moment in time that he left

Earth, a moment when Billy was virtually brain dead, which he will be again if he returns. Nor can the Doctor help him with his dilemma. If he helped Billy cheat possible death, he would be guilty of breaking his solemn Time Lord oath of non-interference. Nor could he answer for the profound effects it would have on the fabric of time itself.

But Billy is willing to take his chances. His home and people is where he belongs. And, like the Doctor says, he wasn't completely brain dead, and where there's life there's hope. The Doctor and Pog exchange a look of weary resignation – at least they tried, the look says . . .

Tessa is alone in Billy's intensive care room. She often comes here alone. She believes that if she wills it hard enough, she can pull her brother back from the brink . . . But even as she tries the hardest she knows how, there are tears in her eyes. Although she's trying, she still hasn't learned not to cry . . .

Tessa hears a sudden bleeping erupt from the battery of support systems and vital sign indicators. Something is happening to Billy. She yells out for help. Her parents and a medical team rush in. It takes everyone a moment to realise that a miracle has happened. Billy's eyes are open and he's smiling at them . . .

The door opens and an odd-looking stranger pops his head inside the room. He appears to have wandered in by mistake. He apologises, smiles at Billy and Tessa and leaves. Tessa feels just the briefest flash of recognition, but it's really too swift to register. Tessa and Billy will never know that it was the Doctor just checking to see that Billy had made it back OK.

The Doctor's only problem now is to explain somehow to the High Council of the Time Lords the monumental screw-up that restoring Billy has caused to the fabric of time. But the Doctor is not too worried. He's pretty good at bending the rules to his advantage – he's got several lifetimes of practice behind him . . .

Notes

1 By 1990, *The Time Lord* script once again evolved. The Native American angle was abandoned. Billy Dreamer has now become Billy Melville, who lives in Anytown, USA. The character of Lyria has gone, replaced by Billy's sister, Tessa.

2 On the other hand, Pog is back. In one presentation, Byrne wrote: 'Pog is established as the long-time companion of the Doctor's travels. Pog will be integral to the interior of the TARDIS, a kind of watchdog/guardian. In the quieter moments, we see him with the Doctor, slumped in one of the library chairs, listening to, perhaps even understanding, one of the Doctor's many one-sided conversations. And don't think of Pog as the Doctor's pet or he'll bite your hand off!'

3 The quest for immortality is still driving Varnax; however, in this version it is accomplished through the 'genetic duplicate', i.e. Billy. Varnax's ship is again dubbed 'Creator'.

4 This change in spelling is deliberate. From this point onward, the story is substantially similar to the previous versions, except where indicated.

5 The dilemma faced by the Doctor regarding Billy's life or death is unique to this version.

6 In this version, the vortex jump becomes an event of incredible magnitude, turning the TARDIS into a virtual reality of its own, as in New Adventure *Cat's Cradle: Time's Crucible*. The nuclear waste burial site is eliminated, and the story climax now takes part inside the TARDIS/Creator.

7 Kernos has now been renamed Kernia, but the sequence with the Kerne remains basically identical.

8 Again, the story reverts here to previous patterns: the Doctor's final confrontation with Varnax in the crucible, Gonjii's sacrifice, etc.

9 The ending, however, goes in a new direction, to take into account, and resolve, Billy's personal plight. It is implied in this version that, as in the original BBC television series, the Doctor's interference is more or less tolerated by the Time Lords.

Review

No matter which version of Johnny Byrne's *The Time Lord* one considers, it represents a daring break with the past, and could have fully justified a big-budget motion picture.

It is the first *Doctor Who* script to flesh out the Doctor's past. It is the first to introduce mature (or adult) romantic concepts. It is the first to consider the genetic consequences of unions between Gallifreyans and Humans. It is the first to hint at the 'special relationship' that exists between the Doctor and Earth.

The story's scope has been made more 'cosmic' by Byrne. In that respect nothing surpasses Varnax's mad and yet seductive dream to recreate a perfect universe, as outlined in Version 1. The subsequent immortality-driven plots were something of a let-down by comparison. At the same time, Byrne managed to explore some very human themes. Version 3, with its remarkable Native American angle, or Version 4, with Billy's moving plight, are excellent examples of how to integrate the human angle into an epic story.

3

LAST OF THE TIME LORDS
by
Johnny Byrne

Background

In 1990 Peter Litten and George Dugdale joined forces with producer Felice Arden. By then the story, while retaining certain elements, had mutated further. Johnny Byrne had begun increasingly to stray away from the original premise devised by producers Litten and Dugdale which had formed the basis for Mark Ezra's *The Return of Varnax*.

Among the new concepts developed by Byrne were (a) the destruction of Gallifrey by Varnax, combining the climax of Ezra's script and Demos's apocalyptic fate from *The Time Lord*, and (b) the introduction of the Doctor as having become the victim of amnesia, an idea which had only been hinted at in *The Time Lord*'s Version 3, and which had the dramatic merit of enabling the spectator to discover the character and his origins in a progressive, suspenseful fashion.

After a few initial outlines, *Doctor Who – The Time Lord* was eventually retitled *Doctor Who – (The) Last of the Time Lords* – both versions of the title were used interchangeably.

Eventually *Last of the Time Lords* required the writing of an entirely new script. In early 1991 Byrne delivered 75 pages, outlined here as Version 2, accompanied by a synopsis covering the rest of the story. But by then a lot of steam had gone out of the project. As a result the script was never completed. Instead a third, half-hearted attempt to develop an entirely new story (*Chameleon*) was tried, but never got past the initial premise.

[To be concluded at the end of this chapter.]

VERSION ONE: *The Fall of Gallifrey*

Story (Synopses by Johnny Byrne)

SUMMARY

He is a Time Lord of Gallifrey, a galactic super elite, the only race ever to master travel in time. But his world is in ruins, his people dead, both destroyed by VARNAX, the dark genius who was once his friend. He was betrayed by ZILLA, the woman he loves, the woman who broke his heart when she chose Varnax. Zilla, whom he still loves. [1]

He is the DOCTOR – the last of the Time Lords – and only the Doctor knows where the TARDIS, the last timeship in existence, is hidden. Varnax wants the TARDIS. His twisted dream is to control the evolution of all other races through genetic manipulation, play God with the forces of creation. [2]

Varnax wants the Doctor as fervently as he wants the TARDIS. He has perfected a genetic implant that will restore him to prime physical immortality. But he lacks the means to energise the implant, a rare source of energy present only in the unique regenerative powers of a living Time Lord, [3] and the Doctor is the only living Time Lord in existence. It spells a horrific death for the Doctor and a fitting revenge for Varnax, whose hatred of his one-time friend knows no bounds.

After the destruction of Gallifrey the Doctor sought refuge on Earth and hid the TARDIS to prevent it ever falling into Varnax's hands. But Varnax, even without a timeship, tracked him down and, through his agents, began to take the Doctor's mind apart in his efforts to locate the TARDIS.

BACKSTORY

Imperial Rome at its zenith believed itself invulnerable, the eternal hub of the civilised world. In another time and place, the ancient, highly advanced world of Gallifrey also believed itself invulnerable. Unlike Imperial Rome, whose power was based on military might, Gallifreyan power was benign, based on knowledge. From it had flowed their mastery of time travel, the Gallifreyans being the first and only race to have achieved this.

The Gallifreyans jealously guarded their monopoly of time travel, but it was a monopoly they exercised in an enlightened way for the benefit of all. To prevent abuse of the awesome power inherent in time travel they enacted the Laws of Time, one of the most rigorously enforced being the Law of Non-Interference. It stemmed from the Gallifreyan belief that other races had the inalienable right to undisturbed historical and evolutionary progression. If accidents or abuse did occur and corrective action was needed, the Gallifreyans relied on the only military force at their disposal – The Time Rangers. [4]

Nor was time travel available to all Gallifreyans. Only their Time Lords – an elected super elite, and few in number – were allowed the privilege of unrestricted time travel. [5] While these Time Lords designed and built their own ships, it was the High Council of Time Lords which granted each one a Time Rotor, the device that transformed their craft into timeships.

Two of the most gifted Time Lords, VARNAX and the DOCTOR, were once close friends. Later they became bitter enemies when Varnax tried to wreck the ancient consensus that governed the control of time travel. Instead of non-interference, Varnax believed the Time Lords should positively interfere. But it was power that Varnax sought for himself. A brilliant geneticist, Varnax's twisted ambition was to control the historical evolution of all other races through genetic manipulation; in effect, to play God with the forces of creation. [2] The Time Lords, if they followed Varnax's way, would control and direct the evolution and history, the very existence of other races and civilisations. The Gallifreyans had it within their power to become, in effect, Lords of Creation.

But Varnax could do nothing without the consent of the High Council of the Time Lords, to whom the status quo had become an end in itself. They had long ceased to quest for new knowledge. They believed that they knew all it was safe and prudent to know. What Varnax proposed was a giant leap into the unknown and it mortally scared them.

The Doctor's fears were more prosaic. He had seen at first hand Varnax's descent into megalomania, an evil clouding of the personality of a man who had been as close to him as a brother. Varnax's friendship with the Doctor died when the Doctor opposed him, eventually resulting in Varnax's banishment from Gallifrey.

For a time, nothing more was heard of Varnax, until he returned with an invading horde of bio-genetic alien warriors, the MORDREAD. Varnax's monumental ship appeared undetected out of the timestreams. Pods manned by the ferocious warriors spewed out of its vast bulk and attacked. Other warriors attacked on foot and in fearsome armoured ground columns. The timeless serenity of Gallifrey was shattered for the first time by the catastrophic violence of a barbarian invasion.

Gallifrey was invulnerable to everything except an attack led by one of their own Time Lords – an unimaginable event. As shrines of beauty crumbled, halls of knowledge were sacked, and one by one the visible symbols of Gallifrey's advanced and elegant civilisation were destroyed, the Time Lords knew that Gallifrey was doomed. While they could not defeat Varnax, they still had the means to deny him the prize he sought above all, mastery of time.

The Time Lords destroyed most of the existing Time Rotors, along with the means and knowledge to construct more. Only two were left intact, those in the ships belonging to Varnax and the Doctor. The Doctor was ordered to destroy first Varnax's and then his own.

Along with his close friend MENON,[6] the commander of the decimated Time Rangers, the Doctor attacked the Time Rotor in Varnax's ship. They succeeded, leaving Varnax grotesquely injured amidst the debris of his damaged ship.

The vengeful Varnax had the Doctor and Menon hunted through the ruins of once-beautiful Gallifrey. The Doctor now possessed the last active timeship and Varnax wanted it almost as frenziedly as he wanted the Doctor.

The Doctor got to the TARDIS first and escaped. But he still had an agonising dilemma to resolve. Before they had perished, the Time Lords of the High Council had ordered the Doctor to destroy his Time Rotor. If he obeyed their orders, the priceless knowledge of time travel would be lost, perhaps for ever. If he didn't, Varnax might still find the TARDIS and that the Doctor had to prevent, whatever the cost.

The Doctor chose a solution he believed would cover both eventualities: preserve the TARDIS, the only remaining timeship in existence, and at the same time prevent it from ever falling into Varnax's hands. He delivered Menon to the relative safety of his home world, Raquets,[7] and, before they parted, gave him the Imager,[8] the component of a Time Rotor which contains the coded knowledge to construct a duplicate. If anything happened to him or the TARDIS, the knowledge of time travel would survive in Menon's safekeeping.

Next he rigged the controls so that the TARDIS would automatically set off on a pre-timed loop through multi-dimensional time. Here it would be untraceable until it reappeared at a predetermined time and space of his own choosing.

Since the Doctor could not survive travel in multi-dimensional time, he would have to wait for the loop to expire and the TARDIS to reappear. It would be a very long wait. Thirty years would pass before the TARDIS reappeared, which it would do on Earth, somewhere in London in the year 1903, the Doctor's chosen time and place of refuge.[9]

By then the Doctor knew that Varnax would be dead. He also knew that, so long as he lived, Varnax would never stop searching for him. Thirty years was a long time, time enough for a thwarted genius like Varnax to locate his time and place of refuge. And, if he was ever captured, the Doctor could not prevent Varnax from extracting from him the knowledge of the TARDIS's whereabouts. Which is why, before the TARDIS deposited him on Earth and vanished into multi-dimensional time on its thirty-year round trip, the Doctor decided to strip his mind of all knowledge of Varnax,

84

Gallifrey, the TARDIS – everything that he was and had been.[10]

Now if Varnax did find him the Doctor's knowledge would be beyond reach. Only the TARDIS, when, or if, it reappeared, would trigger a return of his memory and true identity, if he survived to rendezvous with it. The Doctor pressed the button and his identity siphoned away . . .

FILM OUTLINE

When the story opens, the DOCTOR is held fast in the grip of a recurring nightmare. Destructive visions of Gallifrey, all without context or meaning, torment him, together with images of being restrained in some kind of primitive, demoniac laboratory where vats bubble, convulsometers spark and charge, and people, human one moment, inhuman the next, are around him. Then images of strange and fantastic machines carousel through his mind . . . The Doctor cries out in terror and wakes up. He hears a sudden, distant lunatic scream which touches off ripples of equally lunatic laughter.

The year is 1903, the place is London and the Doctor is in a secure cell in an asylum for the criminally insane. He does not know how he came to be there, nor for how long he has been incarcerated. Neither is he aware that he is a Time Lord of Gallifrey. What the Doctor does know is that the man he was yesterday is not the man he is today. He keeps the knowledge to himself because he senses danger, a pervasive, intangible menace so acute that he can trust no one but himself, and possibly LOTTE WELLINS.[11]

Lotte is a seventeen-year-old slum urchin, one of the domestic serfs who toil in the asylum. Her humane and cheerful attitude to the deranged patients has attracted the Doctor's interest and once, during the steam-clouded hell of communal ablutions, she courageously saved the Doctor's life when a psychopathic inmate attacked him.

At first she thought the Doctor was loopy. Everyone complains about the things that happen to them in the place behind the mortuary. She has never met an inmate who believed they were insane. All are convinced they have been driven insane by the things people do to them in the asylum, especially in the creepy place the Doctor is complaining about. But somehow Lotte came to believe him. Though mentally disturbed, she does not believe that the Doctor is insane. Nor has she ever understood why he is in the asylum.

The Doctor's memory is returning. Fragments of knowledge and recognition are surfacing from the dark void in his mind. Entertaining some inmates, he discovers the almost frightening extent of his scientific knowledge, a revelation interpreted by the staff as a symptom of the Doctor's insanity. The Doctor's struggle to recover his identity is a lonely one, and Lotte knows about loneliness. Her entire young life has been a struggle to survive, a lonely struggle in which no one ever cared whether she lived or died. But the Doctor cares, and because he does, Lotte has come to care for him. In the Doctor, Lotte has found the emotional outlet for her yearning for the father she has never known.

The Doctor learns that his nightmares are deliberately induced, that, in a hellish Frankenstein laboratory off the mortuary, surrogate inhuman replicates are using terrifying means to destroy his mind as they strive to extract information from him. It happens when the asylum director, PROFESSOR HOLLAS,[12] uses the Doctor to demonstrate his galvanic treatment for amnesia to three distinguished society people. The Doctor, pretending not to know or understand, thinks he recognises the visitors. Hollas switches on his device, but the power source that drives it is not of this time and place. Its effect is to pitch the Doctor into his familiar nightmare, only now it is really happening.

The device charges the air, which acts as a kind of wavering X-ray on the bodies of the visitors, and beneath the façade of distinguished Victorians, the three are inhuman. Images of strange machines once again carousel through the Doctor's mind. The inhuman visitors need him to identify one of them, something called TARDIS. And they are speaking in the voices of VARNAX, ZILLA and NEGLOS.

The Doctor is feverishly drawing in his cell. It is a picture of an old-fashioned, walk-in English police box, one of the

86

carousel images from his nightmares. He knows it is the TARDIS. And, without understanding why, he knows that it will shortly appear in London. He plans to escape so that he will be there to rendezvous with it. He must escape because he knows he is close to breaking point. One more nightmare session might reveal what Hollas and the others want to know, and that he must avoid at any cost.

With Lotte's help the Doctor escapes from his lunatic's cell. They journey through the night madness of the asylum and find Hollas in the hidden lab beyond the corpse-filled inmates' mortuary. Working like a man obsessed, Hollas is creating more replicates, and in three upright, open coffins are the inanimate, fully dressed replicate bodies of Varnax, Zilla and Neglos.

The Doctor learns from Hollas that he is a Gallifreyan, that the TARDIS is a timeship and his enemy is called Varnax. The Doctor discovers that Varnax is still alive on Gallifrey. He artificially prolonged his life and is now a physically grotesque, vengeful psychopath, the very embodiment of evil. He not only needs the TARDIS, he also wants the Doctor. The Doctor does not know it, but he carries the means that will restore Varnax to a prime physical state of immortality.

Varnax located the Doctor's time and place of refuge on Earth. With no Time Rotor, his ship couldn't travel in time. But he devised other means to get at the Doctor. He and Zilla seeded the Time Vortex with manipulated genes cloned from himself, Zilla and Neglos, his murderous strong right arm. On Earth, the genes were fashioned into replicates of their genetic donor by Hollas. The replicates are inhuman automata, remote extensions of the real Varnax, Zilla and Neglos on Gallifrey.

Varnax and Zilla also seeded Earth's evolutionary time-stream with 'Sleeper' genes. These were timed to infiltrate three specific individuals. The first was Hollas, who was 'triggered' to perform two specific tasks: the first was to incarcerate the Doctor and the second was to construct the replicas. [13]

Then, Hollas attacks the Doctor and switches on a device.

It generates a signal that animates the replica of Varnax. The Doctor destroys Hollas in a vat of acid, but the Varnax replicate screams out a command which animates the dripping, half-solidified creatures that Hollas has been creating. These horrors can't be held at bay for long. The Doctor incinerates several with high-voltage power and he and Lotte escape.

Hollas's death raises a hue and cry for the Doctor, who is hunted as an escaped lunatic killer. He finds temporary refuge in a slum tenement with Lotte, whose courage and street-wise cunning help them avoid capture. She is now a fugitive on his account. They are hunted both by the law and by more of Varnax's creatures. Their mutual need to survive draws them closer. But the Doctor fears for Lotte's safety. Her courage and loyalty have made her very special to him.

Lotte and the Doctor make an unlikely team. She is a tough but sensitive slum kid, unsophisticated, uneducated, and brimming with natural intelligence and curiosity. Although she has come to love the Doctor, she finds him a strange and baffling man. He can be funny and frightening by turns. She knows he can be ruthless, yet he is the most humane person she has ever known. And he is fun to be with. His eccentricities and quirky sense of humour trail mischief, misunderstanding and zany complication in their wake. She knows too that his casual, easy-going manner conceals a will of iron, lethally combined with an endlessly resourceful mind. And if she was more educated, the depth and extent of the knowledge the Doctor reveals as his sense of identity returns would terrify her.

The Doctor makes contact with his old friend, JAMES ALWYN, in whose house in the fashionable heart of London he and Lotte go to ground. The upper-class grandeur of her new surroundings fails to impress Lotte. Slum urchins are meant to know their place, a notion that completely escapes Lotte and which causes pandemonium with the staff downstairs. But when scrubbed and decently dressed, Lotte reveals herself to be an extremely beautiful young woman.

James's help is vital in pointing the Doctor towards his time and place of rendezvous with the TARDIS. But danger stalks their heels. Both the law and Varnax are closing in on him. James and Lotte are with the Doctor when he waits for the TARDIS. He has worked out that it is due to reappear on the fourth chime of the ninth hour of Bow Bells. But it doesn't appear. He has miscalculated. It is the ninth chime of the twelfth hour of Big Ben that will trigger the TARDIS's reappearance,[14] which is just as well, because Varnax has uncannily read their intentions. His replicates have laid a trap and are waiting to pounce the moment the TARDIS appears.

They escape, but the Doctor knows that someone has betrayed him. It proves to be James, who is revealed to be the second of Varnax's sleepers, James, who located the Doctor at Varnax's behest and who, along with Hollas, arranged for his incarceration in the asylum.

The Doctor knows by now that James, like Hollas, is an unwitting victim, a disposable strand in the manipulative web spun by Varnax to ensnare him. And he is still a friend. But James knows the new location of the TARDIS and, because he does, the Doctor has to kill him. It is an act that shocks Lotte, who recoils from a chilling darkness in the character of a man she has come to trust.

The TARDIS appears on cue on the ninth chime of the twelfth hour of Big Ben. It is locked into one of its potentially many outward shapes, that of the old, walk-in English police box. Later the Doctor discovers that its chameleon circuit – the mechanism that controls the TARDIS's outward form – has been damaged beyond repair during its mysterious loop through multi-dimensional time.[15]

When the Doctor and Lotte enter the TARDIS the contrast between its small outer size and its relatively vast inner dimensions, potentially infinite in scale, renders the Doctor and even the normally underawed Lotte silent with wonder. Dim understanding of what he has to do next stirs in the Doctor's mind. He fumbles with the controls and sends the TARDIS spinning into the Time Vortex. Instinct draws him to the recall pod, which he enters and switches on.

His mind floods with the recorded information that spills into his consciousness. The confined space of the recall pod expands and the Doctor finds himself back in the vast and beautiful council chamber in the palace of the Time Lords on Gallifrey. The High Council of the Time Lords, in recorded word and image, reveal the harrowing details of his past. The experience almost overwhelms him. The Doctor inwardly weeps as remembered shrines of beauty, halls of knowledge, all the visible symbols of Gallifrey's timeless civilisation, fall under the onslaught of a catastrophic barbarian invasion.

With it comes the knowledge of what Varnax did and the steps he took to protect both the TARDIS and himself, his defiance of the Time Lords when he disobeyed their order to destroy the TARDIS, and the burden of conscience and responsibility he now carries because of it. The recorded memories fade. The discovery of his past has revealed his future. The Doctor buries his anguish and hardens his heart.

When he emerges from the recall pod, Lotte is stunned by the change in the Doctor. The years appear to have rolled back, and he radiates an almost unnatural vitality. He is the Doctor, the sole inheritor of the collective knowledge, mental resources and values of his people, one of the most formidable races in the Galaxy, the Time Lords of Gallifrey. (The one mystery he never solves is how to repair the chameleon circuit, which keeps the TARDIS locked in its existing police-box form.)

The Doctor now bends his power to a single unwavering purpose, the destruction of Varnax. The struggle that began in Victorian London now continues in the starkly contrasting outlaw world of Raquets, the alien melting pot of the galaxy. Here, where anarchic violence seethes and life is the cheapest commodity for sale, they find MENON, the Doctor's old friend.

Menon is an aristocratic soldier, the ex-commander of the Gallifreyan Time Rangers, who were destroyed defending Gallifrey against Varnax. Menon fled to Raquets, where he has carved out a refuge of peace and security for himself and his son, GONJII, [6] amidst the prevailing anarchy. Menon has long been a target of Varnax's lust for revenge. It was Menon, along with the Doctor, who left Varnax a shattered hulk before they both escaped from Gallifrey. The Doctor also entrusted Menon with knowledge about the TARDIS – the Imager. Above all, Menon is able to forge the next vital link in the Doctor's chain of remembrance.

Lotte feels threatened by the Doctor's close friendship with Menon and Gonjii. She feels excluded, once more the outsider she has always felt herself to be. Her familiar world is gone. She has committed herself to the Doctor. Their relationship is all she has left and she resents any intrusion into it. She becomes withdrawn and difficult and takes it out mostly on Gonjii. She instinctively resents his aristocratic bearing and manner. Nor is Gonjii much impressed by Lotte. Her temperamental displays, lack of manners and abysmal lack of knowledge leave him cold.

Then Menon is betrayed. Varnax's agents attack and carry him off to Gallifrey. Varnax has him horribly tortured to death – a sadistic act with a purpose, which is to lure both the TARDIS and the Doctor to Gallifrey.

Gonjii is devastated. His secure world has been shattered by the barbaric death of his father, whom he loved and revered. This arouses Lotte's compassionate nature. She understands how he feels. Varnax has made Gonjii an orphan, but she has been one all her remembered life. Gonjii's grief finds expression in bitter anger, but it doesn't deter Lotte. She understands Gonjii's needs at this time better than he does himself. Her honesty, intuitive wisdom and depth of understanding demolishes the antagonisms that previously existed between them. It has a healing effect on Gonjii and reveals to him just what a very special person Lotte is. It also puts their relationship on a completely different footing. They like what they discover about each other, and their involvement grows.

The Doctor blames himself for the tragedy. It was he who led Varnax to Menon, and it is he who must now shoulder the responsibility for Gonjii's future. This hardens his resolve to destroy Varnax, but he can only do that by going to Gallifrey, where he knows Varnax will be waiting for him.

The struggle against Varnax shifts to the ghostly eeriness

of Gallifrey, where its ruined civilisation, like a futuristic Pompeii, has been frozen at its moment of death. Emotions stir in the Doctor's heart as he travels through the debris of a vanished wisdom and beauty. But the Mordread are still there, and the Doctor's party have to get through them to get at Varnax. As they battle their way to Varnax, the Doctor becomes aware that something very special is happening between Gonjii and Lotte. Respect for each other's courage and character has forged a bond that is growing deeper by the moment. They don't know it yet, but they are falling in love. Then the Doctor is betrayed and all three of them are captured by Varnax. Once again, Varnax has uncannily anticipated the Doctor's intentions.

Varnax now has everything he wants – the TARDIS, which will give him control of time, and the Doctor, whose living being he will use to make himself physically perfect again and, in doing so, also make himself immortal. It means a ghastly, painful death for the Doctor, which intensely pleases Varnax. He wants the Doctor to experience something of the agony he has endured, agony the Doctor inflicted on him when he escaped from Gallifrey, leaving Varnax a grotesquely shattered hulk. It is a desperate prospect. A mortal Varnax was terrifying enough, but an immortal Varnax, deranged, megalomaniacal, the very embodiment of pernicious evil, is too horrible to contemplate. It will grant him colossal power – control of time and an endless life, which he will use to inflict unimaginable chaos and suffering throughout creation.[2]

And among the first casualties will be Lotte and Gonjii, the two people most precious to the Doctor. Varnax has installed them in his genetic laboratory, a nightmare place where Varnax's chilling, genetic visions find experimental expression. The Doctor pins his hopes on Zilla, a wish as much as a hope. Zilla is still beautiful, in every way the woman he loved, and he still loves her, as he discovers when they meet again. In the secret places of his heart, the Doctor hopes that maybe she still loves him. But if she doesn't, then maybe he can reach the nobility of character he knows that Zilla once possessed. It was Varnax's genius that attracted

Zilla. His visionary mind put all others in the shade. A scientist herself, Zilla believed that Varnax's discoveries could be used for the benefit of all. What she didn't see and the Doctor did was Varnax's descent into megalomania, an evil clouding of the personality of a man who had been as close to him as a brother. It was when the Doctor opposed him that Zilla chose Varnax.[1]

Zilla, like the Doctor, grieves for the loss of Gallifrey. But she believes that Varnax had no choice. He had to destroy the Time Lords, otherwise they would have destroyed him. Varnax has convinced her that the loss of one world is a small price to pay for the benefits his genius can bestow on the rest of creation. She knows that Varnax has used terrible means to achieve his ends. But she is convinced he will change. Once Varnax is restored physically, becomes immortal, he will become the Varnax of old, the Varnax they both loved and admired.

The Doctor realises that his efforts to reach Zilla are hopeless. Her blind faith in Varnax is unshakable, and her mind is also on the prize Varnax has offered her – to make her immortal. The Doctor buries his feelings and hardens his heart. Zilla's weakness always was her vanity. She never doubts that the Doctor still loves her, a weakness the Doctor plays on. It provides the means of escape, which he accomplishes with the resourceful help of Lotte and Gonjii.

Varnax is insane with rage. He sees all that he has schemed and suffered for slipping away. He has only one desperate option – to ram the TARDIS when it is in the process of vanishing into time. Two objects occupying the same space and time are a physical impossibility. It promises instant and catastrophic oblivion for both ships if Varnax has mis-calculated.[16]

On collision, a titanic detonation warps the fabric of time. When the debris clears, the tiny TARDIS appears to have absorbed Varnax's huge ship. The inside of the TARDIS has always been a place of almost unlimited dimension. Now the interior is staggeringly vast and a nightmare combination of both ships. This is where the final act of the Doctor's struggle against Varnax takes place. The collision has fractured temporal reality. Time, history, memory even, have been sliced like a salami and now crazily co-exist, sandwiched inside the distorted dimensions of the TARDIS.

Time, history, memory that is relevant to those trapped inside the TARDIS, a warped reality that induces visions unique to each, primal memories that find expression in the form of creatures dredged up from the depths of their darkest subconscious. Some of these creatures are ghostly, unreal. Others are formed or half-formed beings of short existence. One is a beast that surfaces from the depths of Lotte's subconscious – a demented, vengeful being that mercifully vanishes before it is fully formed. But there are also some real enough to kill in the most frightening way imaginable.

The interior of the TARDIS is fraught with other perils too. The fault in the fabric of time has caused illusion and reality to combine to lethal effect – a step onto seemingly solid ground could pitch you into a bottomless void, or when you pass through a seemingly endless open space you find that it retracts to crush you into nothingness. And, ticking away in the background, the fracture in time works to correct itself. Every so often an elemental spasm warps the weirdly joined structures, altering them into ever new, mind-bending combinations. The Doctor knows that the fault will correct itself and, when it does, anything not somewhere else will be annihilated. They must find their way to the control area of the TARDIS and shift to new space-time co-ordinates. [17]

While surviving these hazards, Lotte and Gonjii discover their love for each other. The Doctor is deeply moved by their happiness. It gives him one more reason to destroy Varnax.

They finally reach the control area of the TARDIS, only to find that Varnax is waiting for them. The Doctor never believed that Varnax could find his way there. It is knowledge only a Time Lord would have. It is as though Varnax has read his mind.

The Doctor ends up in the regeneration laboratory. The charging up of Varnax's genetic implant takes place. And as it does, the Doctor's life force, living fuel to Varnax's implant, agonisingly drains away. The grotesque Varnax is being reborn, restored to prime physical immortality. The Doctor realizes that it is all over. He has lost and Varnax has won. But he is wrong. Zilla can't endure what is happening to the Doctor. Seeing him die agonisingly brings back memories of what they had shared before she fell victim to Varnax's deadly lure, memories of the man she loved and, as she watches his death, the realisation that he is the man she still loves.

Zilla reverses the regeneration process. Varnax, held fast in the mechanisms, knows he must act fast if he is to avert the horrific consequences of what she has done. First he destroys Zilla by consuming her being with a charge of high voltage power. [18]

Next he activates the last of his 'Sleepers'. The third and last is Lotte, who has been the source of the Doctor's many recent betrayals. So far Lotte has not been aware of it. But she is now, when Varnax's desperate need for her to correct what Zilla has done rises like a tidal wave of compulsion in her mind. Helpless to resist, she is driven by a frantic, obsessive need to serve Varnax. Buried in the depths of her overwhelmed mind is the horrific knowledge that she belongs to Varnax, and that what he has commanded her to do will destroy the Doctor.

Gonjii belatedly becomes aware of the terrifying change in Lotte. By the time he understands its significance it is almost too late – Lotte is already throwing the switches that will destroy the Doctor and restore Varnax. Gonjii can't reach her. Lotte is beyond all reason. Her love for Gonjii, for the Doctor are as nothing to her imperative need to serve Varnax. In despair Gonjii threatens to shoot her, but in his heart he knows he could never do it, no matter what the consequences. [19]

But Gonjii's intervention has delayed Lotte, and Varnax needs her to act swiftly. Varnax is *in extremis*, his identity and mental power siphoning off by the moment. One effect of this is temporarily to weaken his hold over Lotte, which allows the real Lotte to suface momentarily. She uses this brief time to plead with Gonjii. Lotte wants him to prove that he loves her, and he can do it only by killing her. If he kills her now he will save the Doctor and destroy Varnax. Above all he will grant Lotte deliverance from the horrible thing that has taken possession of her being.

And with Varnax's power reasserting its hold over Lotte, Gonjii has no option but to kill the girl he loves. Filled with a terrible anguish he takes her in his arms and shares her dying moments, a pitifully brief period in which he is reunited with the real Lotte.

Lotte's death has horrific consequences for Varnax. The transformation goes frighteningly awry. He becomes beast-like, a crazed, immortal horror from the realms of vengeful darkness. And is oddly familiar. It is the same creature that materialised from the depths of Lotte's mind. It now has one single purpose – to destroy the Doctor. But he survives because of his knowledge of the time fault. He positions Varnax for the next grinding spasm caused by the fault in time and, when it occurs, he is on hand to send the thing that was Varnax howling into the exposed Time Vortex. Varnax's body is instantly annihilated. But the immortality implant regenerates him and he has to suffer the same agony again and again, until the end of time.

The Doctor rushes back to remove the TARDIS from danger. He has survived, but at the cost of Zilla, who died so that he might live, and Lotte and Gonjii, two people who can now share a future together, one free of the evil of Varnax. But when he rejoins them, he finds Gonjii cradling the dead Lotte in his arms. The Doctor understands too late how it happened. He had seen the signs of Varnax's control over Lotte, but he had blanked them out. He had avoided thinking the unthinkable about the girl he had come to love like a daughter. Lotte, who thought she belonged to Gonjii, and never even knew that all the time she belonged to Varnax – Varnax's ultimate act of evil. All that is left is their shared memory of Lotte, whose beauty, laughter and unique personality is gone forever from their lives.

But life goes on, and in their case it has a purpose. Menon Gonjii's father, escaped from Gallifrey. So did the Doctor. Others could have escaped Varnax's holocaust, Gallifreyans stranded throughout time and space whose priceless skills and knowledge are needed to rebuild what Varnax destroyed. To find them, gather them in and restore Gallifrey is a challenge that ignites the Doctor's hope and optimism. It is a monumental task, one worthy of any sacrifice, and one Menon would have wanted Gonjii to undertake.

Gonjii flatly refuses even to consider the idea. This completely throws the Doctor, who suddenly becomes aware of the change in Gonjii. The youthful Gonjii has come of age. He is now a man, one who knows his own mind, has his own priorities. And Gonjii's number one priority, the first thing he will do, is to take Lotte home to Earth. After that, anything is possible. The slight smile on his face says all the Doctor needs to know. He understands that Gonjii is making his peace with Lotte. Only when he has finally laid to rest everything he shared with her in the past can Gonjii respond to the challenge of the future, a future the Doctor and Gonjii will share as equals. One that will forge enduring bonds when they travel the by-ways of time and space in their quest to restore Gallifrey.

Notes

1 In an earlier version Zilla is a 'ruthless, beautiful alien woman', responsible for the creation of the Mordread. But the character was soon reverted to her previous role of Time Lady in exile and former flame of the Doctor.

2 Varnax's motivation now incorporates both the search for personal immortality (which he also promised to his cohorts) as well as a form of genetic lordship over the universe, which is only slightly less ambitious than the scheme outlined in *The Time Lord* Version 1, *Varnax the Creator*. The genetic thread is obviously carried over from Version 4, *The Genetic Duplicate*.

3 The means to Varnax's end are the Doctor's own regenerative powers, as in *Mawdryn Undead* (6F).

4 'Time Battalion' was also used in an earlier outline.

5 This clearly establishes that not all Gallifreyans are Time Lords, nor do they share their powers, i.e. the ability to

regenerate. This is something that *Doctor Who* fans have speculated about ever since the appearance of the Outsiders in *The Invasion of Time* (4Z). Coincidentally, the same Outsiders will, once again, be singled out in John Leekley's *Fathers and Brothers.*

6 In the first outline, the former Time Ranger was, naturally, named Gonjii. When the decision was made to give him a son, and to name that son Gonjii, Byrne rechristened the character first Manon (which had previously been the same given to the asylum director), then finally, Menon.

7 Now spelled this way.

8 The Imager disappeared from later outlines, in order to streamline the action.

9 1903 was the date selected in the first outline; it was later changed to 1875, and later again to 1934. In another attempt to simplify the action, the concept of the TARDIS stranded in multi-dimensional time was also abandoned (see note 14 below).

10 In one divergent version, which never even reached the outline stage, Byrne hypothesised that the Doctor had merely been hiding as a vaudevillian in Victorian England: 'The public who frequent the Variety Halls know him as "Doctor Tempus – Lord Of Illusion". His stage act is equally strange, his illusions, so unlike anything seen before, not only entertain, they also disturb. Even those closest to "Doctor Tempus" find him an enigma. His stage assistant, EMMY, a forthright seventeen-year-old London girl, finds him fascinating, infuriating and, at times, quite frightening. TOM is the silent, burly man who provides the muscle backstage and drives their coach.'

11 In an earlier version Lotte was called Millie.

12 In an earlier version Professor Hollas was named Manon (see note 6 above). Also, it is stated that 'the Doctor is not just insane, he is criminally insane. Two years ago he killed someone, a traumatic act that brought on total amnesia. But for Manon, the Doctor would have been hanged for murder.'

13 In the same earlier version Hollas/Manon is a plasmoid.

14 When the concept of stranding the TARDIS in multi-dimensional time (see note 9 above) was abandoned, a simpler explanation was substituted: 'The TARDIS was left on a street corner, where it looked like any other walk-in police box, until it was removed and junked by the City authorities, who found it couldn't be opened.' In this version, the Doctor and Lotte have to dig it out of a junk heap.

15 While this remains a story which clearly takes place far in the Doctor's future (in relation to the original BBC television series), the script explains why the TARDIS outwardly looks like a police box.

16 The concept of the Time Ram, previously dubbed 'vortex jump' in *The Time Lord*, Version 4, has survived.

17 The odyssey within the virtual reality of the TARDIS as in New Adventures' *Cat's Cradle: Time's Crucible* has also survived the transition.

18 In an earlier version the Doctor has rigged Varnax's machines, knowing full well that the result could go either way. As was the case in *The Time Lord*, by so doing he causes Zilla's death. 'The Doctor still loves her and part of him dies when he destroys her.'

19 Byrne outlined several variations on Lotte's dilemma. 'When VARNAX is becoming beautiful again, Lotte recognises him as the man she believes to be her father – the man in the locket picture. If Lotte is in the position to tilt the odds one way or the other, she would be in conflict between her hero-worship of her father and her love for the Doctor. Varnax could play on this. Or she could pretend to go along with VARNAX when she was weak, but later prove her love for the Doctor when she is in a strong position. In both cases, whatever she did would probably result in her death. And in both cases, Lotte would reveal the good side of Varnax, true Gallifreyan selfless nobility.

'Alternatively, Lotte may be the result of one of the many genetic experiments conducted by VARNAX, not only on Earth but on other worlds as well. The offspring of these experiments could be triggered by Varnax's death to develop into more Varnax(es)! That way, Varnax would have made certain that, if all else failed, others just like him would take up where he left off. If this were the case, by killing Varnax, Lotte would be renewing his evil inside herself. But if she didn't kill him, the Doctor would die . . . The effects of this dilemma are interesting. They may not be right for the story, which at present is going only on Lotte's recognition of Varnax as her father. But it is intriguing. Lotte might choose to save the Doctor and Gonjii but, knowing what is to happen, might vanish never to be found again, or to return in a sequel . . .'

VERSION TWO: *The Mark of Varnax*

Story

We open inside the TARDIS's power chamber, a dark, circular room of seemingly vast dimension. A tiny DOCTOR, dwarfed by the scale, is performing various repairs with his Sonix.[1]

We then cut to a normal-sized Doctor sitting in a futuristic chair, wearing a virtual reality helmet. His gloved hand holds a normal-sized Sonix. He has been using 'Virtual Drift', a VR system, to create a miniature image of himself in order to perform the necessary repairs.

Eventually the repair work is completed. The Doctor steps out of the TARDIS and into London in the year 1934.[2] Later, at the art deco Garden Club, the Time Lord plays a game of fives with his friend JAMES RADLEY,[3] a wealthy, sophisticated man in his late thirties and a prominent surgeon. He passes on the news of the TARDIS's repair to James, along with the fact that he intends to return to Gallifrey, which elicits a sense of disappointment in his friend.

Doctor *I must, James. I've been out of contact far too long.*
James *So there's been no communication?*

Doctor *No. The Matrix link is broken. And that's worrying.* [4]

James would like to see the TARDIS but the Doctor refuses for security reasons. So James invites him to a proper goodbye dinner.

At that moment, the Doctor notices that their WAITER bears the 'Mark of Varnax' tattooed on his wrist. He sets off after the Waiter but it is a trap. He is attacked, then shot with a soporific dart. VARNAX, a man of almost godlike male beauty exuding fanatical evil, materialises in a VeeDrift chair surmounted by two spinners.

Varnax *The TARDIS, Doctor . . . I want it. You will tell me where it is. I shall make you. And while you suffer, I shall . . . enjoy!*

We cut to Varnax's domed genetics chamber where the Doctor is suspended in weightless crucifixion. Clamped to his head is a metallic skull-cap bristling with needles. Varnax attempts to make the Doctor reveal the location of his TARDIS, but fails. In his frustration the renegade Time Lord lashes out at the Doctor – but his arm passes harmlessly through his body. Varnax's form is but an image!

The only way Varnax can destroy the Doctor's synaptic block is to burn out his memory, then wait for his mind to heal. On Varnax's order the needles plunge through the skull-cap and superheat. The Doctor, his identity burning away, screams in agony.

We cut to the secure room of St Audon's Mental Asylum. Two months have elapsed. The Doctor now looks haggard, confused, prematurely aged. He is finally coming to after his long, prolonged mental trauma.

Later, he is questioned by the asylum director, PRO-FESSOR HOLLAS, in the presence of a MATRON and a male nurse named CHARLIE. Showing signs of increased awareness, he is entrusted to the care of LOTTE WELLINS, a confident, capable seventeen-year-old girl. We meet other patients, such as the huge CHALLIS, who lifts imaginary weights, and the crazed, mumbling HEADMASTER.

As the Doctor's faculties start to return, he begins to develop a relationship with Lotte, who cannot quite bring herself to believe that he was incarcerated because he allegedly killed a man. He also starts seeing clues that all is not what it seems – such as the presence of spinners, like the ones on Varnax's Virtual Drift chair.

One day the Doctor is told that he has visitors. Hollas introduces him to INSPECTOR DACRE (who looks like a benign cleric) and two other POLICE OFFICERS.[5] Dacre tells the Doctor he has been confined because he killed a waiter in a seemingly motiveless attack, but the Doctor remembers nothing. Then, in an attempt to elicit memories, Dacre shows him the Mark of Varnax and asks him about the TARDIS . . . Gallifrey . . . The Doctor becomes intensely suspicious and denies all knowledge of these things. When he leaves he finally gets a good look at the face of one of the Police Officers – and it is that of the Waiter he allegedly killed!

Later the Doctor confides his suspicions to Lotte and begs her to help him escape, but she is not yet ready to believe him.

The following night the Doctor is violently abducted from his room by Varnax and his shadowy acolytes and, in a nightmarish scene, he is once more subjected to the torture of the skull-cap, but in vain.

> **Varnax (viciously, distorted)** *You said he was ready!*
> **Hollas (cringing)** *I was mistaken . . . The memory pathways are not yet healed. A little more time . . .*
> **Varnax** *There is no time!* **(gasping anguish)** *My labours exhaust what little is left of me! He must talk!*

The next day, the Doctor again begs Lotte for help. This time he manages to convince her of his sincerity. Lotte agrees to help him and uses her sexual wiles on Charlie to get the Doctor out of his cell. They stealthily reach Hollas's office. It is empty, but another spinner is powering up. The Doctor recognises it.

Doctor *I know it as a . . . Virtual Cell Cluster. We use them . . . to project bio-static mass across . . .* (**whisper**) *galaxies?*

As more memories flow into the Doctor's mind, they discover a secret passage leading down to Varnax's domed genetics chamber. Cadavers laid out on slabs sprout organ growths. Monitors control containers in which humanoid foetal beings float. Dominating all is the huge displayed symbol of the Mark of Varnax. Now Lotte is fully convinced that the Doctor was telling the truth.

The Doctor remembers having seen these hellish experiments before. He also recognises the hideous, needled skullcap which was used to break down his mind. They then come across Hollas, capture him and subject him to the skull-cap. The villain chooses to talk rather than undergo the torture. However, before he has time to say much, Matron and two male ATTENDANTS appear. A battle ensues, during which Matron is thrown into Varnax's Virtual Drift chair, which explodes, killing her. Hollas, who has been jerked up into the skull-cap, babbles mindlessly.

Doctor *The TARDIS? What is the TARDIS, Hollas?*
Hollas (**crazed**) *The TARDIS is his renewal!*
Doctor *Whose renewal?!*
Hollas (**babbling**) *The One who brings the power. The Immortal to be, the One who will renew Creation!*[6]

Hollas's brain finally short-circuits and he dies. On his wrist, the Doctor discovers the Mark of Varnax.

The Doctor and Lotte then flee from the asylum. They hole up in Lotte's refuge in the teeming East End slums. They meet MARCUS, a kid whose leg is shrivelled from polio. The Doctor discovers something of Lotte's orphan background and her interest in science. She keeps a picture of the father she never knew in a locket around her neck.[7]

But Dacre and his two fake policemen, the Waiter and the Other Man, discover their refuge. Warned by Marcus, who is shot by the villains, they escape over the rooftops. The Waiter catches up with them and seizes Lotte. He threatens to throw her over the edge unless the Doctor surrenders, but Lotte head-butts him and he is the one who ends up taking a deadly plunge.

In their flight the Doctor and Lotte come across a fascist rally, where a black-shirted DEMAGOGUE is haranguing the crowds. The symbol of his movement is the Mark of Varnax.[8]

An associative freak of memory in a pie shop directs the Doctor to the elegant house of his friend, James Radley. Getting past James's stately manservant, TOMKINS, they gate-crash his glittering party. The Doctor is then reunited with the man he considers a friend. James tells him that he looked everywhere for him, but it was as if he had vanished. The Doctor questions him about his identity.

James *You're . . . the Doctor. The only name you ever gave me. Does the word 'Gallifrey' mean anything to you? You won't find it on any map. It's where you come from. Your home world . . . A place in some future time.*[9]

Doctor (whisper) *I am . . . not of Earth, then?*

James *No. I'm the only one you trusted enough to know.*

Doctor (quietly) *I should have guessed. I've felt the . . . strangeness here. Knew things an Earthman had no right to know . . . Did I tell you why I came to Earth, James?*

James *A little. You didn't want me involved. But I do know your people were concerned about something happening here . . . We met after you arrived. Then, the . . . accident happened. Some freakish event severely damaged your ship. You described it as a . . . destructive command that originated on your home world. You tried to repair it, repeatedly failed . . . but in the end succeeded. On the very day you vanished, in fact.*

Doctor *You knew this ship, James?*

James *I never saw it. Dangerous knowledge, you said. But you spoke about it often. Said it could travel* *through space – and time. You called it the TARDIS, Doctor.*

Later, in what used to be the Doctor's room, James gives him a box he left behind, and which could only be opened by the Doctor, which contains the Sonix. Lotte asks what it is.

Doctor (very calm, remembering) *The Sonix. They give them to people like me. It permits me to own a ... timeship. A privilege they grant only to a ... Time Lord of Gallifrey.* (**Looks at Lotte**) *I know who I am, Lotte ... I know what I am.*

That night the Doctor discovers that Lotte, washed and made-up, her locket glinting on her neck, dressed in a fine, silk gown, is a very beautiful young woman. He also tells James that he now believes that Earth is being secretly infiltrated by a conspiracy of genetically enhanced (or manufactured) humans, fanatically devoted to serve someone who can only be another Time Lord – since he recognised the technology as Gallifreyan. But why another Time Lord would go to such extremes to capture his TARDIS, when he presumably would have one of his own, is still a mystery.

The next day, with memories crowding in thick and fast, the Doctor is able to retrace his steps to St Bertram's Church near Smithfield, one of the city market places, where he had hidden the TARDIS. They drive there in James's Bentley. Lotte asks the Doctor how such a ship could remain in a street without being noticed. The Doctor explains the concepts of the chameleon circuit, as well as the transcendental dimensions of the TARDIS.

When they get there, they discover a police box. However, it is a real police box, with a POLICEMAN inside. The Sonix helps guide the Doctor to another neighbouring police box which is the real TARDIS. But just as he is about to speak, the Doctor notices the Mark of Varnax stamped inside James's cigarette case. His world collapses. He then sees Dacre's car crawling forward in the vicinity, and more of Dacre's men mingling with the passers-by, yet closing in on them.

As the Doctor is considering his options, the Policeman returns, tries to open the TARDIS/police box, fails, then goes away. The Doctor seizes this opportunity to grip James and force him to talk. His orders were to get close to the Doctor and protect their organisation. They knew only the Doctor could repair the TARDIS. After he had done so, if he had told James its location it would not have been necessary to have him committed to the asylum. James finally reveals the identity of the master schemer – Varnax.

> **Doctor (shocked)** *But he's dead! I finished him and that hellish ship of his . . . long ago!*
>
> **James** *He survived. All he needs is you – your TARDIS.* (**Fanatical**) *And not just ours . . . Every world will be redeemed!*
>
> **Doctor (eyes ablaze with terrifying intent)** *We shall see. What I started, I will finish. Finish Varnax. Along with the filth he trails in his wake.* (**Deadly**) *Good-bye, James, whatever you are . . . You were a good friend, but not good enough.* [10]

The Doctor's hand chops with lethal effect and kills James. Moving with blinding speed the Doctor then rushes inside the TARDIS, dragging Lotte with him. Dacre's car hurtles towards them, but the police box dematerialises before it hits it. Instead it crashes into a lamp-post and explodes, killing its passengers.

The Doctor decides to return to Gallifrey. He now knows that Varnax is responsible for the evil things that happened to him. He also hopes to discover why the Time Lords tried to destroy the TARDIS.

We witness the Doctor's joy as he rediscovers the marvellous power and beauty of the TARDIS, a discovery he shares with Lotte, who is completely bowled over by the experience. The lower level is the control area, where the Time Rotor rises and falls with effortless rhythm. Other areas, including the galleried library, are havens of knowledge and relaxation. [11] Through windowed apertures soft natural light spills in.

The Doctor approaches a three-dimensional web-like

artifact, a Matrix Terminal linked to the Master Matrix on Gallifrey.

Doctor (to Lotte) *It began as the map of time. Now . . . it's the heart that pumps the life force of the world that created it.* [4]

The Doctor also explains the Time Rotor to Lotte, and shows her the multi-coloured timestreams among which they are travelling in the Vortex. They visit an enchanting garden, located behind a door in the TARDIS, stretching out into a seemingly endless horizon. When the Doctor closes the door the same garden, seen through a window, seems very small.

As they step onto a bridge crossing a meandering stream somewhere in the TARDIS's fabulous landscapes they meet POG, a small, long-haired humanoid with a grouchy face. He and the Doctor exchange some banter in Latin, then the creature goes away. Lotte asks the Doctor what it was.

Doctor *Something I made. For when I felt the need of a good argument. Nothing like it to pass away time.* [12]

Then the Doctor puts Lotte inside the Virtual Drift helmet and guides her tiny duplicate around the insides of the TARDIS. Later, while he is still trying to puzzle his way around the Matrix, Lotte returns dressed as an eighteenth-century Gainsborough beauty. Taken by her elegance, the Doctor creates a miraculous period dining room where they enjoy a meal (fish and chips, courtesy of the TARDIS's nutrient bank, made especially for Lotte!) served by a funny, intelligent TROLLEY. During the meal, a subtle change takes place in Lotte's relationship with the Doctor. The fun, friendship, mutual respect, genuine affection – all of the elements are still there. But since he recovered his memory he seems to have become more emotionally distanced.

Then the Time Rotor's pitch suddenly changes, indicating that they're about to arrive in Gallifrey's space-time.

The TARDIS appears above the darkened surface of Galli-frey. The Doctor checks the monitors, sensing that something wrong.

Doctor (*fearful whisper*) *It's dark when it should be*
light. Still when it should be active. According to these
instruments, Gallifrey . . . It's dead. An unpopulated
heap of rubble . . . [13]

SYNOPSIS BY JOHNNY BYRNE

They arrive on Gallifrey and discover that it is in ruins. The
ruling Council of the Time Lords destroyed all their time
ships to prevent Varnax from taking control of time.[14] In
doing so, they also destroyed their world. It explains why the
TARDIS blew up on Earth. It also explains why Varnax tried
so hard to get the restored TARDIS – it is the last timeship in
existence. Without it Varnax cannot complete his crazed
purpose.

The Doctor sets out in a vengeful state of mind to find
Varnax. They travel to the outlaw world of Raqetz.[15] Their
search takes them to the glitzy, vice-ridden casino of
MOTHER CAJAJE, an obese, organ-playing alien female.
She is an old enemy of the Doctor, but he manages to con the
information he wants out of her. In revenge, she alerts Varnax
to the Doctor's presence on Raqetz.

GONJII attaches himself to them at the casino. He guides
them across the bewildering landscape on Raqetz and they
locate Varnax's HQ. Here Varnax has set a trap for the
Doctor, but the timely intervention of an exiled Gallifreyan
commando group – of which Gonjii is one – foils it.[16]

They find refuge with the Gallifreyans. Their leader is
ZILLA, a beautiful woman who was once the Doctor's
lover.[17] We discover that they, too, have been hunting Varnax, whose malign power is based on selling the results of
his horrific genetic experiments. These shadowy activities
are the means to achieve Varnax's long-planned end result
which now hinges on gaining control of the Doctor and the
TARDIS.

Gonjii displays a keen interest in Lotte, but her feelings are
still fixated on the Doctor, feelings which have been in
turmoil since the Doctor and Zilla met up. Lotte burns with
resentment at the easy, intimate relationship the Doctor and
Zilla share. She feels excluded, rejected and insecure. She

takes it out on Gonjii, but especially on Zilla whom she perceives as a deadly threat. Zilla's courage, dedication and the high esteem in which she is held by the Doctor and the other Gallifreyans means nothing to Lotte. Her emotions have reached critical mass where the Doctor is concerned.

Zilla comes to understand what drives Lotte. She confronts the Doctor and it emerges that he is on the brink of giving into his feelings for Lotte.[18] Before Gallifrey was destroyed his oath meant something. But Gallifrey is gone and with it everything else that it represented. He has come to feel that there's little purpose in denying happiness to himself and Lotte. Zilla understands and sympathises deeply with the Doctor's plight, but she passionately believes he is wrong. The Doctor is the last of the Gallifreyan Time Lords, a potent symbol of what Gallifrey had once been, what it could become again. He has no choice but to look beyond his individual needs. He is the only surviving symbol of hope for their scattered race and ruined world.[19]

The Doctor and the Gallifreyans attempt to infiltrate the TARDIS into Varnax's fortress HQ. The plan goes wrong and results in the TARDIS and Varnax's concealed, disabled timeship combining in a time-space warp. The collision fractures temporal reality. Time, dimension, history are sliced like a salami and now crazily co-exist, sandwiched inside the distorted dimensions of the combined ships, distortions that are also fraught with mind-bending perils. Ticking away in the background, the fracture in time works to correct itself. Every so often, an elemental spasm warps the weirdly joined structures, altering them into ever new surreal combinations. The Doctor knows that the fault will correct itself, and when it does anything and anyone not somewhere else will be annihilated.

This is the setting for the final lap of the drama. Under the pressure of events Lotte discovers the truth of the Doctor's feelings for her and the sacrifice he has made on behalf of his people. The knowledge has a transforming effect on her. All that matters – all that has ever really mattered – is that he loves her. Secure in that, how it expresses itself is not important. It is Zilla, the woman she feared and resented, who helps her through this crisis – Zilla who later dies, sacrificing herself so that the Doctor may live on to help their people.

Varnax captures the Doctor and we discover the nature of his grand design. A vile travesty of the once handsome man he was, he intends to use the Doctor's life force to restore himself to prime physical condition. In doing so he will also become immortal, and with the TARDIS under his control he will be free to seed all Creation with his genetically altered beings – a master race bearing the Mark of Varnax that will reflect his own evil concept of perfection.

Varnax is on the brink of succeeding when Lotte makes a shattering discovery. Her father, the man whose image she has carried in a locket all her life, and whose memory she reveres, is Varnax. Lotte is the result of Varnax combining his own Gallifreyan genetic material with that of a woman from Earth – a woman who spirited the infant Lotte out of Varnax's clutches.

Lotte discovers this when Varnax is at his most vulnerable. She is confronted with a choice. If the Doctor lives, Varnax, her father, will die an unspeakable death. Lotte chooses to destroy Varnax, a traumatic act that kills what's left of the child in her. [20]

Later, in safety, with Varnax and all his works consigned to oblivion, Lotte ponders the new circumstances of her life. Since she is half Gallifreyan, no barriers now stand between herself and the Doctor. But the emotional parameters of her life seem to have changed. She feels strangely secure in what she and the Doctor have come to share. Besides, the Doctor is going to be a very busy Time Lord. He intends to devote himself to the reconstruction of Gallifrey, [19] a task in which she will also share.

But she has much to learn about the Gallifreyan part of her heritage, and Gonjii wants to help. She remembers how brave he showed himself to be in their struggle with Varnax. What she has not been aware of until now is how very good-looking Gonjii is . . .

110

Notes

1 The Sonix device returns, carried over from *The Time Lord*.

2 Byrne justified the choice of the 1930s because this was when the police box model first hit the streets. 'The '30s was a period of interesting visual contrasts – Art Deco elegance, overcrowded slums, privileged life styles, the ocean of dole-less unemployed . . . Circumstances that nourished the evil of Hitler, and which, in our terms, could conceivably nourish the evil of Varnax.'

3 Hadley in one version.

4 Byrne introduced his version of the Matrix in *The Time Lord*, Version 2. The fact that it is linked to all TARDISes is an interesting concept, one first hinted at in *The Trial of a Time Lord* (7A–7C), where it was shown that the Matrix could record events happening within range of a TARDIS. The notion of a physical link between Gallifrey and the TARDISes eventually evolved into the idea that TARDISes derived their power from the Eye of Harmony (cf. *Fathers and Brothers*, *The Time of My Life*) and, ultimately, that they each carried an Eye of Harmony. Of course, the original BBC television series long established that the Time Lords (or at least the CIA) could remote-control the TARDIS from Gallifrey.

5 In this version, the Doctor's tormentors are no longer replicas of Varnax, Neglos and Zilla, but genetically enhanced servants, a notion which has also replaced the concept of the 'Sleepers'.

6 Varnax's motives remain a combination of becoming the genetic overlord of the universe while restoring his body to its original state and acquiring true immortality in the process.

7 The notion that Varnax is, secretly, Lotte's father has now been incorporated into the plot.

8 Varnax's evil grasp is now seen reaching Earth. Coincidentally, Peter Litten and George Dugdale toyed with the notion of involving the Doctor with Hitler and the rise of fascism in America in the 1930s in their next version, *Chameleon*.

9 An interesting hint that present-day Gallifrey lies in Earth's future, once again previously suggested by *The Trial of a Time Lord* (7A–7C), where contemporary Gallifreyan events (the Trial itself and the relocation of Earth) were stated to happen two million years in Earth's future.

10 More than in any other incarnation this Doctor is shown to have a grim edge of ruthlessness. He shows no hesitation in killing James in cold blood, even though the latter may not be human. One is naturally free to attribute this to the radical brainwashing experienced by the Doctor earlier.

11 This depiction of a more grandiose TARDIS interior anticipates the later, more lavish designs which will eventually take form in *Enemy Within*.

12 Pog makes a startling cameo in this version, but in a modified shape and with radically different origins.

13 This is where Byrne's script ends (script page 75).

14 In this version, it is revealed that Varnax did not physically assault Gallifrey with an army of Mordread (as in Version 1) but tried to take over the Matrix.

15 Note the change in spelling again. Varnax is now headquartered on Raqetz.

16 Gonjii is still a member of the Gallifreyan Time Rangers, but he remains the brash young fighter (not the wizened old warrior) seen in the previous version.

17 Zilla, here, is still a Gallifreyan, and the Doctor's former lover, but she no longer serves Varnax.

18 Unlike the father–daughter relationship outlined in the previous version, the Doctor and Lotte share here a mutual sexual attraction, later validated by the discovery that Lotte is half-Time Lord. The two triangles, Doctor–Lotte–Zilla and/or Doctor–Lotte–Gonjii, would give the script a unique perspective.

19 Byrne indicated in a memo that he saw this plot element as a means to launch a series of *Doctor Who* films based on the Doctor's efforts to restore the glories of Gallifrey.

20 Zilla sacrifices herself to save the Doctor's life. It is likely that most of the 'beats' in this part of the story would have followed the previous version, with the exception of Lotte's fate.

VERSION THREE: *Chameleon*

Story (Synopsis by Johnny Byrne)

Someone hatches a plot to destroy the DOCTOR. Later he will discover that it is one of the powerful elite that rule his home world of Gallifrey, a Time Lord like himself.[1] Time is the weapon used against him. The Doctor's past is manipulated with the skill of a master surgeon, with vital connectors severed and cut adrift. The effect is to shunt the Doctor's life span into a temporal dead-end alley, one that will cause his body and mind to self-destruct in a very short period of time.

Planted evidence convinces the other Time Lords that the Doctor has illegally meddled with the sensitive mechanisms of time, a major crime. He's tried and imprisoned,[2] but the Doctor, elderly, quirky, eccentric, proves far from finished. He escapes and time travels to present-day New York.

There he believes he will be correctly positioned to reintegrate the missing elements into his past, which, like Humpty Dumpty, must be put back together again if he is to survive. It's a delicate, highly complex operation and the outcome is unpredictable. Nor are the Doctor's mental powers at their best – he is already beginning to feel the effects of what's been done to him. The operation goes disastrously wrong and almost terminally damages his timeship, the TARDIS.

Something else happens. In delving into time the Doctor accidentally conjures up a man from the past. The new arrival is a real, living Gallifreyan, young, good-looking, intelligent and the Doctor knows him – it is, in fact, himself, the Doctor's YOUNGER SELF.[3]

Young Doctor is real, a distinct and separate individual from Old Doctor. But circumstance has now linked them together more securely than handcuffs, because their survival is linked. If Young Doctor dies, Old Doctor's present existence will be snuffed out as though it's never been. If Old Doctor dies, the damaged and very tenuous links to his past will disintegrate and Young Doctor will not have existed, which makes it easier for their enemy to destroy them and someone is trying to do just that.

After Old Doctor's escape from Gallifrey, CHAMELEON[4] has been contracted to hunt him down and destroy him. Chameleon has only to kill one of the Doctors to destroy both, and Chameleon is an expert at killing. He is a time-travelling assassin, a sinister alien who can merge at will into local background. He is ruthless, resourceful, highly intelligent and possesses unimaginably lethal skills.

Old Doctor and his living, breathing, independently minded own youthful self are forced to work together for their mutual survival. It's not an easy situation for either of them. Old Doctor is far from thrilled at having to confront and live with himself as he was in his dimly remembered past, and Young Doctor finds a permanent reminder of what he will become later in life less than enthralling.

Mutually dependent they may be, mutually compatible they are not. Young Doctor is at an age where he *thinks* all old men are fools. Old Doctor is old enough to *know* that all young men are fools. If Old Doctor has forgotten what it is like to be young, his younger self cannot conceive of what it is like to be old. What Young Doctor sees as passion in himself he conceives as vice in his older self.

It seems, as Shakespeare says, that 'crabbed age and youth cannot live together'. At times Old Doctor believes that he has spent the first half of his life simply to make the second half miserable. If he thinks that youth is wasted on the young, Young Doctor feels equally strongly that it is better to waste it than (in the person of Old Doctor) to do nothing with it.

Early on they join up with MALLIE JORDAN.[5] Mallie is beautiful, about the same age as Young Doctor, and her well organised existence is turned upside down by the eruption into her life of the two Doctors. Her relationship with the Doctors is fraught with problems, especially after she discovers that, though they look and act differently, they are really one and the same person.

She may have a weakness for Young Doctor's body, but time and again she finds herself bowled over by the sheer vaulting brilliance of Old Doctor's mind. But he can spoil it by displaying the sheer cussedness and irritating certainties of age. And while she goes for the idealism and generosity of Young Doctor, his lack of understanding of people in general, and women in particular, can get her steamed up.

Her big problem is to reconcile how she feels about loving two men, one old, one young, both in reality the same man, but only one of whom she wants to make love to.

Having finally destroyed Chameleon and restored the TARDIS, the two Doctors travel back to Gallifrey, where their Time Lord enemy is unmasked and routed. The time comes for the Doctor's past to be finally corrected, a process that will reintegrate both of them into their correct time-streams. It will also recombine the two into a single individual, one with the past of one and the future of the other.

Old and Young Doctor make their final goodbye. Much has happened in their time together. Both have been changed by what they shared and learned from each other, and from knowing Mallie, who was left behind on Earth.

Old Doctor has a poignant awareness that age, despite all it has brought in status, knowledge and wisdom, still loses out in comparison to youth. And for Young Doctor there is the regard and pride he has come to feel for his brilliant, quirky older counterpart. He has the wisdom to understand that what he likes about Old Doctor is really what he has come to know and like about himself.

On Earth Mallie has struggled to pick up the pieces of the life she had before the intrusion of the two Doctors. But try as hard as she can, she knows that things will never be the same for her again.

One day she returns to a place in the park where she and the two Doctors had spent a particularly happy few hours on the day when she discovered she was in love with Young Doctor. A man is waiting for her when she gets there. He's neither young nor old and, since he didn't know where she lived or worked, he's waited here for her to turn up. Even though she has never seen him before, she instantly knows that it is the Doctor.

Notes

1 Probably Varnax, motives unknown . . .
2 One notes the reappearance of the Doctor-tried-and-exiled theme.
3 The 'Two Doctors' concept was totally new, launching the story in a radically different direction. At one point the notion of incorporating Hitler and the rise of fascism was put forward by Peter Litten and George Dugdale.
4 No obvious relation to Kamelion, the Xeraphin shape-changing android from *The King's Demons* (6J).
5 A new companion for a new Doctor, with a clearly delineated romantic sub-plot.

Review

Leaving 'Chameleon' aside, for obvious reasons, *Last of the Time Lords* is based on two remarkable premises. The destruction of Gallifrey provides the Doctor with a set of unique motivations and background. His temporary amnesia is a near-perfect way of introducing the character, peeling away the mystery that surrounds him one layer at a time. This is probably one of the most successful reintroductions of the character.

Dramatically, the script reads like a stylish suspense action thriller, with a real emotional bite thanks to the various interplays between the Doctor, Lotte, Zilla and Gonjii. As with *The Time Lord*, Byrne was the first to tackle head-on the concepts of the Doctor's romantic life and Gallifreyan-Human unions.

Byrne's Doctor is also the prey of superhuman emotions, never revealed in the original BBC television series. His crucifixion in the asylum eerily anticipates *Enemy Within*. He is fully capable of killing James Radley in cold blood, and the fiery anger directed at Varnax is not faked. On the other hand, he is capable of great love and immense nobility. This is, truly, a Time Lord.

Had *Last of the Time Lords* been produced, there is little doubt that it would have changed the course and the perception of *Doctor Who*.

Background

By late 1991 Litten and Dugdale had taken a break from *Doctor Who* to make a low-budget horror feature entitled *Living Doll*. Byrne wrote a feature film, *Brothers of Siam*, about the original nineteenth-century Siamese twins – still unproduced to date. The original Daltenreys partners, who had already negotiated various term extensions with BBC Enterprises, agreed to a final extension, now committing themselves to begin filming a *Doctor Who* movie by 6 April, 1994 or have all rights revert to BBC Enterprises, and thus see all their efforts turn out to have been in vain.

During the intervening years BBC Enterprises, and indeed the whole BBC, underwent various changes in policy as well as personnel. The original *Doctor Who* television series had been definitively cancelled in 1989, yet the new management was under political and financial pressure to exploit the BBC's 'assets'. Well aware of the money made by *Doctor Who*, BBC Enterprises was keen on finding new ways to exploit its franchise, even attempting to produce its own direct-to-video feature, *The Dark Dimension* (see Chapter 5). When approached by Philip Segal – a former executive of the American ABC television network and, at the time, an executive at Amblin Television, Steven Spielberg's production entity and a major force to be reckoned with in Hollywood – BBC Enterprises immediately saw the possibility of resurrecting their television franchise at little risk to themselves, since most of the production costs would be covered by the American licence fee (see Chapter 6).

Meanwhile, in 1992, Litten, Dugdale and Arden had come up with a shining white knight. Having failed to attract a major Hollywood studio, they nevertheless succeeded in securing a co-production agreement. This meant reselling the rights that they themselves had acquired from BBC

Enterprises to Lumière Pictures, a French production company with various interests in Britain. Lumière saw the potential for turning *Doctor Who* into another *Star Trek*-like franchise of successful, big-budget pictures, and had the means to spend the necessary money to hire the required Hollywood 'big names' to enable them to attract a major studio's interest.

One of Lumière's first decisions was to abandon Byrne's *Last of the Time Lords* and instead seek an established Hollywood writer, one connected with the type of movie they were trying to sell. They approached Nicholas Meyer, writer of *Star Trek* II, IV and VI, but eventually ended up with Meyer's writing partner, Denny Martin Flinn.

Interview with Johnny Byrne

Question: Your Doctor Who *script(s) were the first ever to attempt to flesh out the Doctor's past. What was the thinking behind this?*

Johnny Byrne: It flowed from the inherited notion of the Doctor and Varnax being close friends in their earlier, even pre-Time Lord, years. The same applied to Zilla and her various incarnations. Looking at the more symbolic aspects of the relationship, the Doctor and Varnax seemed to represent the duality inherent in *Doctor Who*. Here we saw Good and Evil, Light and Dark, Young and Old, Beauty and Ugliness and so on – a relationship that mirrors the quintessential Manichean order of the *Doctor Who* universe.

Q: You were also the first to introduce mature/adult romantic concepts (Doctor/Zilla, Doctor/Lotte) in Doctor Who, *contrary to the original BBC television series tradition. Again, what was the underlying thought?*

JB: I felt that, to be successful as a high-budget movie, *Doctor Who* had to expand its appeal beyond the perimeters established in the TV show. I stress expand, not cut loose from the universal elements of the show. While some of the set-ups may have inclined too much towards the *Indiana Jones*, I never felt that I had abandoned the Doctor and the universe we all knew and loved so well. In fact, I thought I added to our knowledge and to the show's basic appeal. I should also say that including the Gonjii character (and the early various incarnations) was meant to serve the same function. In Gonjii's case, as an adult and the Doctor's close friend and colleague, I felt we could learn more about the Doctor through a character of this type than we could by the traditional arrangement of having a teenage companion(s) around. I also liked the creation of the Time Battalion – something I hoped to develop in the second movie.

Q: How would you have envisioned the other two Doctor Who *films – since up to three films were planned at one time?*

JB: Depends on which one first appeared. In the earlier versions, more of the same, only bigger and better. In the second phase, a story concerning a time quest to recover and restore lethal and very forbidden knowledge to Gallifrey. And a story which saw the tremendous achievements and triumphs of Gallifrey restored. This one would have been rooted in time conundrums, action (with the Time Battalion), and would have been heavy on feelings.

Q: Which version/elements do you, personally, prefer, or would you have most liked to have seen shot?

JB: If the earlier version had hit the screen in the late 1980s, fine. But since it missed the boat, I very strongly feel that *Last of the Time Lords*, revised, lightened up and so on, would have been my version of choice for the '90s. It would have been very stylish, very strong on thrills, chills and suspense, with less of the mega-big bangs.

Q: In Last of the Time Lords, *the Doctor cold-bloodedly kills his friend James, after it is revealed that he is one of Varnax's pawns, and generally behaves in a rather grim manner throughout. Why this departure from the more traditional view of the character, i.e. Tom Bakerish?*

JB: In reality the Doctor kills something that resembles his friend. Also bear in mind that the Doctor here is not quite sure who or what he is. Discovering his super-civilised Gallifreyan humanity is still some way off. Meanwhile, he's frightened, vulnerable, and desperately fighting to hold it all together. As I said above, the script would have later

119

lightened up considerably along the lines of the Doctor in the earlier versions – mordant, funny, strange and witty, with a sharp edge. As for the Doctor killing people, I mostly kept clear of this – in one version of the story, I had the Doctor displaying phenomenal unarmed powers in his various battles with Neglos.

Q: Would you say that Last of the Time Lords, *unlike its predecessors, was still creatively based on a story by Peter Litten and George Dugdale, or was it, by this stage, mostly yours – from a creative standpoint?*

JB: By this stage it was totally mine – apart from some of the ongoing names (also mostly mine). In fact, since I largely did it on spec and it was not covered by any deal, it's still all mine!

Q: Were you purposefully inspired by any other movies or books in your handling of the various stories?

JB: Not knowingly, but the genre model in the early days – especially when it was slated for a big budget – was along the *Indiana Jones* lines. I still feel that the concept, funny, thrilling, even outrageous, would have worked then.

Q: Who was Felice Arden?

JB: Peter and George met Felice in New York when she was editor (I think) of *MS* magazine. Her background was business and editorial journalism. She liked the boys and came over to England to join them on the *Doctor Who* saga. Felice was good to work with, and very bright and energetic. I liked and respected her very much. She stayed right until the end. It was Felice who set up the deals with Lumière and Leonard Nimoy. During a hiatus I wrote for her and the others *Brothers of Siam*, a spectacular movie based on the lives of the original and amazing Siamese twins, Chang and Eng. I have two posters: one *Doctor Who – The Last Time Lord* and the other *Brothers of Siam*, which Greenlight's movie market people used to drum up business at Cannes. As far as I know the *Doctor Who* poster is the only one produced. Also Peter has (at least he did) a huge amount of artwork and designs.

Q: How would you sum up your collaboration on this project, and what (if anything) did you get out of it?

JB: Fascinating, maddening, and a long exercise in the art of not knowing when to quit – one of my very Irish faults! The most amazing thing is that I'm still friends with all the people concerned. Since then I wrote a very low-budget, with fees going to charity, gay romance story for Peter, which subsequently was chosen to open the 1995 Los Angeles Gay and Lesbian Film Festival, and was seriously complimented by a large review in *Variety*. I did it because a very nice young gay HIV-positive man who worked with us on the *Doctor Who* movie died of AIDS in the most terrible way. As I said, most of the proceeds went to AIDS charities. It cost less to make than Tom Hanks's cab fares on *Philadelphia*!

4

THE JEWELS OF TIME

by

Denny Martin Flinn

Background

In February 1994 Randy and I were invited to be guests at the Gallifrey Convention, organised by Los Angeles-based fan group, The Time Meddlers. We easily convinced the organisers, the wonderfully supportive J. Shaun Lyon and the dedicated Robbie Cantor, to invite Terrance Dicks and Barry Letts as well. Terrance had not attended a *Doctor Who* convention in Los Angeles since 1980, and Barry had never been to southern California at all.

Since this was only a month after the terrible Los Angeles earthquake there was a certain amount of trepidation on the part of all concerned. But in the end to claim that a good time was had by all would be an enormous understatement, as this was truly one of the most pleasant conventions we ever attended.

Two events happened that weekend which reconnected me with the world of *Doctor Who* in ways which I would never have anticipated.

The first was that, unbeknownst to Terrance, Barry, the convention organisers and ourselves, Philip Segal, the executive producer, and Peter Wagg, the then-producer, of what would eventually become *Enemy Within*, were anonymously in attendance. (More about this in Chapter 6.)

The second event was even more fortuitous and complicated. For many years, Randy and I have been friends with Kirk Thatcher, a talented writer and artist, whose credits include the visual conceptualisation of the Henson/Disney television series, *Dinosaurs*, and writing/producing the new Muppet show, *Muppets Tonight*. (Kirk and Randy have co-written an as-yet unproduced feature script based on Moebius's famous comic hero, *Arzach*.) Prior to working for Henson, Kirk was Associate Producer on *Star Trek IV: The Voyage Home* (1986), directed by Leonard Nimoy, in which he also played the punk rocker on the bus whom Spock silences with his famous Vulcan neck pinch.

By this point you might be inclined to ask, how does all this relate to *Doctor Who*? Simple. Kirk has remained good friends with Leonard Nimoy and Kirk also knew of my past involvement with *Doctor Who*, and there the connection was made.

A few months earlier Nimoy had been approached by Lumière Pictures to helm their intended major motion picture production of *Doctor Who* (see Chapter 3). An entirely new script had by then been written by Denny Martin Flinn, who had co-scripted (with director Nicholas Meyer) *Star Trek VI: The Undiscovered Country* (1991), and had eventually suggested Nimoy as a possible director. Nimoy had liked Flinn's script well enough to agree to direct and produce the planned feature. With Nimoy in charge, Lumière knew that their chances of attracting a major Hollywood studio were very good.

It was during one of Kirk and Nimoy's regular conversations that the subject of *Doctor Who* was casually mentioned, as in, 'what are you working on these days?' Upon being told that the director was contemplating bringing the famous Time Lord to the big screen, Kirk brought up my name, which Nimoy recognised through having researched the show with *The Doctor Who Programme Guide* and *The Universal Databank*.

Thus it came to pass that, while Randy and I were showing Terrance and Barry the sights of Los Angeles, we received a telephone call from Leonard Nimoy's office, asking us if we would be available to come and meet with the director. When we told Nimoy that Terrance and Barry were in town for a few days he was overjoyed, and a hurried breakfast meeting was arranged for the next morning.

Leonard Nimoy is a very pleasant, courteous, soft-spoken and generous man, who had already invested a great deal of time in researching *Doctor Who*. He had accumulated a fairly extensive collection of videotapes, covering all seven incarnations of the Doctor. We spent a fruitful couple of hours discussing the very basis of the show – what makes *Doctor Who Doctor Who* – as well as the psychology of its hero, companions, and various off-the-wall casting ideas. (To debunk a rumour, at no time did Nimoy contemplate playing the part of the Doctor himself, Pierce Brosnan being then the actor intended for the role.) Nimoy cleverly picked Terrance and Barry's brains for information about the making of the original BBC television series, in both creative and technical terms.

We stayed in loose contact with Nimoy after that meeting. But meanwhile, in England, BBC Enterprises was facing a dilemma of its own making: could two separate *Doctor Who* franchises cohabit peacefully, one on the movie screen – the Daltenreys/ Coast to Coast/Greenlight/Lumière production – the other on the television screen – the BBC Enterprises/Amblin Television/Universal Television production (see Chapter 6)? The answer would ultimately, and not unreasonably, be no.

As explained in Chapter 3, the producers had to begin filming by 6 April 1994 or else all rights would revert to the BBC. In his interview (see below), Flinn explains how certain contingency plans were made to start filming a scene with the Doctor in an earlier incarnation. (Brosnan would likely not have been available for a single scene on a short schedule.) Yet ultimately the filming of that scene, which technically may have been enough to grant the producers the legal extension of their contract, was not done.

Why such a move was not initiated is still the subject of some argument. Whatever the reasons, Lumière saw the writing on the wall and chose to withdraw. On 6 April 1994 the theatrical rights to *Doctor Who* reverted to the BBC and Leonard Nimoy's involvement with the project came to a rather abrupt end.

What remains of this incarnation of the Doctor is Denny Martin Flinn's script. Even though the script was officially entitled only *Doctor Who – The Movie*, the more distinctive title *The Jewels of Time* was fully endorsed by Flinn.

'Of Treks in Time': Introduction by Denny Martin Flinn

Shortly after I had written *Star Trek VI: The Undiscovered Country* and sometime before I wrote *Star Trek #74: The Fearful Summons* (the first a feature film, the second a novel) writer/director Nicholas Meyer – he of the even-numbered

Star Trek films as well as the inventor of the post-Conan Doyle Sherlock Holmes novels – got a call to write a feature film based on the hugely popular BBC series *Doctor Who*. Wanting to take a break from science fiction, he turned it down but recommended me. Truth be told, I had no idea Who the Doctor was. (I had only slightly more knowledge of *Star Trek* when I got that assignment.) But research is the most fun part of writing. Given an opportunity to write a modern action picture or the story of Charlemagne's third mistress, I'd much prefer the latter, for one gets paid to read up on the most exotic back alleys of history.

So it was that I came upon Jean-Marc Lofficier's wonderful books on the Whoniverse. With little time to screen each and every episode (preferably in order) that had been created in the 30 years since the introduction of the great Doctor – every producer spends months deciding upon a writer, and then wants a first draft 'as soon as possible' – I acquainted myself with a few of the most popular, rentable, adventures on videotape, but with the entire canon through his books.

And what a great acquaintance it was. Having been limited to specific star dates while working on *Star Trek*, I was ecstatic to discover that *Doctor Who* could travel everywhere and anywhere, not only throughout the cosmos, but back and forth in time as well. The Doctor was not saddled to an environment in which anything could be replicated and 'all problems were solved' (as Gene Roddenberry once described to me his idea of the future), a concept which severely handicaps the writer's search for the conflict that forms the foundation of drama. On the contrary, *Doctor Who*'s many galaxies were as topsy-turvy as a *commedia dell'arte* performance. So many interesting aliens, so many dark and dangerous culs-de-sac. Surely if there is any avenue down which a writer can search for a lightning bolt to strike his imagination, it's a time corridor!

I set about thinking about all those places I had always wanted to visit. Shakespeare's England? A future planet? The Impressionists' Paris? King Arthur's Court? But which one? And then it hit me. On Nick's advice ('Never worry about the budget, that's the producer's job'), I decided not to restrict myself to one particular time or place, but to write a story that travelled hither and yon with a speed only the TARDIS could provide. Then I decided that time itself had to be in jeopardy, for what could be more climactic than saving the highway upon which all civilisations travel. Once I stumbled upon the 'Key to Time' in a past episode, I was on my way.

Shortly after I had written the first draft, Tim Van Rellim, a talented line producer, and I had breakfast with the producer of the film. We urged that offers go out to director Leonard Nimoy, with whom I had been much impressed, not only by my own experience in the *Star Trek* world but by his dramatic film *The Good Mother* (1988), and to actor Pierce Brosnan, with whom we had both worked and who we felt was ripe for the role. (This long before we were proved to be correct, considering his later success as James Bond.) Leonard, I heard through the grapevine, liked the script. Alas, in one of those many contractual circumstances that influence the art of film far more than Eisenstein and Welles ever did, the producer lost the rights just as we were ready to go.

Thanks to the diligent scholarship of Jean-Marc, however, you can now imagine, as I once was privileged to do, another *Doctor Who* adventure, a film that never was, that didn't star Pierce Brosnan. A film that had the boring, working title of 'A *Doctor Who* Film' until Jean-Marc dubbed it *The Jewels of Time*.

Story

The script opens with a quote from *The Five Doctors* (6K), 'A cosmos without the Doctor scarcely bears thinking about.'

The film fades in on the Death Zone on Gallifrey. A middle-eastern man (RACHMED) is making his way through the Death Zone in a blinding dust storm and howling winds. Red laser rays from above strike the ground near him, but he manages to avoid them. He encounters a rock-like beast and 'evil-looking snakes, some with two heads, with tusk-like fangs'.

Finally, he reaches a 'giant, craggy, stone edifice'. It is the Dark Tower, the Tomb of Rassilon.

Inside, he moves cautiously and succeeds in avoiding several death traps, a corridor with ground that turns to quicksand and an invisible electric grid, until he finally reaches the Tomb itself. In its centre is a great stone coffin bearing a carved relief of Rassilon. The image of the body has a great ring on the finger of one of its hands. The thief touches it greedily before attempting to lift the lid off the sarcophagus.

Slowly the dark exterior is exposed – 'a cold light emanates from within, bathing him [the thief]. He is horrified. He takes on a look of great pain. His mouth opens slightly, but can't form the cry. He staggers back. But at once his movements are slowed, then stopped. He whimpers. His skin and clothes turn grey. Within a few seconds he has been turned completely to stone, his eyes wide, his face a frozen mask of horror.'[1]

We then cut to Bread Street, in England in 1593, at the 'Sign of the Mermaid' tavern, a rowdy, bohemian establishment. A handsome young nobleman (the DOCTOR)[2] enters and spots a table of young men engaged in passionate conversation. They are SHAKESPEARE, BEAUMONT, FLETCHER, GREENE and MARLOWE, and they are arguing about whether the public liked *Romeo and Juliet*.[3] The conversation soon turns to the reasons for writing. Fletcher categorically states that he writes for posterity, while a young Shakespeare says that he is writing to earn a living.

At that point, the Doctor butts into the conversation to tell the Bard that his play was a masterpiece. He goes on to deliver a rave review, one that makes reference to other Romeos and other Juliets, and women playing the part on stage, comments which pique Fletcher's and Marlowe's curiosity. The Doctor ends with an assertive declaration.

Doctor *Will here is writing for posterity. His writing will make him . . . immortal.*

Marlowe and Fletcher start questioning this stranger who seems to know so much about the future, when suddenly an evil-looking, black-clad, trimly bearded man (the MASTER, a.k.a. the MANDRAKE)[4] passes behind their table and purposefully knocks into Shakespeare, causing him to spill his drink. An argument starts, which soon evolves into the Master challenging Shakespeare to a duel.

Marlowe steps in and offers to duel the Master instead. By now, the whole tavern is shouting. Everyone is on their feet, forming a circle. The Doctor tries to change Marlowe's mind.

Doctor *Don't do this. You are a writer, not a soldier.*
Marlowe *My honour is at stake.*
Doctor *Your life is at stake.*
Marlowe *My honour, stranger, is my life.*

The duel is furious and deadly. The Master is an excellent swordsman, relentless. Additionally, he fights dirty. At one point he sneakily pulls a stiletto out of his boot and stabs Marlowe, who falls dead into Shakespeare's arms.[5]

The Master then attacks the young playwright, who is hopelessly outclassed. As the villain is about to plunge his blade into Shakespeare's throat, the Doctor's sword flashes out of nowhere and disarms him.

Doctor *I think that's enough for tonight.*
Master *My quarrel is with this man, not with you –*
Doctor *Your quarrel is with all mankind, I think.*

After a brief standoff, the Master leaves, stating that he won't forget the slight.[6] Shakespeare profusely thanks the Doctor, who advises him to be more cautious with his words in the future.

Shakespeare *Well advised, sir. I am William Shake-*
speare. What are you called?
Doctor (he turns and heads for the door) *The Doctor.*
Shakespeare (shouting after him) *Doctor? Doctor*
Who?

The Doctor then walks to his TARDIS – which is in the shape of the traditional blue London police box[7] – and vanishes while MAIN TITLES play.

The inside of the TARDIS is described as combining 'the most futuristic materials with mechanical and deco designs'. A Study Room: 'combines the Victorian penchant for comfort and collections with a futuristic design. It is laden with artifacts from many times and places throughout the universe.'[8] The Doctor enters, hangs up his cloak ('leaving him more Victorian than Elizabethan'), makes a chess move on a board, then records an entry in his diary.

He then turns towards K-9[9] and starts discussing their next destination when, suddenly, a bell tolls. A message from the Celestial Intervention Agency[10] – in the form of a ticker tape – orders him to return to Gallifrey at once, setting a meeting at the Tomb of Rassilon. The Doctor briefly ponders whether to obey or not, but finally decides to give in.

Doctor . . . *The Agency can cause us a lot of trouble . . . And perhaps we could repair our chameleon circuit while we're there . . .*[11]

We then cut to the Tomb of Rassilon. Several Time Lords ('humanoid, patrician') and CIA Agents ('working class') stand around the petrified man when the Doctor arrives.

At first the Doctor thinks that they are accusing him of having interfered with history by saving Shakespeare's life and he mounts a passionate defence, without leaving the time for the CIA Agents to explain that this is not at all why they summoned him. But they manage to steer him towards the petrified man, the sight of which stops the Doctor's ramblings.

Doctor *Good lord, that's ugly. Redecorating?*

The Time Lords explain that the man was turned to stone while trying to steal Rassilon's Ring of Immortality.[12]

While the Doctor examines the 'statue' of Rachmed, the camera angles on the shadows at the far end of the room and reveals the Master, watching surreptitiously.

The Doctor completes his study. The Time Lords are eager to find out what he has discovered.

131

Doctor *He is not from this planet. He is not from this solar system. He is not from this galaxy.*

Time Lord *Where is he from?*

Doctor (smiles) *A long time ago and a galaxy far far away.* [13]

The answer is Ancient Egypt, Earth, late third century BC, around the time of King Cheops.[14] The Time Lords are unfamiliar with the planet.[15]

Doctor *It's a heavily populated but under-developed planet in the Sol system, Milky Way galaxy.*

Time Lord *Do they travel?*

Doctor *They commute long distances to work. They like to spend their vacations in enormous cars with refrigerators and televisions and every—*

Time Lord *I mean, do they travel in space? In time?*

Doctor *This civilisation did not. By their twenty-third century they wandered a few parsecs from their own galaxy, but that's all. And they never understood the space/time vortex at all.* [16]

The Doctor senses something and turns to the shadows, but the Master is gone. Meanwhile the Time Lords wonder how an Ancient Egyptian managed to get to Gallifrey. The Doctor agrees to investigate.

We then cut to Ancient Egypt, circa 1800 BC. After much excavating, three GRAVE ROBBERS manage to force their way into the Great Pyramid of Cheops. They eventually locate the King's Chamber, filled with a mountain of gold and jewels. While his men are filling their sacks, the ring-leader comes across a unique jewel: 'it's an odd, unidentifiable shape, pulsing with a gold light from within.'

Suddenly there is a wind which blows out the thieves' candles. When they again strike a light, they discover they are no longer alone. The Master is now with them. He grabs the ringleader by the throat. 'A sparkle of electricity, as well as great strength, runs down his [the Master's] arm and through his hand.' [17] Before dying, the thief manages to grab and tear a metal button off the Master's coat.

The Master keeps the other two thieves away with his electric bolts, then grabs the Gold Jewel from the dead man's hand. He then leaves, sealing the thieves behind a stone wall, condemning them to death by suffocation.

We cut to the cockpit of a 1937 Lockheed Electra as it flies over the Pacific. The skies are clear and blue, with fluffy, white clouds. Simultaneously we see the hands of the Master placing the Gold Jewel on a gothic oak table. Suddenly, the clouds turn black and a storm erupts. On the plane's instrument panel, the dials all go wild.

We cut to the TARDIS control room, which has begun to tilt. Much to the Doctor's and K-9's surprise, they have unexpectedly dropped out of the timestream. On the scanner the Doctor notices the Lockheed being buffeted by the storm. He realises the pilot is not going to make it unless he intervenes, but they have to re-enter the Space-Time Vortex or they, too, will be in trouble. The Doctor comes up with a clever plan.

> **Doctor** *If we dematerialise the TARDIS, then rematerialise around the co-ordinates of that flying device, we could bring it aboard by opening the Zero Room in the same time frame . . .* [18]

After the intricate manoeuvre is executed the Doctor rushes to the Zero Room, where he and K-9 help put out the engine fire which now engulfs the plane. The pilot steps out. It is a young American woman, wearing aviator clothes, goggles and a long white scarf. She is AMELIA EARHARDT, except that she is introduced only as AMY at this point in the script. [19]

The Doctor explains to an incredulous Amy that she is aboard the TARDIS, and what the TARDIS really is [20] – a concept that she has difficulty grasping at first, even though she has read Jules Verne's *From the Earth to the Moon*. But she eventually comes to accept her situation.

> **Amy** *So you're from outer space, then? Is that right?*
> **Doctor** *I'm a Time Lord from the planet Gallifrey, in the constellation Kasterborus.* [21]

Amy *In other words, I've been abducted by an alien.*

Doctor *That's the gist of it.*

Amy (smiles) *Well . . . Wait until* Ripley's Believe It or Not *hears about this.*

We then cut to the Androsterone Strain night club on an unnamed alien planet. The Master locates a glowing Red Jewel, obviously similar to the Gold Jewel he has already stolen, on the costume of an alien belly dancer – Milky Waye. He uses his blasting powers to get past a bouncer and to Miss Waye's dressing room. There, after pretending to be a talent agent to gain the dancer's confidence, he blasts her and steals the Jewel.

As the Master places the Red Jewel next to the Gold one there is another disturbance in the timestream, which is felt in the TARDIS. The Doctor is puzzled by this phenomenon. He compares the timestream to a placid river, but when Amy suggests that 'maybe someone threw a rock into the river' it sets him thinking.

They land in a souk, in Ancient Egypt, circa 2500 BC. To explain the TARDIS's incongruous appearance, the Doctor tells Amy about the chameleon circuit being stuck.

Amy *How'd it get stuck?*

Doctor *That's a funny story, actually. As it happens, I was staying in Totter's Lane in 1963 when a couple of school teachers and I went to visit the Stone Age . . .*[22]

As he keeps telling her the story, she links her arm through his.

We then come across AMAN, a lower-class Egyptian peasant who looks just like Rachmed, the 'petrified man' who tried to break into the Tomb of Rassilon. He is going around pilfering food from various merchants. More interestingly, he wears a sleek digital wristwatch on his arm.

The Doctor and Amy bump into Aman. The Doctor immediately notices his resemblance to the Petrified Man, and starts questioning him. This is when we find out that the intruder was not Aman, but his brother Rachmed, whom Aman has not seen in days.

Aman then leaves, thinking himself well rid of the two bothersome strangers, and is about to return to his pilfering when the Doctor grabs him again, this time exposing the digital watch. Now the Egyptian tells the truth. He stole the watch from the Master, who previously hired his brother as a guide. The Doctor asks Aman to take him to the place where he last saw his brother and the Master and, thanks to Amy's enticing beauty, Aman agrees.

They eventually reach the Great Pyramid of Giza. There indentations in the sand help the Doctor determine that the huge stone block Aman remembers seeing the last time he was there was, in reality, the Master's TARDIS. The Doctor now knows that it is another Time Lord – a renegade Time Lord – who hired Rachmed to steal the Ring of Immortality.

All three return to the TARDIS, where the Doctor finally breaks the sad news of his brother's death to Aman. Realising that the man they are looking for was responsible for his brother's fate, Aman begs the Doctor to let him join them in their quest. Having fallen victim to Aman's easy, roguish charm, the Doctor accepts.

Based on clues obtained from Aman, the Doctor figures out that their enemy was after something kept in the Great Pyramid. They travel forward in time to AD 1900 and rematerialise in the King's Chamber. Aman is bedazzled by all the treasures, but to the Doctor they are mere 'trinkets'. They find the skeletons of the three Grave Robbers, and discover that 'someone sealed them in'. The Doctor also realises that something (the Gold Jewel) was taken from the site.

Doctor *Something's missing here. Only one object from all this treasure.*

Aman *Pharaoh should have taken everything with him to his next life.*

Amy *Maybe he wanted to travel light.*

Finally Amy discovers the metal button still held in the thief's clenched fist. The Doctor identifies it as being from fifteenth-century Eastern Europe. As they leave the Doctor orders Aman to leave behind the treasures he was carrying.

The disgruntled Egyptian puts them all back on he ground, next to the dead robber.

Aman (confidentially) *You've done very well for yourself.*

They rematerialise in Transylvania, in the mid-fifteenth century. There they find sinister, foggy roads, lined with the heads of hundreds of people impaled on stakes. Aman's mouth drops open. Amy turns away. But the Doctor continues marching towards a forebidding castle. A local peasant informs them that it is the residence of the notorious VLAD THE IMPALER (a.k.a. DRACULA).

They cautiously enter the castle, which appears deserted but for a few bats. It is filled with cobwebs and looks as if it has not been inhabited for a long time. A pack of mastiffs come out, but the Doctor pacifies them with some candy bars.

Eventually, they reach a great hall in which a huge oil portrait is hanging above a throne. Aman sees it first and recognises it as that of the man who hired his brother – the Master. Amy holds the button up to the portrait. It matches the others on his coat. The Doctor looks pensively at the portrait.

Amy *Vlad the Impaler?* [23]
Doctor *He goes by many names. The man in the portrait is a Time Lord. Like myself.*
Amy *You know him then?*
Doctor *I have known him for thousands of years.* [24]
Amy *How old are you, exactly?*
Doctor *Time Lords live hundreds of years, Amy. And we can regenerate twelve times.*
Aman *Hundreds of years?*
Doctor *Times twelve.*

The Doctor then embarks on a FLASHBACK.

Doctor *Many centuries ago, when I was a young Time Lord studying quantum field theory and space/time dynamics at the Academy . . .* [25]

We meet the YOUNG DOCTOR, eager, curious, naive, and the YOUNG MASTER, already knowing and conceited. They are both bored with all the theoretical scientific information their TEACHER[26] is forcing them to learn, and intensely curious about the practical applications of space-time travel – something normally forbidden by the Time Lords. Yielding to their relentless curiosity, the Teacher admits to having travelled through space-time himself a long time before, and inadvertently tells them about Earth and its charms. The Teacher soon realises that, propelled by his own memories, he has talked too much, but it is too late. He admonishes the two students before leaving.

Teacher *You have a good deal to learn still. We all do. Learning is the greatest adventure you can go on. I'll see you in class. Tomorrow.*

After the Teacher leaves, the two students make a rash pact to steal a TARDIS and take an unauthorised trip to Earth.

Young Master *I'm going to steal a TARDIS and travel throughout the Cosmos. Come with me.*
Young Doctor *But ...*
Young Master *Are you afraid?*
Young Doctor *No, but ...*
Young Master *Then it's a pact?*

And indeed, soon after that pact is sealed, the Young Master steals a TARDIS's trionic key and plots their first expedition through space-time, to Earth. The Young Master goes into the borrowed TARDIS ('a mirrored door which hangs virtually in space') first. Before the Young Doctor joins him, the Teacher steps from the shadows and draws his attention to the moral aspects of space-time travel.

Teacher *You will find yourself in a position of great responsibility. You may be required to exercise moral judgment. Do not undertake this lightly.*
Young Doctor *I'll ... be careful.*

The Teacher studies the Young Doctor's face for a moment, then steps back into the shadows.

This first journey takes the two young Time Lords to the Ottoman Empire, during the thirteenth century. There the two young Gallifreyans watch as a young man is unjustly accused of stealing. The local police are about to chop off his hands.

Young Doctor *Shouldn't we do something?*
Young Master *Yes. I mean, no. No. We shouldn't.*
Young Doctor *He's innocent.*
Young Master (entranced) *I suppose he is.*
Young Doctor *Perhaps if we gave evidence, spoke up for him. They might listen to us.*
Young Master (happily remembering) *We're not supposed to interfere.*
(. . .)
Young Doctor *This is terrible.*
Young Master (enjoying it) *Isn't it?*

The man has his hands chopped off, and the Young Doctor throws up, while the Young Master waits impatiently.

Young Master (disdain) *Finished?*
Young Doctor *That punishment was awfully severe.*
Young Master *A leader has to have a strong hand. It sends the right message to the people.*
Young Doctor *The man was innocent.*
Young Master *A minor detail.*

After that the two young Time Lords went their separate ways.

Doctor *Eventually, I borrowed a TARDIS for myself. The lure of adventure was simply too great . . .*[27]

They did not meet again until a fateful night aboard the *Titanic*, in AD 1912.[28] An 'Older Young Doctor'[29] is having a fine time with a companion named VICTORIA,[30] when he suddenly spots an 'Older Young Master'. There is now something visibly sinister about him. The Master reveals that the ship is soon going to hit an iceberg, and advises the Doctor to leave.

(Older) Young Doctor *I read up on this voyage in the Time Lord library, and it didn't say anything about a shipwreck. How is it again you knew this was going to happen?*

(Older) Young Master *Never mind that now. And by the way, let's not mention this little meeting to the Time Lords, eh? You know how they frown upon our messing about in things.*

The disaster – 'a glorious thing to see' according to the Master – occurs as predicted. As the Doctor tries to help people aboard lifeboats, he once again confronts the Master.

(Older) Young Doctor *You caused all this! Why? Why?*
(Older) Young Master (smiles evilly) *Because I can!*

The Master then pushes the Doctor overboard. The Doctor dies in the icy waters – triggering his very first regeneration. [31]

Eventually, a New Doctor and the TARDIS are washed ashore on a deserted coastline. After that experience, the New Doctor decides to spend some time in peaceful retreat at beautiful Dora's Fields, in the Lake District in England in the nineteenth century, in the spring when the daffodils are in full bloom. [32] There he comes across another Time Lord – THE MONK [33] – who asks him about his adventures.

Monk *No regrets?*
New Doctor *Regrets? What about?*
Monk *Leaving Gallifrey?*
New Doctor *Never.*
Monk *And the Master?*
New Doctor *What about him?*
Monk *We keep tabs, you know. Some of us. He took your life.*
New Doctor *Oh, I'm all right. It was only my first.*

Then, the Monk suggests that the Time Lords would like the Doctor to intervene.

Monk *The Time Lords would not care to see the Master do harm.* [34]

New Doctor *They sent you? (. . .) I'm not an assassin.*

Monk *Victoria drowned, you know.*

New Doctor (pales) *Victoria? My first companion . . . Still, let them do it themselves.*

Monk *Impossible.*

New Doctor *Too dirty?*

Monk *They can't give you an order.*

New Doctor *I shan't take one.*

Monk *Just something to think about.*

New Doctor *Not me. I want only cheerful yesterdays, and confident tomorrows. (. . .) The time may someday come, as time always does. But not now.*

We RETURN TO SCENE. The Doctor muses about later encounters with the Master,[35] then adds that he came across him recently – an allusion to the earlier scene that took place in Shakespeare's time.

They are then attacked by the Master's legion of headless bodies – the bodies whose heads are on the stakes outside – armed with scythes, staves and clubs. After a hair-raising chase through the castle and an apocalyptic duel inside the castle bedroom, they manage to escape in the nick of time through a secret passage and eventually rejoin the TARDIS safely.

Because Aman feels that they need a break and some food, the Doctor offers to take them to 1891 Paris next.

We then cut to the HERMIT's lair.[36] The Hermit is the Old Time Lord Teacher of the Academy, many centuries older, now living alone on a lonely world. His greenhouse-like home is 'crammed with a magnificent collection of colourful, exotic plants and flowers'. The Master shows himself. Behind him are a couple of his Headless Henchmen.

Hermit *Young Master? Well, well, come in, come in out of the wet. My old students don't visit me very often. Not many want to come to this obscure corner of the cosmos.*

The Master tells the Hermit that he has come to collect a glowing jewel that was left with him for safekeeping.

Hermit *I don't believe you're the one who left it with me.*
Master *No, sir. But I'm the one who needs it.*

Eventually, the Master blasts the Hermit and steals a Blue Jewel from the cupboard where it was kept.

As the Master deposits the Blue Jewel next to the Red and Gold ones, there's another, stronger time disturbance which causes the TARDIS to rematerialise not in nineteenth-century France but on a bleak, far-future Earth inhabited only by cockroaches – an image which severely shakes Amy.[37]

They then travel back to their intended destination, the Moulin Rouge cabaret in 1891 Paris, where the Doctor and Amy watch famous singers La Goulue and Aristide Bruant perform, while Aman dances the cancan with the girls. The Master is there too, unseen, watching them from the shadows.

The Doctor finally realises what his opponent is after: THE KEY TO TIME!

Doctor *It's a device the Time Lords created,[38] then found far too dangerous to use. It was broken into six fragments, and hidden through time and space, so that it could not be reassembled. He's already stolen the first fragment. Right here, on Earth. It was given to King Cheops with the knowledge that he would take it with him to his grave.[39] That's the jewel that was missing from the shelf in the tomb's treasure room.*
Amy *How do you know?*
Doctor (suddenly sombre) *Because I'm the one who gave it to the King.*
Amy *You?*
Doctor *Yes. It was I who hid the six fragments.*

As the Doctor remembers where he hid another jewel, we cut to that very location, a campsite on an alien world surrounded by AMAZON WOMEN straight out of a Frank Frazetta painting. The Master and his Headless Henchmen attack one of the women and steal her Green Jewel. She stabs one of the walking corpses, but to no effect.

We cut back to the Moulin Rouge where the Doctor detects

another time disturbance as soon as the Master brings the four Jewels together. This time, the disturbance causes the brief materialisation of several medieval knights among the dancers.

Amy asks the Doctor how the Master can have found the segments if he is the one who hid them. The answer finally occurs to the Doctor. Because Time Lords are telepathic, the Master is using his powers to deviously pick the information from the Doctor's brain. [40]

The Doctor, now aware that the Master was there, stands up. They are walking along the streets of Montmartre. The Doctor says that they must reclaim the other fragments, because if the entire Key is assembled, there is no telling what could happen to time. Before he can focus on where the other fragments are, Amy tries to distract him by kissing him passionately. [41]

Doctor *Amy?*
Amy *You mustn't think about it.*
Doctor *About what?*
Aman *I think it worked.*

As they keep walking back to the TARDIS, Amy feels the need to explain that the kiss was purely a tactic, that she 'really didn't mean anything by it', that she's 'happily married', and while the lady doth protest too much, we can see that the Doctor is clearly disappointed. The 'pregnant, romantic silence' that ensues is broken by an alarm from Aman's digital watch (formerly the Master's), reminding them that it is time to get back to saving the universe.

We then cut to the Hermit's lush, tropical planet. The Doctor and his companions arrive in time to find the Hermit gravely hurt but still alive. His lair has been totally ransacked. He is happy to see his former student.

Hermit (to Amy and Aman) *He was my worst pupil.*
Doctor *I was your favourite pupil.*
Hermit *That too. It is not a contradiction.*

The dying Hermit tells them about his previous encounter with the Master, who stole the Blue Jewel. The Doctor vows revenge.

Hermit *No. My poor life needn't cause such trouble. Revenge is an unworthy motive.*

Amy *He sure blasted your lovely hydrangeas.*

Hermit (looking at the blackened plants, then back to the Doctor) *Kill him.*

The Hermit then passes away. Back in the TARDIS's Zero Room, the Doctor and Amy share some emotional moments while he helps her fix her plane.

Doctor *I'd better take you back.*

Amy *No! I mean, not yet. I couldn't leave now. I'm not a quitter. I'm going to see this thing through. Whatever it is. Besides, now that I've flown with you, this little plane doesn't seem like much . . .*

The Doctor decides they should go after the final segment. Meanwhile, the Master steals the fifth, Amber-coloured Jewel from a space pirate's ship.

We then cut to London's Carnaby Street in the 1970s. The Doctor, Amy and Aman have come here to get the sixth and last Jewel before the Master can get his hands on it. They enter a crystal shop and wait. Only a few minutes later the FOURTH DOCTOR comes in with the Jewel, intent on hiding it among the other crystals in the shop. [42]

Doctor *Doctor?*

Fourth Doctor *Yes? Don't I know you?*

Doctor *You will. I'm you. Later.*

Fourth Doctor *Great Heavens! Is this safe?*

Doctor *Not for long, I don't think.*

Fourth Doctor *What are you doing here?*

Doctor *I'm looking for a crystal.*

Fourth Doctor (whispers) *The Key!*

Doctor (nods) *The Sixth Fragment.*

Fourth Doctor *I was about to hide it. Thought it would go entirely unnoticed here.*

Doctor *How clever of me.*

Fourth Doctor (eyes light up) *Yes!*

After the Fourth Doctor has deposited the Jewel among the other crystals, he and the Doctor share a moment, talking about the future.

Fourth Doctor *I have so much to ask you. Did you ever run into those frightful Daleks again? Are the Time Lords giving you a hard time? And what of the Cybermen?* [43] *Have you . . .*

While they talk, two female customers take the Jewel, buy it and go out. However, Aman catches up with them, distracts them with his glib chatter and manages to steal it back.

Doctor *. . . Indeed, you'll have a splendid time. Watch out for Logopolis, however.* [44] *The calculations there are fiendishly complex. Now I think I'd better go . . .*

The Doctor, Amy and Aman eventually go out for a cup of tea, waiting for the Master to show up, so that they can follow him and find out where the rest of the Key is. While watching the crystal shop from a café across the street they talk. Amy asks the Doctor about the cockroach-infested world they saw earlier.

Amy *Is that the Earth's future?*
Doctor *What? Oh, you mustn't worry about that.*
Amy *But . . . What about my children? And my children's children?*
Doctor *They're going to inherit a very different Earth, Amy.*
Amy *Then it's all . . . useless.*
Doctor *No, no. Not at all. Look, I am sorry you saw that. You don't want to know your future. In life, it's the journey that counts, not the destination.* [45]

Eventually the Master shows up. He walks into the crystal shop and comes across the Fourth Doctor, who has returned. The Master attacks him from behind, using surprise and his blasting powers. When the Doctor comes in, he sees the Fourth Doctor, 'all his hair standing straight up', his eyes wide, being held by the throat by the Master, whose arm is extended, electricity crackling along it. The shop is in disarray, the crystal bookshelves shattered.

When he sees the Doctor, the Master throws the now-unconscious Fourth Doctor casually away, and turns to face the latest version of his arch-enemy.

Doctor *You can't assemble the Key to Time. It simply isn't safe.*

Master *Playing safe is your method, not mine. You never understood the powers we have.*

Doctor *You use them for your own evil enjoyment.*

Master *And where would the universe be without me?*

Doctor *Better off, I'm afraid.*

Master *No. You can't have good without evil. We've existed side by side forever.* [46] *Why, how could you recognise the very best in life, without the worst to compare it to?*

The Fourth Doctor comes to a sitting position on the floor.

Fourth Doctor *Still a bounder, I see . . .*

Aman arrives and joins the fray on the side of the two Doctors, but the Master easily dispatches him. The Master struggles with the Doctor(s). Amy enters and hits him with a brass hookah. However, he recovers and quickly seizes her, taking her hostage. Before he leaves, he tells the Doctor that he will trade her in exchange for the last Jewel. Before travelling to the Master's rendezvous, the co-ordinates of which have been transmitted telepathically, the two Doctors say goodbye.

Fourth Doctor *I'd be glad to go with you, but . . .*

Doctor *Yes, you'd better carry on. No telling what might happen if we chum around too long.*

Fourth Doctor *It's been a pleasure. I'm sorry I couldn't be more help.*

Doctor (smiles) *To the contrary, you've done a great deal.*

Fourth Doctor (alone) *Handsome chap. If I do say so myself.*

We cut to a Fillmore West concert in San Francisco in the 1960s. This is the mecca of '60s rock. The Who are advertised on the marquis. The Master has left tickets for them at the gate. They go in and find the Master and Amy who is hypnotised, under the villain's spell. The Doctor daringly recaptures her. He and Aman then use the confusion and chaos generated by the concert to escape from the Master and his Headless Henchmen.

Afterwards, in Golden Gate Park, the Doctor tries to free Amy from the Master's mind-control, but fails until Aman suggests he tries kissing her. That does the trick. It is clear that Amy has now fallen in love with the Doctor.

> **Amy** *It's funny, you practically live forever, you've seen it all, yet the one thing I've learned travelling with you is how temporary everything about life is. And there's no second chance. (...) I guess I'll have to face that when I get back. It's going to be very anti-climactic, my little adventures, compared to your exciting life. Imagine having all eternity to go adventuring in. Do you ever get lonely?*
>
> **Doctor** *Lonely? I suppose I do. I'm the perennial outsider. But then, I'm always coming across wonderful friends. Like you two.*
>
> **Amy** *A girl in every solar system?*
>
> **Doctor** *Oh, no, nothing like that . . .* **(pause)** *Some planets don't have any women at all. Some don't even have humanoids.*

Meanwhile, flower children have been passing out cups of wine. But it turns out that they are under the Master's control, and that the wine has been spiked with LSD.[47] As a result, the Master is finally able to steal the sixth and final Jewel.

However, the Doctor has been able to use his own telepathic powers to probe his enemy's mind and has located his secret base – the City on the Asteroid, far away in space. There they face the Master once more. He reveals that he tried to steal Rassilon's Ring of Immortality, and now needs the Key to Time in order to stop time and start a new life cycle – he has run out of regenerations.[48]

Master *Stop* (time)*? Yes, Doctor, that's precisely what I am hoping. You see, my life has required more regenerations than yours. (. . .) I have no more lives left to me. And when I die, I will be forgotten. Unlike your precious William Shakespeare . . . You see why I despise him so? His work will make him immortal. My last hope is to stop time.*

The Master 'reaches to his chin and slowly peels off his handsome, bearded, if sinister face, and exposes the real one underneath: chilling, collapsed, ancient with harsh age lines'.

He then starts assembling the Key, causing all sorts of chaos and havoc throughout time. Indians appear on 5th Avenue. Space ships from different eras cross in the time-stream. A huge hole in the fabric of the continuum opens.

Doctor *He's opened a hole in the universe! To the Space-Time Vortex! Time is collapsing in on itself!*

The Doctor, Amy and Aman attack the Master and his headless zombies. Amy causes the Master to lose his grip on the Key to Time. Aman grabs it. The Master frees himself of Amy and blasts Aman with electricity. The three of them fight while the Hole in Space grows ever larger. Having dispatched the Headless Henchmen, the Doctor rushes to the rescue, but he is too late to prevent Amy and the Master from falling to their dooms in the Hole, with the Key.

Amy manages to grab the edge of reality, but the Master has his arms wrapped around her waist. They are both dangling over infinity.

Amy *Master, the universe doesn't need the likes of you.*
Doctor *Amy, don't!*
Amy *Goodbye, Doctor. Thanks for the ride.*

She lets go and he only manages to hang on to her scarf. Amy and the Master, the Master screaming, fall into the Vortex and disappear into all eternity.[49]

But the threat to the continuum is not yet over. Dodging collapsing walls and jumping over holes opening to the

147

universe, the Doctor and Aman rush back to the safety of the TARDIS. There, the Doctor tells Aman he needs to make 'stitch in time'.

We cut back to England, AD 1593, the 'Sign of the Mermaid' tavern. It is the same scene as in the beginning, except that Aman is in the room, and this time the Doctor does not disarm the Master but instead engages him in a fierce sword duel.[50] The Master dies by falling on his own dagger as he was preparing to kill the Doctor treacherously. Ironically, the Doctor has 'tripped the Master precisely as the Young Master had tripped the Young Doctor off the *Titanic*'.

Having run out of regenerations, the Master's body crumbles, leaving a set of empty clothes behind.

> **Doctor** *'For old unhappy far off things, And battles long ago.' (. . .) Although the Master left this life convinced that he would be forgotten, that wasn't true. 'The evil that men do lives after them. The good is oft interred with their bones.'*
> **Aman** *You say the cleverest things.*
> **Doctor** *I? No, I'm just one of life's messengers.* (**Looks up at young Shakespeare**) *But I steal from the best.*

In an epilogue, Aman expresses the wish to stay with the Doctor; the Doctor welcomes him aboard. The Doctor then takes the TARDIS to 1937, when they again pick up AM (Amelia Earhardt) – except that, for her, it is the first time, of course, as time has been repaired.

After the Doctor has introduced himself and Aman, he invites her to follow them to the control room.

> **Amy** *I'm in the middle of a round-the-world flight! I can just . . . I don't have time for this!*
> **Doctor** *On the contrary, we have all the time in the world.*
> **Amy** *Wait a minute. Hey, wait . . . Did you say Doctor? Doctor who?*

We CLOSE on the TARDIS travelling through the Vortex to the tune of 'All we have is Time'.

Notes

1 The descriptions of the Death Zone and the Dark Tower are remarkably faithful to the concepts outlined in *The Five Doctors* (6K). Even the fate of the unfortunate grave robber, while not totally similar to that of Borusa in the original television episode, nevertheless clearly draws its inspiration from it.

2 The role is not written with any specific physical description; however, we know from Denny Martin Flinn that he, personally, visualised Pierce Brosnan as the Doctor.

3. As acknowledged in the interview below, Flinn took some artistic licence with the ages of his historical protagonists. In 1593, both Shakespeare and Marlowe would have been 29, Greene 35 and Fletcher 45. The play *Romeo and Juliet* was apparently first performed in 1594 or 1595, a year after this scene takes place. However, such liberties are small and unobtrusive.

4 In the script, the villain is called the Mandrake, even though his physical description, relationship with the Doctor, and modus operandi completely match those of the Master. Flinn explains in his interview why it was felt preferable to feature a 'new' villain rather than use an existing one. We believe that this decision may have ultimately originated with the BBC, or that the producers at Lumière may have misunderstood something the BBC said. It is a well-known fact that the BBC cannot freely dispose of certain characters which appeared on *Doctor Who*, usually those created by freelance writers, such as the Daleks, the Sontarans, etc., without first securing some form of permission (and possibly paying some kind of royalty) to the original writers. On the other hand, characters created by story editors while on staff, such as the Master, the Time Lords, etc., belong entirely to the BBC. When the BBC grants a licence on *Doctor Who*, this licence does not automatically extend to every character that appeared on the show (e.g. the Daleks), which can sometimes cause problems for licencees. When Randy and I worked for Philip Segal we were told that the BBC had compiled for

Segal a list of approved characters that could be used freely. Segal later negotiated a separate agreement with Terry Nation in order to be able to use the Daleks. We believe that, in this instance, the same principle operated, and while Lumière could have, in our opinion, used the Master without any legal problems, it chose to play it safe and asked Flinn to come up with a 'new' villain. Because of the overwhelming similarities between the Master and the Mandrake, and the clear intent in Flinn's mind, we have taken the (rare) liberty of restoring the Master to his rightful place in the story. Had the script been actually produced with the name 'Mandrake', it would, in any event, have been relatively easy to postulate that this was just another alias for the Master, perhaps his first 'real' name . . .

5 Marlowe was indeed killed in a duel on 30 May 1593. This is what the *Encyclopaedia Britannica* says: 'Marlowe was killed by Ingram Friser, in the dubious company of Nicholas Skeres and Robert Poley, at a tavern in Deptford, where they had spent most of the day and where, it was alleged, a fight broke out between them over the tavern bill.'

6 Throughout this scene the Doctor and the Master fail to recognise each other in spite of their telepathic powers. It is stated later that they have not seen each other in many years, and have regenerated (possibly several times?) since then. We must therefore assume that such powers must be activated by a conscious effort of will in order to become operative. In *Terror of the Autons* (EEE), the Doctor and the Master did not seem to have any trouble recognising each other. However, in the original BBC television series, as well as in *Enemy Within*, more often than not the Doctor fails to recognise the Master, especially when disguised (e.g. *Castrovalva* (5Z), *Time Flight* (6C)), implying again that telepathic recognition is not automatic.

7 The TARDIS is already in its traditional police box shape – it was felt that this 'icon' did not need any introduction. *The Jewels of Time* is clearly written as a 'future' adventure of Doctor Who, one that takes place in an undetermined time after the end of the original BBC television series in 1989.

8 Coincidentally, this eclectic approach to the visual design of the TARDIS interior was the same as the one that was actually used in *Enemy Within*.

9 K-9 is described in the script as 'a mechanical version of the RCA dog', i.e. more real dog-like and yet still mechanical. In his interview, Flinn states that he put K-9 in the story because he liked the character, but in this early draft had not yet settled on any single specific thing for him to do.

10 The use of the CIA is a reference to *The Deadly Assassin* (4P), a story which clearly influenced *The Jewels of Time*, as well as *Enemy Within*.

11 In this version, the chameleon circuit is mentioned without further explanation. Later scripts made use of the term 'cloaking', more familiar to *Star Trek* audiences.

12 This is another accurate reference to *The Five Doctors* (6K). Note that it is actually more sensible to have the Ring on Rassilon's fingers inside the sarcophagus, as portrayed here, rather than outside on the relief, as shown on the television story.

13 Other than paying homage to *Star Wars*, this line indicates that Gallifrey is located in a different galaxy, which sounds more dramatic, yet contradicts the information given in the original BBC television series in *Pyramids of Mars* (4G). Curiously, the same thing was stated in *Fathers and Brothers*. And in *Enemy Within*, Gallifrey is said to be located 250 million light years away, which is well outside our galaxy. Perhaps the Osirians' information was out of date, and the Time Lords decided to move their planet (star system?) to another galaxy when the presence of war-like races such as the Daleks, who threatened Gallifrey in *Resurrection of the Daleks* (6P), and the Sontarans, who actually invaded it in *The Invasion of Time* (4Z), made remaining in the Milky Way too dangerous. Certainly, we know from the events in *The Mysterious Planet* (7A) that the Time Lords have the means to move planets. The debate continues. Also see note 21 below.

14 The desire to use Cheops and the Great Pyramid is a hard one to resist in *Doctor Who*. In this version, we discover that the Doctor knew Cheops and, as we will discover, entrusted him with a segment of the Key to Time. Later the John Leekley script *Fathers and Brothers* revealed that Cheops was the Doctor's father, a Time Lord stranded on Earth. The two versions do not necessarily conflict. It is not too far-fetched to postulate that the Fourth Doctor, knowing full well that he had once rescued his father (and whatever happened thereafter is still unknown), then chose to travel back in time and entrust him, without revealing his own identity, with a segment of the Key to Time.

15 The alleged unfamiliarity of the Time Lords with Earth is used here primarily for comic effect. One may choose to believe that these specific Time Lords have simply been poorly briefed. Or maybe more time has elapsed on Gallifrey between *The Jewels of Time* and the original BBC television series.

16 While we never saw mankind master time travel the way the Daleks did, the Doctor's assessment of its ultimate advancement is somewhat brutal, and relatively inaccurate, to the extent that it ignores the Empire (thirtieth century), the Federation (thirty-eighth century), etc. Perhaps the Doctor is merely trying to make Earth look less important, a wise decision if one remembers what the Time Lords did to Earth with the Ravolox Stratagem (*The Trial of a Time Lord* (7A–7C)).

17 The Master has, in this script, acquired the ability to project deadly bolts of bio-electricity. Since there is no explanation to bridge the gap between *Survival* (7P) or *Enemy Within* (which had not yet been written at the time) and *The Jewels of Time*, other than the notion that a fair amount of time has elapsed between the two, we are free to hypothesise that this is just one more skill that the Master developed, perhaps due to artificial enhancements, or thanks to his Keepership in *The Keeper of Traken* (5T). (The ability to alter one's biochemistry or rearrange one's DNA would probably have been within the scope of the Keeper's powers.) Because *The Jewels of Time* probably takes place after Matthew Jacobs's *Enemy Within*, we know that, by then, the Master had already acquired some strange powers.

18 The Zero Room is a reference to *Castrovalva* (5Z), although its purpose here is markedly different, implying that this room has more functions than the ones displayed (in 5Z). The use of the TARDIS to rescue Amy and her plane is particularly clever, and might have been inspired by some of the Doctor's actions in *Logopolis* (5V). Also see note 44.

19 To make sure that everyone figures it out, the end of the script shows a period newspaper spinning into camera range, as in old cinema newsreels, with the headline 'Amelia Earhardt Disappears'.

20 Among the explanations he gives the Doctor mentions that the TARDIS runs on mercury (B), zyton–7 (6V) and artron energy (4P).

21 This is a reference taken from *Pyramids of Mars* (4G).

22 This is a reference to *An Unearthly Child* (A), which doubles as an explanation for the shape of the TARDIS for the uninitiated viewer.

23 The revelation that the Master may have been the infamous Dracula (or Genghis Khan as hinted at in *Enemy Within*) is somewhat similar to the assumption made in *Battlefield* (7N) that the Doctor was/will be Merlin. (Although this may have happened in an alternative universe.) Obviously we cannot be certain if the two Time Lords just impersonated real historical figures for a limited time, or if they always were those figures.

24 This serves as a convenient way of introducing and explaining the concept of Time Lord regeneration. Note the 'thousands' (not hundreds) of years, which would imply that the Doctor's life has been a lot longer than heretofore suspected.

25 This entire flashback scene offers us yet another version of the Doctor's 'origins', certainly a more conservative one than that later postulated in John Leekley's *Fathers and Brothers*. It is, however, interesting to compare, and attempt to reconcile, the two scripts. Clearly, this entire flashback (including the later scene on the *Titanic*) takes place before the events described in Leekley's script. It has been established that the Doctor and the Master studied together at the Time Lord Academy (cf. *The Deadly Assassin* (4P), *The Five Doctors* (6K)). The fact that they may have been related certainly was not public knowledge. In *Fathers and Brothers* the Master later claims to have known – but he could have learned that fact after this flashback. As to the Doctor, he certainly was unaware of it until told by 'Borusa' in *Fathers and Brothers*. The major continuity clash is that the two scripts appear to offer two mutually exclusive stories of the Doctor's first journey to, and discovery of, Earth. I think we can accept Flinn's version of a student breaking the rules and simply assume that, in *Fathers and Brothers*, our hero is older, has just been shaken by the revelation about his half-human ancestry, and as a result is in effect rediscovering Earth through new eyes. Another possible explanation is that, as a punishment for running off to Earth with the Master, the Time Lords erased the Doctor's memories of the incident. It certainly would not be the first time!

26 The Time Lord Academy Teacher mentioned here is clearly not Borusa, if only because of what happens to him later in the script, although his character is certainly drawn from the version of Borusa portrayed in *The Invasion of Time* (4Z).

27 The Doctor's 'borrowing' of his TARDIS has often been referred to throughout the series. In this version it is motivated purely by the 'lure of adventure'.

28 In *The Invasion of Time* (4Z), Borusa is shown reading a newspaper in the TARDIS, with a headline about the *Titanic* disaster. Upon noticing it, the Doctor insists that he had nothing to do with it. He was not lying! Coincidentally, Randy and I used the sinking of the *Titanic* as well as the Key to Time in our proposed outline, *The End of Time* (see Appendix), even though we had not read *The Jewels of Time* at that stage.

29 In total, five Doctors would have appeared in *The Jewels of Time*: (i) the 'present-day' Doctor (Pierce Brosnan); (ii) the Young Doctor at the Academy (played by an actor in his early twenties); (iii) an Older Version of the same Young Doctor on the *Titanic* (possibly played by the same actor); (iv) the 'New Doctor' who regenerates after the *Titanic*

scene (see below – played by a different actor); and finally (v) the Fourth Doctor (played by Tom Baker – see below).

30 This Victoria bears no relation to the Second Doctor's companion, Victoria Waterfield (LL-RR).

31 This may well have been the most controversial continuity clash with various bits of information stated in the original BBC television series which, *The Brain of Morbius* (4K) and *The Power of the Daleks* (EE) notwithstanding, takes some pains to establish that William Hartnell was the Doctor's first incarnation, and that the regeneration in *The Tenth Planet* (DD) was his first regeneration. Obviously the original BBC television series contradicted itself before, and this would just be one more contradiction to be retroactively reconciled by the fans. Even assuming that the 'New Doctor' (or 'Lake District Doctor') eventually ages to become the Hartnell Doctor, and that there are no other unrevealed regenerations, this would still make Hartnell the Second Doctor, not the First. Dramatically, the fact that the Doctor lost his first life to the Master is certainly justified and effective. One might retroactively explain away this contradiction by the Doctor's desire to erase from his memory (but not from Morbius's brain scanning machine!) his first life, sadly cut short at the hands of a fellow Time Lord whom he considered a friend and – if one takes into account what he later discovered in *Fathers and Brothers* – a brother.

As to the Time Lords' records referring to Hartnell as the Doctor's first incarnation, they may just have been edited by the CIA. We certainly know that, at various times, the Doctor has been an agent, willingly or unwillingly, of the CIA, even prior to his official arrest and trial in *The War Games* (ZZ). We prefer to believe that the CIA was always aware of the Doctor's movements, and did not hesitate to use him when it suited their needs. In *The Two Doctors* (6W), when the Second Doctor tells Dastari that he is 'a bit of an exile', the scientist observes that he nevertheless 'still act on their [the CIA's] instructions', to which the Doctor replies, 'The price I pay for my freedom,' and goes on to insist that the fact he is a 'pariah', an 'exile from Time Lord

155

society'. This gives him what is called in intelligence circles 'deniability'. In the same fashion as the American CIA is allegedly said to have hidden certain covert operations from the Presidency, one might then easily assume that the Gallifreyan CIA was keeping some of its carefully orchestrated meddlings in time from the High Council's prying eyes. Also see notes 33 and 34.

32 Denny Martin Flinn explains in his interview why this scene was inserted here (see below).

33 The sudden presence of the Monk acting for all intents and purposes as an agent of the CIA raises the possibility that he might have once worked for that organisation and then simply defected. His appearing and vanishing here without a TARDIS (like the Time Lord in a bowler hat in *Terror of the Autons* (EEE)) makes his appurtenance to the CIA more credible. This would certainly account for his later familiarity with William Hartnell in *The Time Meddler* (S). In fact, one might be led to suppose that, long ago, the Doctor too may have been a full-time CIA agent, if not one of its founders, and defected too. He could have been initially driven to this line of work by the events chronicled in the flashback, and his general desire to do good. He may even have been offered extra regenerations, which we know is within the Time Lords' power (cf. *The Five Doctors* (6K)), since it stands to reason that a CIA agent would burn through his lives faster. The Doctor's role in the creation of the CIA might even explain Lady Peinforte's cryptic remarks about the Doctor's 'secrets' in *Silver Nemesis* (7K).

Why the Doctor eventually chose to resign from the CIA remains a matter of speculation, making him a Gallifreyan version of the notorious Number 6. A matter of principle? Discovering horrible abuses of power like the Ravolox Stratagem (cf. *The Mysterious Planet* (7A))? Betrayal? The death of a friend or loved one? Certainly, whatever the cause, the Doctor could never give the real reason for his defection to the High Council, because he himself would then be implicated in the CIA's horrendous interference with time. And surely the CIA would similarly 'clean' the Doctor's records accordingly. Indeed, we already know from *The*

Deadly Assassin (4P) that the Doctor's Matrix bio-data has been tampered with.

34 The fact that certain parties within the Time Lords' hierarchy – probably the CIA again – would like to get rid of the Master but obviously cannot do it openly would accord with Robert Holmes's as well as John Leekley's assumptions about Time Lord society, as well as help bring credence to the theory that, were the Master a descendant of Rassilon (as postulated in *Fathers and Brothers*), he could not be officially executed. In any event, if one accepts the events depicted in Leekley's story, the Master eventually overcame his opponents and rose to become Gallifrey's Minister of Defence.

35 This is framed in terms general enough that all the Master's appearances could be comfortably included, from *Terror of the Autons* (EEE) to *Survival* (7P), to *Enemy Within* (which, logically, would take place prior to *The Jewels of Time*).

36 While the idea for this Hermit may have come from the mention of the Gallifreyan hermit who once taught the Doctor (cf. *The Time Monster* (OOO) and *State of Decay* (5P)), there is no need to suppose that they may be the same characters.

37 Interestingly enough, this may well be the polluted future Earth mentioned in *The Sunmakers* (4W) and *The Curse of Fenric* (7M).

38 The script states that the Key to Time was actually created by the Time Lords themselves – perhaps at the behest of the Guardians? Being pure conceptual entities, the embodiments of Order and Chaos, the Guardians may have had to rely on the assistance of corporeal beings (such as the Time Lords) to create the Key. While stating that the Key is used by the Guardians to maintain the universal balance, *The Ribos Operation* (5A) does not, after all, exactly state who created it. In any event, one is free to hypothesise that, after successfully bluffing the Black Guardian at the conclusion of *The Armageddon Factor* (5F), and before the events of *Destiny of the Daleks* (5J), the Fourth Doctor physically travelled through space and time to re-hide the six segments, now in the form of six

Jewels. It then follows that the Doctor lied when he stated (admittedly not very clearly) that one of the segments had been reincorporated as Princess Astra of Atrios. After all, once the location of one of the segments was known, the danger to the universe would have been too great. One might further speculate that Romana later sacrificed one of her lives and assumed the form of Princess Astra as, perhaps, a way of expiating the real Princess's sacrifice. In view of Romana's later dedication to the Tharils' cause in E-Space (cf. *Warriors' Gate* (5S)), this act of contrition would indeed be in character.

39 Possibly the Doctor's father, the Time Lord explorer known as Ulysses (see *Fathers and Brothers*).

40 This is one of the few times when the Time Lords' telepathic abilities have actually played a substantial part in the plot. The opening would imply, however, that such abilities must be purposefully focused in order to be effective.

41 As noted elsewhere, most 'Nth Doctor' versions of *Doctor Who* entertained the idea of greater intimacy between the Doctor and his female companion, expanding rather than contradicting the type of relationship displayed between, say, the Fourth Doctor and his companions. Also see the later scene in Golden Gate Park.

42 This surprise guest appearance by the Fourth Doctor was purposefully intended by Denny Martin Flinn as a homage to Tom Baker (see interview below), and would probably have been very popular with the fans. It also helps validate the theory mentioned in note 38 above that the Fourth Doctor went and took personal care of hiding the six segments of the Key to Time after *The Armageddon Factor* (5F).

43 Why would the Fourth Doctor be concerned about the Cybermen? Wouldn't we like to know . . .?

44 A nice bit of retroactive continuity, anticipating the Seventh Doctor's hints that he receives messages from his future self/selves . . .

45 This Doctor does not have the innocence of the Eighth Doctor, nor the dark, manipulative nature of the Seventh Doctor. He seems a more integrated personality, one who has clearly survived many trials by fire on the various battlefields of time and space, and has come through them all happy to live for the moment.

46 The dual nature of the Doctor *vs* the Master, Good *vs* Evil, the two sides of the Eternal Coin, which has been a running theme of Doctor Who from the Third Doctor's adventures to *Enemy Within* and *Fathers and Brothers*, not mentioning the duality of the two Guardians, is once more reaffirmed.

47 As mentioned by Denny Martin Flinn in his interview (see below), the BBC objected to this scene.

48 Clearly, since this takes place long after *Survival* (7P) and *Enemy Within*, we must assume that the Master 'got better' (as they say in comics), probably by extracting himself from the TARDIS's Eye of Harmony and borrowing new bodies, until he finally ran out of luck.

49 This was the original ending intended by Denny Martin Flinn (see interview below), leaving the door open for an always possible return of the Master. The final duel which echoes back to the beginning of the script was added later. Curiously, in *Enemy Within*, the Doctor also returns to a previous moment in time to prevent a crisis from happening.

50 In a gag bit, when the Master asks the Doctor how he learned to fence so well, the Doctor responds by slashing a 'Z' across the Master's chest.

Review

The Jewels of Time is an excellent script, strong on both pacing and character. The story jumps from place to place without respite. The Doctor, Amy, Aman and the Master are well written and really come alive. There are many genuinely funny lines in the script. On the other hand, the presence of K-9 in the story is not fully integrated, and contributes little.

The plot is not wholly original, borrowing as it does from the sixteenth season, but it does make full use of the concepts of space-time travel. The pay-off is good, and the final time paradox clever.

The flashback scenes to the early days of the Doctor and

the Master are particularly interesting. However, continuity references are unobtrusive and whether the villain is named 'Master' or 'Mandrake', the prospective audiences would not have needed to be familiar with *Doctor Who* in order to enjoy the story.

Interview with Denny Martin Flinn

Question: Whose idea was it to incorporate a part for Tom Baker in the script?
Denny Martin Flinn: Entirely mine. I had watched a lot of Tom Baker episodes. I thought he was the most charming of the seven Doctors, and to me that charm is a great part of the success of *Doctor Who*. When I found by watching the *Baker Years* tape that he was not only still alive but very much working, I decided that I had to find a way to use him in the film. I thought of the 1970s and of his virtual identification with that decade, and that it would be a nice touch to place him there. It would be something that the fans would enjoy. Obviously, I had to write something that would be accessible for the millions of people who may have had no familiarity at all with *Doctor Who*, but I also wanted to write a film which wouldn't bore the fans, a film that the fans would like, and having the Tom Baker Doctor suddenly show up unexpectedly in a couple of scenes was a way to accomplish that.

Q: Were you given any elements by Lumière that had to be included in the script, or did you have carte blanche?
DMF: I pretty much had carte blanche. But the BBC had overall approval of everything we did. For example, one argument we had that frustrated me greatly was about a scene that takes place in the 1960s, when the villain slips the Doctor some LSD. The BBC nixed that scene because they felt it besmirched the image of the Doctor to take drugs. We argued that he did not take drugs, it was the villain who fed them to him, but they wouldn't budge so I had to rewrite that scene, which I felt was a great shame because it was a very visual, very photogenic sequence. I was surprised to see how nervous they were about that sort of thing, but I couldn't do a thing about it because they had that total approval power.

160

Q: Why did you have K-9 in the film when he does virtually nothing?

DMF: You're absolutely right. The producers remarked on that too. That's one of the things that I would have fixed later, in the rewrites. In fact I seem to recall that I did come up with a scene for him towards the end, a couple of drafts later, but I can't remember what it was all about now. I put K-9 in the script because, honestly, I liked him and I always wanted him in there. And then, when I wrote the first draft, I didn't come up with anything for him to do. But had we gone on to production, we would have fixed that.

Q: Why did you call your villain the Mandrake instead of the Master, when for all intents and purposes, they appear to be the same characters?

DMF: Well, they were, sort of. I mean, the Mandrake is taken from the image of the Master. I don't recall exactly why we changed the name now. I have a vague memory that, when I started plotting the story, he was the Master. Then someone, the BBC or the producers, I don't recall, told me that we couldn't use any of the villains from the television series, so we decided to start from scratch and come up with a new villain, which in many ways suited me much better.

Q: I liked the many historical references: Amelia Earhardt, Shakespeare, Dracula, the Titanic . . .

DMF: That's one of the things I wanted to do from the very beginning, which was not to confine myself to any single location in space or in time. This was written purposefully to be a big-budget feature, a roller-coaster ride, and it would have been a little boring to restrict myself to only a couple of sets. So I wrote into the story every location that I always wanted to visit. Most of them just came out of my head, then when I started to write my first draft I did some historical research to ensure that I didn't have any inaccuracies.

The only thing that I cheated with was that group of British writers who meet in the tavern. I cheated with their ages, by making them all about the same age, when in reality one of them would have been, like nine, and the other, say, forty-five. But as far as I know, that's the only cheat. Everything else is pretty accurate, from Amelia's disappearance to the *Titanic*. I checked all the facts.

I like history and historical accuracy. In fact in the British tavern scene the poets say things that they did say in real life, although I made up some of their dialogue, obviously. Marlowe's death remains somewhat of a mystery, one that has never been solved satisfactorily. Yes, I took some artistic licence with the facts, but we do know that he was attacked by an assassin and died in a duel in a tavern at a young age. Nobody is really sure why he was killed.

Q: The flashback scenes to the youth of the Doctor and the Master were also very interesting . . .

DMF: I didn't want this story to be just like any other episode of *Doctor Who*. I thought of it as sort of a genesis story, in which many people would learn about the Doctor. I wanted to show who he was and where he came from. The idea behind these scenes was that we are all programmed in some fashion. The Doctor and the Master are the two sides of the same metaphorical coin; he is Good and the Master is Evil. That compulsion is embedded into them from early on. You could say that it's in their character, part of their genetic make-up. This explains the choices that they make and the lives they eventually go on to live. It was important to me to go back to their youth and show that they started like mirror images of each other, like two sides of the same coin. We saw that all that power, the ability to travel in time, to go anywhere, corrupted one, and energised the other.

Q: In your script, the Young Master pushed the Young Doctor off the Titanic *and the Doctor ends up regenerating, which meant that William Hartnell's was not the first regeneration. Why did you do this?*

DMF: In the first draft, for dramatic reasons, of course; because it helped establish the point at which time the Doctor and the Master chose their respective paths and became alienated from each other. But later, Lumière asked me to expand that scene, because they needed to start principal photography sooner in order to not lose their option. So they came up with the idea of shooting a scene that would involve the Doctor, and yet at the same time not require any stars in it! So I came up with this scene in which the Doctor is obviously not the same actor who plays him during the film. Because we were in May, I wrote it to take place in Dora's Fields, that beautiful field of flowers which an English poet – Wordsworth, I believe? – wrote about.

Q: Don't you think that the final time paradox – the 'stitch in time' – is a little of a cheat?

DMF: I do, I do, and I struggled over that ending for weeks and weeks, and I argued over it with the producers. I said, if we go back through time and wipe out what we did, then the movie doesn't exist. It's one of these things that we didn't have time to satisfactorily resolve. In my initial story ending, the Master fell through that crack in time, and that was the end of it, and the Doctor went back in time only to get Amelia back. Also, that way, we hadn't really killed off the Master, and the character could have been re-used for a sequel.

Q: Did you know that, coincidentally, they used the same type of device in Enemy Within?

DMF: Really? I haven't seen the new movie yet. But I suppose it's a conundrum that you face every time that you use a story with time travel in it. I mean, the hero can always turn back the clock to make sure he wins.

Q: In the television series, they came up with a bit of technobabble called the Blinovitch Limitation Effect to explain why the Doctor couldn't just go back in time and change everything again . . .

DMF: I really wish I'd known that at the time I wrote the script. I certainly would have worked it in!

5

THE DARK DIMENSION

by

Adrian Rigelsford

Background

In 1992 BBC Enterprises, well aware of the commercial success of its *Doctor Who* merchandise, in particular the pre-recorded reissues of the original BBC television series episodes on videotape, decided that, in view of the then forthcoming 30th anniversary of the series in 1993, it made sense to produce and release a special direct-to-video feature film.

They commissioned *Doctor Who* fan scholar Adrian Rigelsford to write a script, eventually entitled *The Dark Dimension*. The story principally featured the Fourth Doctor (simply referred to as 'the Doctor' in the script) and found a clever way to explain his ageing – Tom Baker's last *Doctor Who* performance being *Logopolis* (5V), thirteen years earlier.

Unfortunately the production of *The Dark Dimension* ran into some unanticipated obstacles which ultimately prevented it from being made. The logistics of the production, especially with respect to the division of responsibilities between the BBC and BBC Enterprises, proved difficult to overcome. In particular, the BBC itself is in charge of production, whereas BBC Enterprises' mandate is to generate revenue from licensing and exploiting the BBC's productions. Consequently, BBC Enterprises is not normally set up to do productions itself, and lacks the appropriate facilities and staff.

In the same fashion that the scripts for *The Three Doctors* (RRR) and *The Five Doctors* (6K) had to be rewritten to accommodate last-minute changes in casts, e.g. William Hartnell's failing health or Tom Baker's unavailability, *The Dark Dimension* script would probably have had to be changed to take similar factors into account. In view of the 'cameo' nature of their roles, arranging for the appearance of some of the other 'Doctors' in the feature would probably have required complicated juggling, both in terms of rewrites and production schedule. Such things require time and tight planning, a challenge that became even more insurmountable considering the pre-set release date of November 1993 to coincide with the 30th anniversary.

Finally, having recently decided to join forces with Philip Segal, then of Amblin Television, and Universal Television to co-produce a new television series of *Doctor Who* to be sold to the American market, BBC Enterprises faced a legitimate conflict of interest. Ultimately, it decided to pull the plug on the project, and *The Dark Dimension* became one more script to add to the growing pile of unproduced *Doctor Who* stories.

However, unlike all the other 'Nth Doctor' scripts covered in this book, it is unique in that it does not introduce a new Doctor, but in effect recounts a 'missing' adventure of the original Time Lord, or of five original Time Lords, to be accurate.

Story

We open on Earth in the year 2525. This is a heavily polluted planet, scarred by the remnants of a post-industrial civilisation and plagued by electrical storms. Four uniformed ECO-TROOPERS (EVERITT, FLEMYNG, MASON and SANDERS) – all women – led by SUMMERFIELD[1] are making their way into the zone, clearly looking for something. They finally locate the object of their search, a body lying face down in the mud. It is the corpse of the SEVENTH DOCTOR, seemingly dead.[2]

The Eco-Troopers conduct a Viking-like funeral, setting fire to a raft bearing the TARDIS and the Seventh Doctor's body. Summerfield then orders her crew to proceed with the operation. They set up four pylons (voltron-wave transmitters) which, once activated, create an opening into the Time Vortex, going all the way back to creation itself. It becomes clear that their purpose is to use this makeshift time tunnel to kill an as-yet-unseen Creature, and that it is their last chance to do so. We learn that the Doctor lost his life while trying to accomplish this very goal.

Not far away, in the flaming ruins of an ancient building, the CREATURE rises. It is described as a 'featureless humanoid' with a 'death-like face'.[3]

The Eco-Troopers are planning to lure the Creature

between the four pylons, then activate the time tunnel and thus get rid of it forever. But the Creature finds them first and attacks before they are ready. Still, the resourceful Summerfield manages to draw the monster into the trap. The time tunnel opens and the Creature is sucked into it. However, instead of being propelled all the way back to the beginning of time, the Creature manages to escape from the tunnel in the year 1936.[4]

After the OPENING TITLES, we cut to a bleak and gritty London street in the year 1999.[5] We are at 76 Totters Lane, near a junkyard owned by one I.M. Foreman. The street is being patrolled by two para-military police officers, DEAVISH and HAMMOND. They come across a man lying in the gutter, clearly exhausted. He had been trying to force his way into the junkyard. His clothes are tattered rags, his burgundy coat faded, his long scarf caked with mud, but we still recognise an older FOURTH DOCTOR.[6]

The almost delirious Fourth Doctor rambles on about having to save someone – a woman – from something which is coming. The two police officers decide to take him to a hospital. There the Fourth Doctor is attended by a female physician, DR KELLER, who reports to a cold-hearted, immaculate businessman named FRELANE.

Dr Keller makes various discoveries about her patient: a dual cardio-vascular system, the ability to store small quantities of air, needles breaking when they touch his skin, etc.[7] But the Fourth Doctor appears to be no stranger to Frelane, who reports his presence to an as-yet-unseen figure. The man orders Frelane to silence the witnesses and deliver the Fourth Doctor to him. However, when Frelane moves to execute his instructions he discovers that he is too late. The Fourth Doctor has come to and escaped into the night, still obsessed with the notion of finding and saving 'her'.

We cut to a library where DOROTHY McSHANE,[8] a young teacher in her late twenties, is reading H.G. Wells's *War of the Worlds*.

Meanwhile, television journalist TONY McCABE interviews the famous entrepreneur, millionaire scientist

PROFESSOR OLIVER HAWKSPUR, a cigar-chomping Howard Hughes who is running for Prime Minister on the platform of the so-called 'Evolutionary Party'. Hawkspur claims to have all the answers to Mankind's survival, but his private conversations with his chauffeur reveal that he is lying.

As she exits the library, Dorothy runs into her boyfriend, ALEX STEWART,[9] a young man in his mid-twenties. After some light romantic banter Dorothy catches a glimpse of the Fourth Doctor watching her. This elicits a flurry of strange visions, sounds and images of another life in her head. Alex takes her home but the visions persist. In a dream she sees herself younger, her hair pulled back, wearing a bomber jacket, fighting an odd assortment of creatures. When she wakes up, she goes to her closet and, from an old, dusty box, she pulls out the bomber jacket from her dream. Emblazoned on its back is a logo reading 'ACE'.

The next day Dorothy and Alex lead an ecology demonstration in front of Hawkspur's headquarters. Dorothy has loaned the jacket to one of her students. Hawkspur himself watches the demonstrators as he drives by in his Rolls-Royce. He eventually comes outside and addresses the protesters, charming them with his eloquence. Suddenly the Fourth Doctor appears in the crowd. He is trying to warn Dorothy to get away. When Hawkspur sees him a weird flux of raw power passes between the two men.

Suddenly, several CYBERMEN emerge from the sewers and scatter the demonstrators.[10] Dorothy falls to the ground. The silver giants close in on the Fourth Doctor, who runs away. Dorothy comes to, but the Cybermen are gone, and no one but her, not even Alex, seems to have noticed anything wrong. The protesters are still entranced by Hawkspur's words. Fleetingly, we see the face of the Creature briefly superimposed on that of Hawkspur.

Later, in a park, Dorothy is once again fighting against her 'visions'. Suddenly, she is attacked by three DALEKS: the SPECIAL WEAPONS DALEK and two WHITE DALEKS.[10] They are obeying Hawkspur's orders to capture her. But as they are about to corner the young woman, a time

tunnel opens and Summerfield and her Eco-Troopers step
out.

A battle is joined, during which the Daleks stun and
capture Flemyng and Sanders. Dorothy escapes to find Alex
who was searching for her. He puts the 'Ace' bomber jacket
on her shoulders. She is thoroughly confused by what is
happening to her. Meanwhile, Summerfield and the two
surviving Eco-Troopers are puzzled by the presence of
Daleks in 1999, but they attribute it to the Creature's powers.
Summerfield has a hunch that if they follow Dorothy, they
will find the Doctor.

At Hawkspur's HQ, the villain confers with two of his
top executives, SWIFT and SNYDER, who report on the
progress of their various ventures, which are all draining
Earth of its vital resources.[11] Frelane enters to report the two
Eco-Troopers' capture, but Hawkspur is not pleased by the
Daleks' failure.

Alex is now comforting Dorothy on a railway station
platform. She heads off to find a telephone. Alex is attacked
and captured by a YETI.[10] Dorothy hears his scream, but
before she can rush to help him, the Fourth Doctor steps out
of the shadows and intercepts her. Exhausted, her head still
filled with alien images and sounds, she faints.

At Hawkspur's HQ, the villain interrogates the two Eco-
Troopers. They know that they are really facing their arch
foe, the Creature, the entity responsible for the Seventh
Doctor's death in the year 2525.

When the Creature was exiled into the past, it remembered
its encounter with the Seventh Doctor, whom it knew to be a
time traveller, and deduced that the Doctor must have visited
Earth in the past. It waited for him and eventually located
him in 1980, when the Fourth Doctor fell to his death
from the radio telescope at the Pharos Project.[12] Instead
of letting the normal regenerative process take place, the
Creature intervened and saved the Fourth Doctor, while
simultaneously capturing him and wiping out his memories.
As a result, the Creature gave rise to an alternate dimension
of time, a 'Dark Dimension', one in which it now has a
second chance to eradicate Mankind. But the Fourth Doctor

escaped and, for reasons unknown to Hawkspur, has been seeking Dorothy.

While Hawkspur explains all this to the two Eco-Troopers, two Yeti arrive and deliver Alex wrapped in a webby cocoon. The villain is disappointed that the monsters did not succeed in capturing the girl, but he has no doubt that, thanks to Alex, he will find Dorothy, and through her, the Fourth Doctor.

At the railway station, OFFICER SPAULDING finds the debris left by the Yeti and an ID card in Alex's name. It turns out that Alex is the son of the former head of UNIT, BRIGADIER LETHBRIDGE-STEWART. The news of his disappearance makes the headlines, and the Brigadier returns from Geneva to look into it.

We cut to the study in the Brigadier's house. It is a comfortable room with a collection of UNIT memorabilia: a Yeti silver sphere, an Auton plastic daffodil, the head of Azal's gargoyle, etc. Dorothy, still unconscious, has been taken there by the Fourth Doctor. The various names that she muttered during her delirium (Cybermen, Autons, Daleks, etc.) convinced the Brigadier that the Doctor is using her to ask for help. But which Doctor?

The Brigadier tells Dorothy how, in 1980, UNIT rescued the Fourth Doctor after his deadly fall from the Pharos radio telescope.

> **Brigadier** *It was the Doctor . . . He should have regenerated. Something held him . . . It wouldn't let his body die . . .* [12]

A few days later, the Fourth Doctor was kidnapped from the UNIT hospital and never seen again – until Dorothy showed up. The Brigadier decides that the two of them should try to find the Fourth Doctor.

Outside, thanks to her sophisticated tracking systems, Summerfield and her two remaining Eco-Troopers have managed to follow Dorothy to the Brigadier's house. They watch as the Brigadier and the girl leave the house in a souped-up, vintage yellow Edwardian roadster – BESSIE. They shoot a homing beacon into the spare tyre. The Brigadier, who has looked after the car since the Doctor last

171

worked for UNIT,[13] uses its own monitoring systems to pick up the signal of a twin heartbeat.

At Hawkspur's HQ, the villain is notified by Snyder that his quarry has been located. Pleased, Hawkspur dispatches two ICE WARRIORS to capture them. Later, in a deserted street, the Ice Warriors come across Summerfield's group and stun and capture Mason and Everitt. Summerfield barely manages to escape.

Meanwhile, the Brigadier and Dorothy have arrived at an ordinary-looking country church with a graveyard. They enter the church and discover that, behind its heavy wooden doors, is a library larger than that of the British Museum. The strange alien noises in Dorothy's head – recognisable as TARDIS-like sounds – increase in volume. They walk down a seemingly endless line of bookshelves, until they come across the Fourth Doctor, who is reading from a large, dusty tome. This finally proves too much for Dorothy, who falls to the ground.

When Dorothy awakens, she discovers that the Fourth Doctor now claims that he wants to be left alone. He behaves in an abnormally rude and antagonistic fashion towards the Brigadier, putting down their old friendship. The Brigadier naturally lashes out at the Time Lord, which causes the Fourth Doctor to grab his head suddenly, as if in great pain.

Indeed, at Hawkspur's HQ Snyder and Swift immediately notify the villain that something – a powerful emotional appeal – is reaching deep down into the Doctor's personality and has finally succeeded in tearing down the mental blocks that they erected when he was their prisoner.

At the church, the Fourth Doctor is now free of Hawkspur's conditioning. He reverts to being his old self with amazing speed and welcomes the Brigadier in his traditional cheery style. He explains that he fought against the conditioning, which drove him into an almost schizophrenic state. He used Dorothy to summon the Brigadier to help him break it. He has also deduced that Dorothy's visions come from the future, that alien memories have been implanted in her mind, and that the strain is proving too much for the girl to handle. When the

Brigadier asks who could have done this to her, the Doctor sheepishly replies, 'Me.'

Outside Summerfield has finally caught up with Bessie. At Hawkspur's HQ, the villain has decided to send his three Daleks to recapture the Fourth Doctor. We also discover that Hawkspur has just won the election and is now Prime Minister.

The Fourth Doctor leads the Brigadier and Dorothy down into the catacombs of the church. The Time Lord is now fully aware that he should have died at Pharos, and that 'someone' managed to keep him alive, for its own reasons. They then walk into an ancient crypt. Inside is a metal pyramid with electric cables attached to it and a jumble of 1930s technology. One of the sides of the pyramid appears to have been exploded from the inside, as if something had broken through from within. It is the primitive, static-electricity-powered, time travel device built in 1936 by the 'real' Professor Hawkspur (i.e. before he was taken over by the Creature) which opened a hole in the Vortex, and which the Creature used to escape his intended fate.[14]

(Fourth) Doctor *The side of it was smashed open from the inside . . . Something wanted to get out . . . And as a result, time's been manipulated . . . History altered . . . I'm not meant to be here . . . Neither are you . . . We're trapped in an alternative reality . . . A dark dimension . . .*

The Fourth Doctor theorises that, since he has been removed from the normal course of time, entropy will set in and ultimately erase each of his future incarnations. At that moment, Summerfield crashes in, but Dorothy hits her on the head. The Fourth Doctor recognises the devices Summerfield carries as 'open-ended voltron-wave transmitters' and deduces that she comes from the future. Furthermore, a hieroglyph stamped on the machine and identifying its maker turns out to be – the Doctor's own (Gallifreyan) signature! A homing beacon tuned into the Doctor's thought waves indicates that the Eco-Troopers travelled to the past to look for the Doctor in one of his earlier incarnations.

The Fourth Doctor sets up the voltron-wave transmitters and opens another time tunnel. He then travels back to 1936 to find out what really happened. There, he is invisible because of time displacement. He watches as Professor Hawkspur and REVEREND MERRICK set up their initial time experiment, using the static-electricity-powered metal pyramid. Hawkspur believes that unlocking the secrets of time is akin to finding immortality. A highly religious Merrick is incensed. He thinks that Hawkspur has betrayed him. He calls him a heretic and a Satanist, and pulls a gun on the professor.

But before the confrontation can be resolved, the Creature drawn from the Vortex rematerialises inside the pyramid. We hear its heartbeat and see the shape of its claws indenting the metal. Merrick, believing it to be Lucifer, fires at the pyramid, causing it to shatter and release the Creature. The monster kills Merrick and takes over Hawkspur (or assumes his shape). But it also becomes preternaturally aware of the Fourth Doctor watching him.

Meanwhile, in 1999, the three Daleks have arrived and attack the Brigadier and Dorothy, forcing them to flee into the time tunnel. They come out in the polluted wasteland of the year 2136, an alternative future where a gun-toting FIFTH DOCTOR is helping human soldiers fight the Cybermen.[15]

In Downing Street the newly-elected Hawkspur, or rather the Creature, has seen the Fourth Doctor watching his emergence in 1936, and is concerned that the Time Lord may marshal the help of his future selves. So he mentally orders his Daleks to enter the time tunnel and hunt them down as well. Summerfield, who has come to, follows them.

In 1999, the Fifth Doctor takes the Brigadier and Dorothy to a fortified camp where the soldiers stand guard around a captive CYBERCOMMANDER. (It can extrude claws from its hands.) The Fifth Doctor attempts to convince the Cybercommander of the ultimate futility of the Cybermen's goals. Once the entire universe has been filled with Cybermen, then what?[16] They discuss the disruption of the time continuum, the threat of the growing entropy and how to rescue the Fifth

Doctor before he is erased from existence. Suddenly the Cybermen attack, freeing the Cybercommander. But just at the same time the time tunnel opens and Hawkspur's Daleks burst upon the scene. While the Daleks engage the Cybermen, the Fifth Doctor encourages the Brigadier and Dorothy to use the tunnel to return to the past. As they do so, they see the Daleks closing in on the Fifth Doctor. [17]

Meanwhile, the Fourth Doctor has returned to the time tunnel and left 1936. He steps out in a surreal White Void where he meets the THIRD DOCTOR who claims to still live – inside the Doctor's head. [18] The Fourth Doctor deduces that their meeting has been caused by a scrambling of the time tunnel, meaning that the Brigadier and Dorothy have tried to follow him. A sense of despair almost overwhelms him, but the Third Doctor brings him back to his senses.

Third Doctor *Have you forgotten about Gallifrey? Think of the Dark Times . . . The turmoil in our mind . . . Your decision was to leave. Do you remember the reason why? (. . .) Think of that reason . . . Don't ever let it die. That would be too easy. Whatever kind of crusade it is we've been leading . . . You cannot let it end like this . . .* [19]

The Brigadier and Dorothy become separated in the time tunnel. The Brigadier arrives in a trial chamber in some undetermined future, when the SIXTH DOCTOR is defending a group of ICE WARRIORS, led by COMMANDER AZZLYX, who are being accused of having purposely delivered contaminated supplies to the Jassix Five colony. With his usual flair, the Sixth Doctor exposes the true villains – a Mining Corporation [20] – but is taken aback when the Brigadier makes his entrance. The Brigadier delivers his warning, just as Hawkspur's Daleks burst onto the scene. The Sixth Doctor and the Brigadier run away, and are intercepted by Summerfield. She opens another time tunnel. The Brigadier leaves with the Eco-Trooper while the Sixth Doctor allows himself to be captured by the Daleks.

Meanwhile, Dorothy rematerialises in the White Void where she finally comes across the Seventh Doctor, who calls her 'Ace' and stirs memories of their past adventures together. He tells her that she was one of his companions, 'Ace by name, ace by nature.' [21] He finally explains that he met his match when he encountered the mysterious Creature in the year 2525. During their ill-fated encounter, the Creature attempted to steal all his knowledge. Before he died, the Seventh Doctor projected a portion of his mind into Ace. Then he suspects that the Time Lords must have intervened to send her back to the point she would have reached in her life had she never met him. [22]

> **Seventh Doctor** *I knew that wherever I was, your mind would act like a beacon . . . Calling me to you, even if I didn't know it . . . My instinct would be to save you, guard the knowledge of the Creature I put in your head . . .*

The Seventh Doctor gambled on the Eco-Troopers being able to open the Vortex without him, thanks to the voltron-wave transmitters he had made for them, and thus dispose of the Creature. Unfortunately, because of Professor Hawkspur's ill-timed 1936 experiment, the monster was able to escape back into the past and retroactively change the future.

Summerfield and the Brigadier come out of the time tunnel into the church's impossibly large library. But they are suddenly confronted by the other Eco-Troopers, their glowing yellow eyes an indication that the four women are now possessed by the Creature. At Hawkspur's HQ, the Creature gloats as the bodies of the Fifth and Sixth Doctors are placed in suspended animation.

Back in the White Void, the Seventh Doctor frees Dorothy of the burden of the memories he had implanted in her mind and transfers them to the Fourth Doctor who has walked into the scene. The Fourth Doctor now knows everything the Seventh Doctor knew about the Creature. The Seventh Doctor then fades away. When the Fourth Doctor starts apologising to Dorothy for the stress that his latter incarnation caused her, she corrects him, saying that her name is – and always was – Ace.

The Fourth Doctor and Ace return to the church in time to

join the Brigadier and Summerfield as they face the four, possessed Eco-Troopers. Summerfield recounts the tale of the Eco-Troopers sent to reclaim the wastelands and confronted by the mysterious Creature, who began killing them, playing cruel cat and mouse games. As hope almost faded, the Seventh Doctor appeared and turned the tide of battle. Looking at the Fourth Doctor, Summerfield recognises that he does not look like her Doctor, yet she can tell they are the same man.

At Hawkspur's HQ, the Creature is preparing to play host to a royal party including visiting dignitaries from other countries.

In the churchyard, the Fourth Doctor has realised that the church's library, which is bigger inside than outside, must be part of his missing TARDIS.

> **(Fourth) Doctor** *Hawkspur must have tried to dimensionally displace it . . . But even he wasn't powerful enough to do that to a TARDIS . . .* [23]

However, the possessed Eco-Troopers manage to capture Summerfield and Ace and vanish, but not before having succeeded in damaging the voltron-wave transmitters. A resolute Fourth Doctor and the Brigadier decide it is now time for them to confront the Creature directly.

At Hawkspur's HQ, the banquet is being held. Much to everyone's surprise, Hawkspur – the Creature – drops all pretence of humanity in a blistering speech. He then lets his three Daleks into the banqueting hall and orders them to exterminate everyone, including Swift and Snyder.

In the TARDIS library (formerly the church's), the Fourth Doctor consults an ancient map showing that, in addition to its four main consoles, the TARDIS is also equipped with secondary consoles in the engine room, the power room – and the library. Following the map's instructions leads him through a maze of bookshelves and eventually to a large area occupied by a three-foot-high mountain of books. After pushing the books aside, the Fourth Doctor triumphantly reveals a TARDIS console. He uses it to re-energise the voltron-wave transmitters. The Brigadier returns, dressed in full battle uniform. He has also brought with him a new floppy hat, scarf and red jacket for the Fourth Doctor, who beams at the sight.

At Hawkspur's HQ, Ace awakens, strapped to an operating table. Alex is there, but he is clearly possessed, just like the Eco-Troopers. The Creature reveals that the various monsters it has been using (Daleks, Cybermen, Ice Warriors) are not the real thing but shape-shifting, bio-morphic clones made of his own substance from images he stole from the Seventh Doctor's mind. The Creature seeks to cleanse Earth of Mankind's presence in order to repopulate it with his own life forms.

The Fourth Doctor and the Brigadier leave the church in Bessie. They carry with them the re-energised voltron-wave transmitters. As they drive away, Cybermen, Daleks, etc., all created by the Creature, start attacking London en masse. Tony McCabe is killed reporting the assault.

The Fourth Doctor and the Brigadier arrive at Hawkspur's HQ. The Time Lord finally confronts the Creature, which he describes as a being 'composed entirely of chronal energy'. The Fourth Doctor asks the Creature how he located him at Pharos. Having found out about the Doctor's previous regenerations from the Seventh Doctor's mind, the Creature explains that it was a matter of elimination. The First Doctor's body was inaccessible at the South Pole, the Second was on Gallifrey,[24] the Third at UNIT's HQ . . . The Fourth was the easiest to seize and control.

The Fourth Doctor finally challenges Hawkspur to a duel by slapping him on the face. (His blood is revealed to be green.) Ace and Summerfield are there, watching the impending confrontation. The Fourth Doctor has seen the bodies of his Fifth and Sixth Incarnations as prisoners inside glass tubes. During this time the Brigadier has secretly positioned the voltron-wave transmitters in the courtyard.

The duel takes place outside. It is an old-fashioned sword fight. Meanwhile the possessed Eco-Troopers morph into white Daleks, which monitor the Brigadier, Ace and Summerfield. But, pressed to respond to the Fourth Doctor's furious attacks, the Creature cannot hold his concentration and the companions are able to escape from them. However, Ace is being held back by her desire to rescue Alex. The Creature reclaims its hold on Alex and the Daleks, but by then the Brigadier has used a rocket launcher to destroy two Daleks. He and Summerfield jump into Bessie and race back to the church.

Meanwhile, in order to defeat the Fourth Doctor, the Creature realises that it needs more energy. It concentrates and the two remaining Daleks vanish. The resulting floating spheres of bio-energy are reassimilated by the Creature. The duel continues. The fight progressively moves to the mansion's roof. There, the Fourth Doctor discovers that energy is drained from the Creature when the monster hits a lightning rod. A now-weakened Creature hisses defiantly:

> **Hawkspur** *You can never defeat me, Doctor . . . You don't know what I am! . . .*
> **(Fourth) Doctor** *A creature of chaos and death . . .* [3]

The Fourth Doctor delivers a final blow that sends the Creature flying over the edge of the roof. But it is Hawkspur who falls to his death, not the Creature, who rises from the Professor's body, his face 'the image of Death itself'.

In order to reach the TARDIS console inside the church, the Brigadier and Summerfield run a gauntlet of Creature-controlled Cybermen.

Inside Hawkspur's mansion, the Creature is pursuing the Fourth Doctor, shooting energy bolts at him. Meanwhile, Ace is trying to help Alex, but it is too late for the young man and he dies in her arms. Enraged, Ace challenges the Creature and intercepts a bolt meant for the Fourth Doctor. She falls to the floor. The Fourth Doctor lunges at the Creature.

While the Creature and the Doctor are locked in a desperate struggle, inside the church, the Brigadier and Summerfield manage to reach the TARDIS console in spite of the Cybermen. The Brigadier succeeds in activating the console which in turns energises the voltron-wave transmitters previously hidden in Hawkspur's courtyard. Another time tunnel opens. The Creature is momentarily distracted, enabling the Fourth Doctor to gain the upper hand. He is thus able to force the Creature into the tunnel. With a last burst of strength, he sends the monster spiralling down towards its doom.[25]

Ace struggles back to her feet. Alex's body is gone. The voltron-wave transmitters are gone too. The Fourth Doctor staggers into scene, looking badly injured, then collapses. Ace rushes to him. Her words – 'don't let it end like this' – echo those of the Third Doctor. The Fourth Doctor smiles and regenerates into, successively, his Fifth, Sixth and finally Seventh Incarnations.

The Seventh Doctor's eyes open and he smiles as he sees Ace. They hug, happy to be back together again.[2]

In an epilogue taking place in the church's graveyard, the Seventh Doctor and Ace pay their respects to the grave of Professor Oliver Hawkspur (1890–1936). The church is now a normal church, and the TARDIS, back in its London police box mode, stands inside. Ace has many questions, none of which the Doctor is inclined to answer. She asks about Summerfield.

> **Seventh Doctor** *Back on her right timeline, back where she belongs . . . As are we all. Who knows, we might even meet her again one day . . .*[1]

Ace has forgotten about Alex and the momentous events they have just lived. Time has returned to normal. The Doctor ushers her into the TARDIS, which dematerialises with its characteristic sound.

Outside, the Brigadier stops and listens for a moment, before depositing a wreath on a grave that reads 'Alexander Lethbridge-Stewart 1969–1979'.[9]

Notes

1 Clearly, the 'Summerfield' character of *The Dark Dimension* is intended to be the 'Bernice Summerfield' of Virgin's series of New Adventures novels. However, since the copyright to that character belongs to Paul Cornell, it is interesting to note that it could not have been used by the BBC in this film without his permission. On the other hand,

the script never refers to the character as 'Bernice', only as Summerfield. There is also a conspicuous lack of any physical description in the script, other than introducing Summerfield as 'a striking young woman with a cropped haircut', which may easily have led any director to cast an actress with a look different from that of the NA character. The dating is somewhat inconsistent with the New Adventure *Love and War*, which states that Bernice Summerfield is from the twenty-fifth century, and *Falls the Shadow*, which states that she was born in 2422. On the other hand, people may just live longer in the future, and later NAs have moved Bernice into the twenty-sixth century.

2 *The Dark Dimension* is deliberately a continuation of the original BBC television series, taking place in some undetermined time after *Survival* (7P), but obviously before *Enemy Within*. If there is a conflict, it is not with the series but with the New Adventures. *The Dark Dimension* appears to open on what might well be an alternate timeline where the Seventh Doctor, alone, comes to the rescue of the Eco-Troopers in the year 2525. Ace has already left (the script remains silent on the circumstances of her departure), and yet the Seventh Doctor has not yet met Bernice. Indeed, the Bernice he meets is not that of *Love and War*. (And later in the story, Summerfield fails to recognise Ace as well.) Because this is supposed to occur before the Creature has had the opportunity to alter the timelines, one is led to conclude that this future diverges from the one depicted in the New Adventures.

On the other hand, in a laudable, and perhaps futile, attempt to force *The Dark Dimension* into the continuity of the New Adventures, Rigelsford hints at the end of the script that a now reunited Seventh Doctor and Ace may still someday meet Summerfield on her 'right timeline', thereby virtually invalidating everything that was supposed to have happened prior to the Creature's meddling. This is the same type of circular logic that was used to introduce Mel in *Trial of a Time Lord* (7A–7C). One has to wonder why Rigelsford chose to deviate from the New Adventures' continuity in the first place, only to then try to 'retcon' it back together. One might argue that, since timelines were altered in *The Dark Dimension*, the same sort of 'memory loss' which occurred in *The Three Doctors* (RRR) or *Mawdryn Undead* (6F) ended up happening to Bernice as well as the Seventh Doctor and Ace, since they clearly do not recognise her in *Love and War*.

3 The true nature and origins of the Creature are shrouded in mystery. The script occasionally drops cryptic hints that the Seventh Doctor knew its true nature, but other than offering the description 'a creature of chaos and death', and 'a being composed entirely of chronal energy', no hard evidence is offered. The fact that the Creature did not know the Doctor before he met him (in his seventh incarnation), and stole his memories, would indicate that the two have never met before, ruling out avatars of the Master, the Shadow, Fenric, etc. In the end, the Creature remains an enigma. Since it is made of 'chronal energy', perhaps it is connected in some fashion with the chronovores of *The Time Monster* (OOO).

4 Interestingly, 1936 was also the year when the Second Doctor faced the Great Intelligence in Tibet in *The Abominable Snowmen* (NN). While no connection is drawn between the two stories, one cannot help but speculate if the Intelligence was not, in some mysterious fashion, connected with the Creature.

5 The bleak near-future depicted here is not inconsistent with that offered in the New Adventures (*Warhead*, etc.). The nefarious activities of the Creature might, in fact, explain the global devastation of the planet, and its subsequent demise the hypothesised clean-up which occurred in the early days of the twenty-first century.

6 *The Dark Dimension* intelligently accounts for the fact that the Fourth Doctor (i.e. Tom Baker) looks older today than he did when we last saw him in *Logopolis* (5V).

7 This is consistent with what has been revealed so far about Time Lords' physiology.

8 While Ace's surname, 'McShane', is never once used in the dialogue of *The Dark Dimension* – and therefore its

182

production would not have established it as part of official BBC series continuity – this nevertheless constitutes a semi-official recognition of its existence. For the record, it was first mentioned in the New Adventure *Set Piece*.

9 *Downtime* introduced the notion that the Brigadier had a first wife called Fiona, who gave him a daughter called Kate, born in the 1970s, and that Doris, mentioned in *Planet of the Spiders* (ZZZ) and seen in *Battlefield* (7N), was his second wife. The identity of Alex's mother is not mentioned but, according to information provided later in *The Dark Dimension*, Alex would have been born in 1969. Even though this date internally conflicts with his description as being in his 'mid-twenties' in the script, one would therefore be inclined to assume that his mother was Fiona. The reason that Kate does not mention the existence of an older brother is probably due to Alex's (traumatic?) death in 1979 in the regular timeline, restored at the end of *The Dark Dimension*.

10 As the script eventually explains, these monsters and images have been pulled out of the dying Seventh Doctor's mind by the Creature, hence their quasi-archetypal appearances in the story. This allowed for a fair amount of freedom for the design teams to update the original BBC television series designs.

11 Another indication consistent with Earth's ecological breakdown projected in the New Adventures. See note 5 above.

12 This reference to the fatal conclusion of *Logopolis* (5V) becomes a crucial plot element, since it is from that point that the timelines diverge, resulting in the creation of the eponymous 'Dark Dimension'. The script does not actually explain how the Creature was able to prevent the Fourth Doctor's regeneration, especially in light of the formidable presence of the Watcher. Since the script states that UNIT was called in and rushed the Doctor to a hospital (from where he was later kidnapped), any intervention by the Creature must have been fast and immediate. The concept that an outside force could prevent a Time Lord from regenerating is an interesting one, and throws new light on

the regenerative process. It suggests that regeneration is an artificially-triggered phenomenon that could be inhibited with some kind of electro-magnetic field, for example.

13 Since this is 1999, one would assume that the Brigadier is referring to *Battlefield* (7N) which took place in the early-to-mid-1990s.

14 Even though no connection is made in the script, this is obviously consistent with Edward Waterfield's own static-powered time travel experiment conducted seventy years earlier, in 1866, in *Evil of the Daleks* (LL). One may even hypothesise that Professor Hawkspur somehow found notes left by Waterfield which inspired him in his ultimately fatal enterprise.

15 This would be a new encounter with the Cybermen, after their attack on Space Station W3 in *The Wheel in Space* (SS) and, in 2070, on *The Moonbase* (HH), but prior to the First Dalek War of 2160 (cf. *The Dalek Invasion of Earth* (K)). As in *Earthshock* (6B), the Fifth Doctor is leading Earth soldiers in battle. Since Earth was arguably not, at that time, a 'wasteland', this description may only apply to that specific location.

16 A new type of Cyberman is introduced here. The interesting dilemma posed by the Fifth Doctor is, regrettably, left unanswered.

17 In the age-old fan debate about the respective strengths of the Daleks and the Cybermen, Rigelsford backs the Daleks, although the script makes it clear that the presence of the Special Weapons Dalek tipped the odds in their favour.

18 The concept that the Doctor somehow carries within him his previous incarnations which can appear or be summoned in case of emergencies would seem inspired by John Peel's New Adventure *Timewyrm: Genesis*, in which the Seventh Doctor is able to evoke the mind of his third incarnation. Generally, the New Adventures novels have definitely favoured the idea that the Doctor's previous incarnations still exist in his mind – also cf. *Timewyrm: Revelation*, *Love and War* and *Head Games*. One might theorise that the

ability to semi-materialise entities such as the Watcher from *Logopolis* (5V), or Cho-Je from *Planet of the Spiders* (ZZZ), which stem from future incarnations, is derived from the same process. Curiously, this anticipates Robert DeLaurentis's concept of individual timestreams in *The Time of My Life*.

19 The connections between the Dark Times and the motives behind the Doctor's self-imposed exile from Time Lord society are developed at greater length in the notes on both John Leekley's *Fathers and Brothers* and Denny Martin Flinn's *The Jewels of Time*, which both deal with various aspects of the Doctor's earlier life(ves). In spite of some superficial differences, it is remarkable to see how coherent a pattern ultimately emerges . . .

20 Likely IMC, from *Colony in Space* (HHH), but not identified as such.

21 The Seventh Doctor implies that Ace had left him by the time he went to fight the Creature, but gives no details. 'It doesn't matter how, why or when . . . They always [leave],' which would appear to conflict with the New Adventures' continuity.

22 One may see the hand of the CIA at work again here . . .

23 The fate of the TARDIS here is somewhat reminiscent of what happened in *Frontios* (6N).

24 The script does not actually mention the second regeneration, but one assumes that it would have been beyond the Creature's reach.

25 The Creature is supposed to be annihilated in the 'hydrogen inrush', 'the point when creation began'. It is interesting to speculate that, if the Creature managed to survive, it may have ended up becoming the evil entity dubbed Fenric, who was supposed to have been created when time began. This seems otherwise to be a fitting end, since the first *Doctor Who* adventure that was disrupted by the Creature's meddling was *Castrovalva* (5Z), which featured the hydrogen inrush as a major plot point.

Review

The Dark Dimension is, by far, the most faithful of all the 'Nth Doctor' scripts, in terms of being a continuation of the original BBC television series. Like *The Five Doctors* (6K), it is based on the cumbersome premise of having to incorporate as many Doctors and classic foes (Daleks, Cybermen, etc.) as possible. Rigelsford rose to the challenge and managed to spin a yarn which accomplished it all, even though some fans may have eventually been disappointed to discover that the Daleks which appeared therein were not real Daleks, etc.

In style, *The Dark Dimension* reads like one of Virgin's earlier New Adventures. The Seventh Doctor is as ruthless and devious as usual, forcing a heavy burden upon Ace without her consent. The Fourth Doctor, who certainly exhibited an occasional darker side (according to Terrance Dicks (cf. *Doctor Who The Handbook – The Fifth Doctor*, p. 227), he was the one initially meant to be a prime suspect in *The Five Doctors* (6K) because 'he was the one you could believe would go bad'), is also darker and grimmer, in spite of the occasional flash of humour. Even the sets alternate between the wastelands of the future and the decay of the near-present. This sense of familiarity is compounded by the presence of Bernice, making *The Dark Dimension* the first almost-produced New Adventure.

The Dark Dimension cleverly manages to appeal to both fans of the Fourth Doctor and, because of its style, fans of the Seventh Doctor. While it may not have been able to reach a larger, more mainstream audience, it certainly could have been very popular with *Doctor Who* fans.

Interview with Tony Harding

Question: Can you tell us a little about yourself? And what was your involvement with The Dark Dimension?

Tony Harding: I am the senior designer and manager of the BBC special effects department. My connection with *The Dark Dimension* was as special effects designer and supervisor leading a team of effects technicians. It would have been our role to design and manufacture the props, the monsters, including a special Dalek, etc. and stage the special effects sequences. I was present at two meetings before the project was dropped.

Q: Did Adrian Rigelsford submit other storylines than the one that was actually scripted?

TH: I believe that there were at least two variations of the script. One was co-written by a lady called Jo McCaul. I, personally, only had access to one version of the script, which I believe was the final one.

Q: The Dark Dimension tries to be consistent with Virgin's New Adventures books; was this a deliberate BBC policy?

TH: I'm afraid I'm unable to answer this question as I have no knowledge of the facts and politics involved.

Q: I've read somewhere that Adrian Rigelsford would have liked k.d. lang to play Bernice Summerfield? Did the producers actually contemplate casting her?

TH: I believe that the casting of k.d. lang was pure fantasy.

Q: Would the classic monsters (Daleks, Cybermen, etc.) have been redesigned for the show?

TH: The Cybermen and the Daleks would have remained the same, but there was to be a one-off special Dalek and a one-off Cybercommander – redesigned.

Q: Had The Dark Dimension been greenlighted, what changes are likely to have been made in the script?

TH: There would almost certainly have been alterations as the meagre budget was insufficient to finance the project as it stood.

Q: Was the decision made from the start to centre the story around Tom Baker's Doctor?

TH: Yes, I believe that the story was to be based around the Tom Baker Doctor.

Q: What truth is there to the rumours that the other Doctors weren't happy about the size of their roles?

TH: I know of at least one Doctor who was unhappy with his contribution.

Q: Also, is there any truth to the rumour that the powers-that-be at the BBC objected to BBC Worldwide physically producing the show?

TH: You mean the rumour that BBC Drama Department objected to Worldwide producing the show ... I can't substantiate the rumour.

Q: *Finally, do you think that the signing of the deal with Philip Segal in 1993 was the last straw that torpedoed the project?*

TH: No. I think the project had already been dropped before the Segal deal had been signed. I myself only found out that *The Dark Dimension* had been abandoned from a newspaper article. I wasn't officially informed for several days.

6

FATHERS AND BROTHERS

by

John Leekley

Background

As mentioned in Chapter 4, Terrance Dicks, Barry Letts, Randy and I were invited to be guests at the Los Angeles-based Gallifrey Convention in February 1994. Unbeknownst to Terrance, Barry, the convention organisers and ourselves, Philip Segal, the executive producer, and Peter Wagg, the then-producer, of what would eventually become *Enemy Within*, were anonymously in attendance.

At that time, the news of Amblin's possible involvement in producing a new *Doctor Who* television series had just hit. Most people legitimately associated Amblin with its founder, the award-winning feature film director, Steven Spielberg. Furthermore, Amblin's track record in the field of television production was, at the time, admittedly far from impeccable. Although it was reasonably successful in commercial terms, *Seaquest DSV* was not popular among science-fiction fans. Many people in attendance had, therefore, leaped to the conclusion that 'Spielberg was going to ruin *Doctor Who*'.

During the first panel of the convention several questions on this subject were asked. Terrance, Barry and I attempted to reassure a visibly worried audience. We outlined the daunting challenges that any producers would face in trying to relaunch *Doctor Who*, especially in the ultra-competitive American television market. We explained the economics of television production: the costs of producing a science-fiction show that would be expected to compete against the best, the reasons why it made financial sense for the BBC to seek co-producing partners, etc. But above all we pointed out that fans should wait for hard news before jumping to conclusions.

Little did we know that we were performing before the two men who were, at the time, in charge of the destiny of *Doctor Who*.

Philip Segal, a British expatriate, had previously worked as an executive for the ABC television network, where he had been involved in the development of series such as *Twin Peaks*, *Thirtysomething*, *Young Riders* and *Young*

Indiana Jones. At Amblin Television he had been one of the executives responsible for the creations of *Seaquest DSV* and *Earth 2*. This type of job can be one of the most frustrating in television, as what reaches the screen after the network's 'input' is rarely what was originally envisioned when the series was first developed. For example, Segal's 'Bible' – the name given to the 50+-page document written to describe a television series and sell it to the network – for *Earth 2* was a superb document, well written and much superior to the blander programme that eventually made it to the screen.

It had been Segal's lifelong dream to produce *Doctor Who*, and he had worked tirelessly since the cancellation of the original BBC television series in 1989 to bring it back. In 1993, thanks to his position at the well-known and respected firm of Amblin, Segal had eventually succeeded in convincing BBC Enterprises to join forces with him in the first-of-its-kind television co-production agreement between BBC Enterprises (later BBC Worldwide), Amblin Television and Universal Television, Amblin's then-partner in the television and film business.

Peter Wagg, another British expatriate, who had previously produced the American version of *Max Headroom*, produced by Lorimar for ABC in 1987-8, and a sci-fi pilot for CBS entitled *Cyberforce*, had been hired by Segal to produce the new television pilot. (Wagg eventually left the *Doctor Who* production in 1995 to return to England to take a job with one of the independent television companies.)

In July 1994 we received a call from Amblin and were invited to meet Segal who, it turned out, had been impressed with our performance at the Gallifrey Convention. At that time the Daltenreys/Lumière project had collapsed and the rumour mill was working overtime, fuelled by ridiculous British press reports about Amblin (e.g. the castings of David Hasselhof, Pamela Anderson and, later, Eric Idle), inaccurate or grossly-deformed leaks from alleged insiders, dubious reports published in various genre magazines, and a growing Internet community of vocal *Doctor Who* fans, especially on rec.arts.drwho and America OnLine.

After the meeting, we volunteered our services to offer technical comments and advice, and to act as 'fan liaisons' with an eye towards debunking rumours while putting out official news from Amblin. Segal gladly accepted our offer, and our first official 'release' came out in September, 1994.

Segal had previously hired writer/producer John Leekley – whose credits include the acclaimed US Civil War novel *The Blue and the Gray*, scripts for *Miami Vice*, *Knight Rider 2010*, *Nightmare Cafe* and *Private Eye*, as well as the pilots for *Kindred, The Embraced* and *The Omen* – to write first a 'Bible' and then a script for the proposed new show, with an aim towards selling it to an American television network. The favourite target in this case was the fledgling Fox Television Network, which had already displayed its inclination towards science-fiction/fantasy programming with *Alien Nation*, *X-Files*, *The Adventures of Brisco County*, *Sliders*, *VR5*, etc.

A few words here to explain the basic economics of American television production. For a variety of legal reasons having to do with anti-trust laws the networks (ABC, CBS, NBC, Fox and now UPN and Warner Bros.) do not actually 'buy' or 'produce' a series, they 'licence' it, meaning that it remains the property of its producers. The networks pay a 'licence fee' which gives them the right to broadcast the show a limited number of times, before all rights (including syndication, i.e. future reruns, videocassette and foreign) revert to the producers. When the amount of the licence fee paid by the network is actually less than what it costs to make the show, the producers finance the difference out of their own pockets – this is called 'deficit funding' – in the hope of recouping that money, and more, from lucrative syndication, foreign sales, etc.

In the case of *Doctor Who*, the licence fee paid by Fox would be expected to cover most, if not all, of the costs required to make the programme. After its initial broadcast on Fox, BBC Worldwide would then be the owner (co-owner in this case with Universal Television) of a state-of-the-art and (mostly) paid-for programme, which it could then resell to foreign countries, merchandise, and broadcast on

BBC1, without it costing much in terms of British investment money, a much appreciated fact at a time when the BBC's resources were said to be stretched.

John Leekley's script was eventually delivered in September 1994. Even though the script was officially entitled only *Doctor Who*, the more distinctive title *Fathers and Brothers* was fully endorsed by John Leekley.

[To be continued in the following chapter.]

Story

ACT ONE:

We open on Gallifrey, located 'in a distant galaxy, one million light years from Earth'.[1]

The home planet of the Time Lords is described as 'strange' and 'majestic', 'stark' and 'solemn'. It is a desert world of quiet mesas and sun-burned canyons, without grass or water, orbiting around a binary sun system. The sky is 'vivid shades of red and orange'. The rocky landscape is littered with ruins of an ancient civilisation.

The script then reveals the presence of a huge, domed city, a perfectly controlled oasis housing crystal spires, flowery gardens and fountains of running water.

The action moves inside the Domed City, into what is dubbed the 'Time Lord Temple', a majestic amphitheatre in which the Time Lords conduct their affairs. 'Floating in the air, just above them, is an amazing display of the galaxy.'[2]

The Time Lords are gathering for an emergency session. They are described as 'humanoid like us, but ... a little strange to our eyes ... clearly not from Earth.' They arrive by stepping out of a 'transmat', which is a floating 'obelisk of light', eight feet high, four feet wide and one foot deep, seemingly made of black marble – 'but on closer inspection, the black is swirling around inside the obelisk.'[3]

We are then introduced to some of the story's main protagonists. The first is the MASTER, who is Gallifrey's Minister of Defence. He is in his forties, with 'eyes like black lasers ... a face like Iago'. Next to him is the CASTELLAN,

Gallifrey's Chief of Security, a 'rugged hawk-faced man', wearing a uniform similar to those worn by the Chancery Guards. And then we finally meet CARDINAL BORUSA, the President of the Time Lords.[4] He is a 'tough old man', who wears the Sash of Rassilon, the insignia of the ruler of the Time Lords.

Borusa is angry because the Master clearly overstepped his authority by calling this meeting without consulting him first as the law requires. The Master claims that he was told that the President was gravely ill, but Borusa challenges him on that point, and the Master eventually backs down, claiming to have been 'misinformed'.

> **Borusa** *Yes.* (**In a loud, stern voice**) *Did everyone hear that?! The Master tells us he was 'misinformed'. Are there any other Time Lords present here who are 'misinformed' about who rules this Council? (. . .)*
> (**To the Master, bitter**)
> *I'm still wearing the Sash . . . You will have to be patient awhile longer.*

The Master then yields the floor to the Castellan, who presents a disturbing report. Gallifrey is threatened . . . by the DALEKS.

> **Castellan** *We are under attack from the Daleks, at all frontiers. These mindless killing machines have slaughtered colonies at the far reaches of our Dominion . . .[5] They have even sent their scouts to probe our own defences . . .*

The Castellan wants the President to declare martial law, but Borusa opposes such a measure, because it would cause rebellions in their colonies and strife with their allies.

> **Borusa** (**glaring**) *How do you think the Elders built this Republic? It is held together with peace treaties between the planets, not the threat of your Demat weapons.*[6]

Borusa prepares to leave, but the Master still has an ace in his sleeve. He reminds the President that they dispatched a

194

fellow Time Lord, Zorbra, to the remote mountain areas of Gallifrey to check for signs of Dalek invasion. He then instructs two guards to unwrap a mysterious package which dramatically reveals Zorbra's corpse, 'sucked dry, like a fly tossed out of a spider web'.

The Master explains that they found an entire village of Outsiders[7] murdered by the Daleks. Shocked by this grim news, Borusa agrees to declare martial law and, in an act of virtual surrender, asks for the Master's advice. The latter seizes this opportunity to remind the gathered Time Lords that they used to be a conquering race.

> **Master** *Look out there, across the mesas . . . And you will see the ruins of the temples of our ancestors. They ruled by the sword. They built our empire planet by planet . . . And their great cities are solemn proof that we are descendants of a proud warrior race . . . A race that has proven itself superior . . . In the thousand years since we harnessed the Black Hole,[8] and with that power found we could travel in time, we have not been forced to pick up the sword . . .*

The Master goes on to state that the Daleks are just what was needed to return the Time Lords to their previous glories and force them to expand their dominion to the farthest reaches of the galaxy.

Borusa knows that he is nearing the end of his twelfth and final regeneration and he has seemingly lost the will to fight the Master, who by now has secured the other Time Lords' support. He publicly bequeaths him the Sash of Rassilon, which will make him ruler of Gallifrey.

> **Borusa** *According to our ancient custom, upon my death, my heir,[9] the Master, will wear the Sash of Rassilon . . .[10]*

But softly, and to himself, he wonders about the Doctor's absence.

The script then shifts to the rugged mountains of Gallifrey – the same mountains where Daleks have been reported – and at last we meet the DOCTOR. He is described as a young man, 'ruggedly handsome . . . with piercing sky blue eyes – while all others of his race have dark eyes'.[11] He wears a long jacket, a duster with many pockets and buckles. He and two OUTSIDERS, dressed in crude woven clothes, are exploring dark, forbidding mountain caves. A transmat obelisk stands on the trail behind them.

Inside the caves, they find various Gallifreyan carvings and relics, bearing the symbols of the Time Lords. From inside a jar the Doctor pulls out scrolls, which turn out to be the long-lost Scrolls of Rassilon.

Doctor (reading) *'These are the Words of Rassilon, Father of Gallifrey, First Time Lord. He has written and foretold that whoever finds these Scrolls shall be the One to lead the people of Gallifrey out of the Time of Darkness. Following the path of the Spirit Guide, the New Leader shall heal the planet, defending it from its enemies . . .'*[12]

The Doctor's excavations are disturbed by the sudden scuttling, metallic sounds of DALEKS (heard but not seen at this stage). Instead of fleeing, like the Outsiders, the Doctor's curiosity proves too strong and he heads deeper into the caves to investigate.

When we come across a Dalek it is described as a 'monstrous creature . . . as much spider as human . . . As it rises up, we can see the armour separate from the body, revealing the insect abdomen . . . The claw-like hand and arms unfold . . . Its feet, which are pointed hooks, extend out . . . It is eight feet high . . . Its red eyes and face, which is barely humanoid . . . Gnashing mouth with fangs . . .'[13]

The Doctor manages to escape the Dalek by blinding him with a flare. He runs for his life out of the cave, with the Dalek hot in pursuit. As the Dalek is just about to snatch him, the Doctor leaps out, flying straight through the Transmat.

He lands right inside the Time Lord Temple, where his dishevelled and impromptu appearance draws disapproving remarks from the other Time Lords, most especially the Master.

Master *This is the typical behaviour of a bastard* . . . [14]

Borusa berates the Doctor for his entrance, then asks for his opinion on how to deal with the Daleks. The Doctor responds with a flippant remark, suggesting that the Time Lords hire the Daleks to collect their taxes. This draws further ire from the Castellan. Both he and the Master emphasise in their speeches that the Doctor is 'young'.

Master *Our young Doctor has no idea what it takes to rule. He wouldn't even be a Time Lord if it weren't for the permanent seat which is provided for the Prydonians . . . A clan which is now extinct, and has no votes in this chamber* . . . [15]

The Doctor urges the Time Lords to investigate who is behind the Daleks. At first, they listen to him, but then they turn against him when he criticises them.

Doctor *What have we become? The perfect bureaucrats. Cold efficiency has replaced wisdom . . . The Master is brilliant, it is true, but he is also cruel and ambitious. He is the perfect embodiment of our worst as a race . . . without feeling or affection. I will not serve the Time Lords while he rules* . . . [16]

The Castellan asks for the Doctor to be placed on trial, but as chaos erupts in the Temple, Borusa's hearts suddenly fail. The meeting is put on hold; the dying President is taken away.

Later, the Doctor has a quiet meeting with the dying Borusa in his chambers.

Doctor *I'm sorry for all the trouble I have caused you. You gave me a home when no one would have me. This is not the way I should have repaid you* . . .

He then shows Borusa the Scrolls of Rassilon.

Doctor *They seem to foretell the future* . . .
Borusa *Why didn't you tell the Time Lords? It is written than the finder of the lost scrolls* . . .

Doctor ... *Will lead his people out of Darkness. Yes, I know. But it is also written that the finder of the Scrolls will be descended from Rassilon, as you are, and your son, Ulysses ...* (**Bitter**) *And his son, the Master ...* [17]

This leads Borusa to reveal to the Doctor the secret of his origins.

Borusa *Until we perfected time travel, many of our early explorers were lost. My own son, Ulysses, never returned ... [He] had a second child while exploring the Blue Planet, Earth ... by a woman of that world ... You are that blue-eyed child ... When your mother died, your father sent you back to Gallifrey, to be raised among his own people.* [18]

The realisation that the Master is his half-brother hits the Doctor badly. He asks Borusa why he was never told the truth.

Borusa *Because your mother was from Earth, you were of mixed race ... and would have never been allowed to be a Time Lord. Everything you have to offer Gallifrey would have been lost. Without a clan to protect you, you would have been sent to the wilderness, to live among the Outsiders ...* [19]

Borusa encourages the Doctor to find his father, fight his brother and help Gallifrey. Then he dies.

The Master immediately takes over, and sends the Castellan to arrest the Doctor. The Doctor manages to escape to the space port, but all the TARDISes, which are in their natural shapes of black pyramids, are locked. In an adjacent museum he finds an old Type 40 from the early days of Gallifreyan space exploration. It looks like a Victorian armoire with ornate brass handles and polished wood veneer. Inside, it contains the traditional console with, in its centre, 'gigantic crystals extending upward into the awesome space of the ship'. [20]

The Doctor hijacks the TARDIS and dematerialises. At the same time, Borusa's departing 'soul' merges with the crystals of the TARDIS. The Doctor realises that his late grandfather has become the 'Spirit Guide' foretold by Rassilon.

Doctor *Pure life force . . . Resonating with the ship . . .*

Borusa *The crystals are even more powerful than we ever imagined. They can maintain my existence . . . Here, in this ship.*

Doctor (realising) *You are the Spirit Guide . . .* **(Slight smile)** *We should make quite a team . . . A condemned fugitive and a ghost.* [21]

Borusa reveals that this TARDIS was Ulysses' TARDIS, mysteriously returned to Gallifrey.

They then escape a tractor beam from Gallifrey and set course for the last co-ordinates registered in the TARDIS's memory banks – London, England, 8 September 1944, 10:00 p.m.

Behind on Gallifrey the Master is furious at the Castellan for losing the Doctor. He swears to kill his brother with his own hands, but the Castellan reminds him of Gallifreyan Law.

Castellan *My Lord. It is forbidden for Time Lords to kill. You would relinquish forever your title.* [22]

Master *Then you will be my sword, Castellan. Find him. Don't fail me again . . .*

The Castellan then adds that, since all TARDISes use power drawn from Gallifrey's Black Hole, the Eye of Harmony, every time the Doctor travels through space and time, they on Gallifrey will know of his location. [23]

We then cut to a view of London during the Blitz. The Doctor surveys the destruction from inside the TARDIS, drawing a parallel with the situation on Gallifrey.

ACT TWO

We return in front of the British Museum, where we meet LIEUTENANT LIZZIE TRAVIS, an American WAC from Kansas. She passes an ordinary London police box on her way to a meeting with her colleague (and presumed boyfriend), Intelligence officer JOHN YEATS, who is helping the British with the famous Enigma machine. They are reporting directly to WINSTON CHURCHILL himself.

Inside the TARDIS, the Doctor and Borusa discuss Earth. It is the Doctor's first visit to the Blue Planet.

> **Borusa** *When you were a boy on Gallifrey, you would stare for hours into the night sky. You never knew why the Earth called out to you. And I couldn't tell you . . .* [24]

Then the TARDIS rematerialises right next to the police box and assumes its shape. The Doctor goes out to investigate the origin of the Gallifreyan signal which the TARDIS detected. It comes from the Egyptian section of the British Museum, whose many artifacts have been stored away to preserve them from the Blitz.

Meanwhile, the newly-decoded Enigma message informs Prime Minister Churchill that the Germans are about to launch a new hail of V2s at London at 11:00 p.m. Lizzie pleads to release the information in order to evacuate the civilians. But John and the British point out that if they do so, they will reveal to the Germans that their code has been broken. It is a heart-wrenching decision, and one Lizzie cannot stomach. John reaches out to her and embraces her.

Elsewhere in the Museum, thanks to an old JANITOR, the Doctor has found the source of the signal. It emanates from the burial mask of the ancient Egyptian pharaoh CHEOPS, builder of the Great Pyramid and, in reality, Ulysses the Explorer.

> **Doctor** *The fall from the bomb hitting must have caused the crystal in the mask to begin its signalling again, after thousands of years of silence. The mask is a transmitter . . . It led us here . . .*

On the sarcophagus the Doctor discovers some hieroglyphics.

> **Doctor** *This was written in 2500 BC. It tells the story of a man from a distant planet, who came to Egypt and taught them wonderful things . . . Hieroglyphics . . . How to build the great pyramids . . . I need to open this. I think my father may be inside.*

Janitor *You'll need one of the professors to come down here and give the nod.*
Doctor *It's OK. I'm next of kin . . .*

Once opened, the sarcophagus is found to be empty, but on the underside of its lid the Doctor discovers more hieroglyphics.

Doctor *It's in Gallifreyan.* (**Reading**) *'To my son, who will search for me. If you receive this signal, you will know where to find me. Forgive me for leaving you behind. Ulysses.'*[25]

The Doctor now knows that his father lived the rest of his natural life and died in Ancient Egypt – his next destination.

On his way out he meets Lizzie, who has overheard part of his conversation with the Janitor. She is the first Earth Woman he has ever met and he falls under her charm. This is somewhat reciprocal.

Lizzie *Who are you?*
Doctor *I am the Doctor.*
Lizzie *What are you the 'doctor' of?*
Doctor *Many things. Temporal engineering, metaphysics, archaeology, history, quantum mechanics, astronomy, medicine . . . The things one must know.*
Lizzie *I have a PhD in physics and I have never heard of temporal engineering.*
Doctor *It hasn't been invented yet.*

Lizzie is suspicious of the Doctor – his knowledge of supposedly top secret matters such as V2 rockets, and his familiarity with coded languages, etc. All this makes her suspect him of being a Nazi spy.

The Doctor strides towards the door. Lizzie pulls her gun and orders him to stop. At that moment a V2 falls barely half a mile away, causing her to stumble. The Doctor seizes this opportunity to race out of the museum. Lizzie runs after him.

The Doctor rushes to the TARDIS, Lizzie hot on his heels. She follows him inside, and then discovers the seemingly impossible immensity of the TARDIS.

Simultaneously Yeats, who was running after her, sees her step into the police box. But at that very same moment the V2s start falling, causing a huge explosion which destroys the entire street.

Inside the TARDIS Lizzie tries to get out but discovers that she cannot. The doors will not open. The Doctor tells her that it is too late. They are on their way to Egypt, 4652 years ago. A frightened Lizzie fires her gun, but being in a state of temporal grace, its bullet just floats harmlessly in the air.[26]

ACT THREE
The Doctor attempts to make friends with Lizzie, and engagingly and candidly tells her his story. She does not believe him.

> **Doctor** *I'm looking for my father. He was a Pharaoh, called Cheops by the people of Egypt.*
> **Lizzie (shakes her head)** *I must have gone nuts. Is this a nut house?*
> **Doctor (frowns)** *Nut house? I'm not familiar with the expressions of Earth, yet.* **(Studies her face)** *My mother was an Earth woman, like you. I hope you have an opportunity to meet her . . .*

He is fascinated by her, and the Earth culture he is discovering first-hand for the first time. She, on the other hand, remains both hugely sceptical and more than a little hostile, even after being introduced to Borusa.

Some of that incredulity vanishes when they arrive in Ancient Egypt, circa 2500 BC, near the Sphinx and the Great Pyramid of Giza. (The second Pyramid is still under construction.) They rematerialise inside Cheops' burial chamber – a room full of treasures, painted with scenes of Egyptian life and odd drawings, reminiscent of Gallifrey. The Doctor reiterates the urgency of his mission.

> **Lizzie** *If he was the Pharaoh and he died, ah, 4,500 years ago, what's the urgency? I'm sure he's still dead . . .*

Doctor *You don't understand . . . We, of Gallifrey, are capable of twelve regenerations. We are nearly immortal, by Earth's standards. My father is in his first life. To be entombed would be like being condemned to hell . . .* [27]

When they step out, they discover that the V2 explosion caused the chameleon circuit to stick. The TARDIS still looks like a London police box. Borusa thinks it looks undignified, but the Doctor likes it.

Doctor *The chameleon cloaking circuit seems to be jammed, Cardinal. It's going to seem a little odd to the Egyptians to find a London police box in their tomb . . .* [28]

Borusa *It's humiliating. This exterior hardly rises to the dignity of a Time Lord's ship . . .*

Doctor (grins) *I'm starting to like it.*

From a hidden observation post inside the Great Pyramid, they watch as Egyptian PRIESTS place Cheops' body inside the royal sarcophagus, and then cover his face with the same signal-broadcasting mask that the Doctor saw earlier in London. He explains to Lizzie that the Pyramid itself acts as an amplifier for the SOS broadcast by the mask worn by the pharaoh buried in its exact centre.

Doctor *Fascinating. My father didn't build this pyramid to be buried in. He built it because he needed to amplify the mask's radio signal to reach Gallifrey. He had the sarcophagus placed in the exact centre. He is sending out an SOS . . .*

After the Priests have left, the Doctor and Lizzie pull Cheops' – Ulysses' – body out of the sarcophagus. He looks very much like the Doctor, but aged. But, as the Doctor remarks, his body will soon regenerate.

Suddenly the Egyptian Priests return and, upon watching what they consider to be an act of desecration, attack them. During the ensuing battle the Doctor and Lizzie become separated. Meanwhile the Priests outside have triggered the fall of a huge, granite block which seals them alive inside the Pyramid. Lizzie is left alone when Ulysses' body begins to regenerate.

ACT FOUR

Trying to escape the two remaining Priests the Doctor accidentally comes across the sealed burial chamber of Cheops's Queen – his Mother.

> **Doctor (reading)** *'Herein this sacred chamber lies my Queen, mother of my son, love of my life. In her arms, I have forsaken eternity. Herein, my Queen is safe . . . For only the resonating crystals of the Heavens can open this door.'*

The Doctor escapes from the Priests by using a handful of crystals from the TARDIS to enter the tomb.

The Queen is (was) a startlingly beautiful woman with blue eyes. Inside her tomb are toys, which stir distant memories in the Doctor's mind. He finds a locket, a carved alabaster relief of his mother's face, and takes it as a memento. The Doctor eventually gains an understanding of why his father chose to stay on the Blue Planet.

> **Doctor** *I don't remember a great Queen . . . Just a mother who held me and played with me . . . You must have been an extraordinary woman. If you don't mind, I think I'll stay with you a while, and talk . . . Just to let you know how things turned out for me . . .*

Meanwhile Lizzie takes the newly-regenerated Ulysses – now, a thirty-year-old man, 'powerfully built, rugged features, weathered face with dark eyes' – back to the TARDIS. The regeneration has been difficult and, at first, Ulysses suffers from amnesia. Then, with Borusa's help, his memories start coming back. He remembers his son and what happened to him.

> **Ulysses** *I remember holding him, when he was just two years old . . . burning up with the River Fever. We knew he would die, like the others were dying. I had to send*

> *him back to Gallifrey to be cured... Then my wife*
> *became sick with the Fever... and she died. I had lost*
> *everything, and no reason to stay on Earth. But as I*
> *made preparations to leave, my TARDIS was stolen...*
> *and I was trapped on Earth.* [29]

Having finished paying his respects to his mother, the Doctor contacts the TARDIS and asks Borusa to bring him back through the Transmat.

Borusa is in the process of transporting the Doctor when an 'accident' occurs. The Transmat 'explodes' – the Doctor makes it safely back to the TARDIS, but Ulysses is pulled into the Vortex and scattered into a whirlpool of electrons. He is projected out of the TARDIS, randomly lost throughout Earth history.

ACT FIVE:
We cut back to Gallifrey. The 'accident' is revealed as an attempt by the Master and the Castellan to destroy the Doctor and Ulysses from afar. The Master is the one who stole Ulysses's TARDIS and stranded him in Egypt.

> **Master** *I was only a boy, but even at such a tender age, I*
> *could see that without the 'Great Explorer', one day I*
> *would rule this galaxy. I knew that after I got rid of*
> *him, I would only have old Borusa to deal with... He*
> *was even nicely entombed under millions of tons of*
> *rocks, and my baby brother rescues him!*

The Castellan has failed again, which makes the Master very unhappy. He orders the Castellan to hunt down both Ulysses and the Doctor, warning him that his life now depends on it.

Meanwhile, the Doctor is determined to find Ulysses again, but Borusa reminds him that he must first help Gallifrey to get rid of the scourge of the Daleks. When the Doctor refuses, Borusa puts the TARDIS on hold.

> **Doctor** *Why are you doing this? Why won't you help me?*
> *He's your son!*

Borusa *The Daleks will continue to kill our people . . .*
until we stop them. You and I have no choice but to let
go of our own desires . . .

Doctor (shaking his head) *Maybe I'm not the One the*
Scrolls are talking about . . .

Borusa *You'll have to find the answers within your-*
self . . . Your life depends on it. The lives of everyone on
Gallifrey depend on it . . .

Doctor *The Scrolls talk about the 'enemy within' . . .* [30]
How will I know him?

Borusa *The Enemy will reveal himself.*

Doctor *Do you have to be so damn inscrutable? Just*
speak plainly.

Borusa *On Skaro, you will finally meet the Enemy.*

SKARO! Borusa then reveals that his analysis of the
clothes worn by the Doctor during his earlier encounter with
a Dalek on Gallifrey has enabled him to trace them to that
Earth-like world whose population was killed during the
savage Neutron Wars.

While they travel to Skaro, the Doctor and Lizzie share an
emotional moment. She describes her brief meeting with his
father. She softens and puts her hand on his arm, as she
comes to realise how much all this means to him, and that he
may never find his father again. She tenderly hugs him and
very innocently kisses him. [31]

They then arrive on Skaro, a planet once inhabited by a
humanoid race called Kaleds. They land in a city which,
because of the Neutron Wars, is now overrun by weeds,
empty and barren, except for small rodents and insects. [32]

They step out of the TARDIS and soon come face-to-face
with feral, wild-eyed teenagers, clearly mutated: 'blistered
skins, heads with only tufts of hair . . .' The Doctor and
Lizzie are horrified.

ACT SIX
Later. The Doctor and Lizzie have explored the Dead City
and its outskirts. The parallels with Earth, and its own wars,
are obvious.

Lizzie *This kind of madness could never happen on Earth . . .*

Doctor (averting his eyes) *Skaro is more like Earth than you could imagine . . .* [33]

While exploring a network of caves, looking for signs of life, the Doctor and Lizzie are captured by non-mutated Kaled survivors who have been living underground in the hope of someday reclaiming the surface of their world. They are taken before the city's female commander, ARAN, whose soldiers protect their home from the hostile mutants from the surface.

Aran *We are from the state of Pater Nomen. Like all Kaleds, we were forced underground by the neutron missiles. We have lived in this cave system for one hundred and nine years.*

Lizzie *The other Kaleds?*

Aran *In missile silos, abandoned mines, and caves around the world. We teach our children the legends of life in the sunlight . . .* **(grim smile)** *. . .but with each passing generation, it seems more distant.*

When questioned about the Daleks by the Doctor, Aran declares her ignorance. She then introduces the Doctor to their Chief Scientist, DAVROS. He is described as a 'paraplegic; his eyes, ears, face, throat, main organs and left arm have been replaced with bio-mass plastic . . . His whole body seems crumpled down . . . The rest [of his body] is not visible, hidden by his elegant flowing robe.' His name means 'bearer of gifts' in the old Kaled tongue. He is the only man to have lived through the Neutron Wars, making him 125 years old, hence his cyborg appearance. [34]

Davros gives the Doctor and Lizzie a tour of his labs. He tells them about the mutations which afflicted the survivors of the wars.

Doctor *You couldn't stop the genetic changes?*

Davros *Nothing I did worked. So I became determined to create an armour that would protect them from the radiation. What you see here are exoskeletons,*

> *genetically engineered from DNA, taken from the insects above who have survived.*
>
> **Lizzie** *Biological armour . . . to return to the surface . . .*
>
> **Davros** *. . .To the blue skies we once knew. To feel the sun on our faces . . .*

After the Doctor and Lizzie leave, Davros retires to a communications room. There it is revealed that he has been secretly working for the Master, and has been providing him with Daleks.

The Doctor and Lizzie return to the surface to explore and eventually discover that Davros has lied to the Kaleds. Outside the cities, in the mountains, there is no radioactivity. It is safe to live there. The Doctor wonders why Davros is making synthetic armours for his people if he knows that the mountains are safe . . .

They return to the city. There, they see a DALEK harvesting a pitiful mutant and carrying him away. They follow him to an abandoned mine, and down a mine shaft. There they discover the empty dry husks of creatures who have been captured and sucked dry. They sneak through the mine and come across a secret Dalek factory: 'Rows of vat-grown armour for the mutants in thick bio-mass fluid . . . The armour looks like the legs of eight-foot crabs . . .'

They watch as Davros places the hapless mutant in a shell, closes it around him, and injects him with a serum.

> **Davros** *This is your armour. It is your salvation . . . You will wear this all your life. Your body will fuse to the new exoskeleton. Your abdomen will increase in size . . . This [serum] is my gift to you . . . It will help to speed the process. Very soon, the metamorphosis will be complete. Then, you will be one of us . . . You will be invulnerable . . . You will belong to the master race. And together we will rise up and claim the entire universe as our domain.* [35]

Before the Doctor and Lizzie can leave they are detected, pursued and captured by the Daleks. A Dalek throws his sticky web all over them, drawing it with lightning speed from its spinnerets, located on its abdomen. In no time the Doctor and Lizzie find themselves wrapped inside a webby cocoon and hung upside down.

ACT SEVEN
The Doctor tries talking with the Dalek, hoping to reach his buried, human side, but in vain.

> **Doctor** *You are humanoid. In your soul, you are the same as us . . .*
> **Dalek** *Once we were like you . . . weaklings. We hid in the shadows, burned by the radiation. We watched as the others died . . . Now we are immune to radiation . . . immune to heat and cold and hunger. This is the gift of our creator, Davros.*

Lizzie, on the other hand, has some success, evoking the image of a mother figure. But Davros arrives and puts a stop to this.

> **Lizzie** *What has Davros done to you?*
> **DAVROS** *I have given him the gift of freedom. Freedom from choice, freedom from human weakness.*

Davros sends the Dalek away. Lizzie asks how he, a great scientist who worked his whole life for the good of his people, could turn into such a monster.

> **Lizzie** *I have seen the horror caused by those who claimed they are the master race. You're not even human any more . . .*
> **Davros** *What do you find so special about being human? There is only pain and misery. To be sure the serum would work, I used it on myself. I began to experience a life free of pain . . . A life with purpose. You see, I created them in my own image . . .* [36]

Taking off his cloak, Davros reveals that his lower bottom half is that strange combination of insect exo-skeleton and spider-like protuberant belly. He then glides away, cackling like a madman.

Left alone, the Doctor and Lizzie eventually manage to

break free by swinging their cocoons so that they fall in a pit infested with feral rodents. The rodents tear the cocoons; the Doctor then uses his sonic screwdriver to drive them away.[37]

The Doctor and Lizzie manage to escape and return to the underground Kaled city to warn Aran. The commander gives them some explosives, and they go back to the Dalek factory to blow it up.

Then, confronted by Aran, Davros shows his hand and reveals his motivations.

Aran *Why? You, more than anyone, know the horror of war. Why have you started it all over again?*

Davros *Why? After the neutron missiles did their work, I thought life was over . . . But then I began to see life all around me. The bombs destroyed the people . . . But do you know who survived the radiation . . . who prospered? The insects! And it struck me, with such clarity, that humans weren't the superior race. This was my opportunity to create a new life form. Without the pain or desire, or guilt or remorse . . . Only victory and survival. So I helped the mutants to become more like the insects . . . to become the perfect race . . .*[38]

Meanwhile, at the Dalek factory, after shooting a Dalek using Lizzie's gun, the Doctor succeeds in his mission and plants a bomb.

Back at the underground city Davros has just ordered the Daleks to exterminate Aran and her men when a black TARDIS pyramid appears. The Master and the Castellan have come to Skaro. The Master needs more Daleks, as colonies are now revolting. Davros claims he has thousands of victims ready to be made into Daleks, starting with the Doctor.

Suddenly, the bomb planted by the Doctor explodes. The factory is destroyed. The explosion scatters and confuses the Daleks. The Kaleds escape in the ensuing chaos. Davros realises that all his Daleks are gone.

The Master orders the Castellan to shoot Davros with his Demat gun, which he does. The Master than assumes command of the surviving Daleks.

Master *Listen to me . . . Listen to my voice . . . I am the Master . . . You must escape. Come with me . . . now. With me, you will have a purpose. You are the most invincible soldiers that have ever been created. Together, we will conquer the galaxy . . .* [39]

He orders them inside his TARDIS and they follow.

When the Doctor and Lizzie return to the Doctor's TARDIS they are confronted by the Master.

Doctor *Are you here to take me back?*
Master *No . . . I like you better as a fugitive.* [40]
Doctor *How long have you known?*
Master *I always knew you were my little mongrel brother. Like it or not, we are linked together by blood.*

The Master offers the Doctor a dagger and tries to provoke the Doctor into attacking him. But Borusa intervenes, pointing out that the Master is, after all, the Doctor's brother.

The Master tries to make the Doctor accept that he is the same as him, but the Doctor avoids the trap and hands the dagger back to the Master. Had the Doctor used the dagger, the Master would have lost only one life, but the Doctor would have lost his Time Lordship and would have become a true renegade. [41] The Master accepts his defeat and leaves.

Master *I still rule. And there's nothing you can do about that.*
Doctor *We'll see.* [42]

Afterwards, the Doctor asks Lizzie if she is all right. She shakes her head in amazement.

Lizzie *Do you have any more family members I haven't met?*

We then cut to a mountain top on Skaro. We see the happy Kaleds reclaiming their planet. The Doctor asks Lizzie to come with him, but she is unsure.

Doctor *This is your choice, Lizzie. Not mine.*
Lizzie *If we travelled together, we would have the time of our lives. But it wouldn't really be my life . . .*

They reach out and hold each other. The Doctor gives Lizzie the locket he took from his mother's tomb for her to remember him.

> **Doctor** *Now I know why my father was willing to risk being entombed . . . Why he gave up his immortality, for a woman.*

Trying to mask his feelings, the Doctor sets the co-ordinates for the same moment in space-time from which he took her. They rematerialise in 1944 London mere seconds after the V2 explosion. They say goodbye, not knowing when or if they'll ever meet again, then the Doctor 'gives her a gentle kiss on both cheeks'. Lizzie returns to John Yeats and her life in Kansas.

Inside the TARDIS a saddened Doctor sets the controls for the location where Borusa claims Ulysses might be: seventeenth-century North America, Pirate's Cove. The Doctor looks up with a grin.

> **Doctor** *What are we waiting for? Power up the crystals, Cardinal . . .*

'And with an eerie sound, they vanish in time . . .'

Bible

John Leekley's Bible was finalised in the early part of 1994, before the above script was completed. It was a 45-page document which Segal art directed with the help of production designer Richard B. Lewis, illustrators Matthew Codd and Trevor Goring and production assistant Jesse E. Augustine. A dozen or so copies were printed and bound in fawn leather, bearing the Gallifreyan seal-like signature of the Doctor, as seen in *The Deadly Assassin* (4P).

Because the Bible preceded the script, not all its concepts were exactly the same. The Bible purports to be written by Borusa long after his consciousness has merged with the TARDIS and he has travelled with the Doctor:

I have instructed him [a scribe] to write these chronicles in the language of the Blue Planet, in long flowing script, because I believe that is the way the Doctor prefers it. Our own hieroglyphics of Gallifrey can't capture the real adventure of it all, our glyphs are far too precise . . . they are meant to convey the logic of the law, and the science of time travel, which are the two proud hallmarks of Gallifrey. This odd elliptical language of the Blue Planet is far more appropriate to the Doctor, who seems to prefer humour over efficiency.

Borusa then goes on to tell the story of Rassilon, the 'founder of our dynasty, who, millennia ago, harnessed the power of a Black Hole'.

This fathomless power brought the Time Lords mastery over the fourth and fifth dimensions.

He reminisces about the Time Lords of Gallifrey, who spend their eternities recording the history of life throughout the universe in the Matrix:

Until the TARDIS ships were perfected, some of our early Time Lords were lost in time, and never returned. (. . .) The most legendary Time Explorer was Ulysses, a hero among the citizens of Gallifrey. (. . .) Ulysses was my son. And, in turn, Ulysses had a son, who in later lives, was called the Master.

Borusa recalls a time 'of danger and turmoil', when the Doctor and the Master, the 'two greatest minds to emerge in the millennia since Rassilon', fought each other:

After seven regenerations, he [the Doctor] seemed to us, the Time Lords, to be the only leader capable of standing up to the Master. [43]

The concept of regeneration is explained:

Regenerations are triggered in several ways . . . old age . . . mortal accident . . . by decree of Time Lord Council . . . or by will.'

Their impact on one's personality and memory is addressed.

I, for example, in an earlier regeneration, became a megalomaniac. Happily, it was a phase that passed. [44]

Borusa then introduces the Doctor:

Irascible, eccentric, and exasperating (. . .) He can be happy, even giddy, but can quickly turn dark and brooding.

As an example of his character, we segue to a page of dialogue detailing a meeting between the Doctor and Napoleon in 1815, followed by some further dialogue between the Doctor and Borusa touching on the subjects of the TARDIS's appearance, and the rules of time travel.

The confrontation between the Doctor and the Master in the 'Panopticon' over the destinies of Gallifrey, and of the Doctor's discovery of the Scrolls of Rassilon that foretold his role as the future saviour of his people, is then retold. [45] This is accompanied by illustrations of the Domed City, the Ruins of Ancient Gallifrey and the Tomb of Rassilon.

The story continues with the tale of Borusa's 'death', the search for Ulysses and the revelation that the Doctor is Ulysses' son, born on the Blue Planet, and the Master's younger half-brother. The theme of the Doctor's half-human inheritance is explored:

'The Doctor is part of their [Mankind's] history . . . He belongs equally to the Blue Planet and Gallifrey. (. . .) The essential conflict between the Doctor's birth on the Blue Planet and his origins on Gallifrey explains his odd personality contradictions. (. . .) I remember when he was a boy on Gallifrey, after his early and tragic first death, he would stare for hours into the night sky. (. . .) He never knew why the Blue Planet called out to him. (. . .) What he didn't know was that his first regeneration took place on the Blue Planet. (. . .) That his mother was a human, an extraordinarily beautiful and bewitching human from the Blue Planet. Her name was Annalisse. [46]

Borusa then narrates how he and the Doctor found clues about Ulysses' identity as Cheops,[47] but remains vague on what happened afterwards. Instead, it goes on to describe the TARDIS, a Type 40, in great detail. This is accompanied by illustrations of the Steering Controls with their central five-sided console,[48] the Engine Room,[49] the Cloisters, the Science Laboratory and the Living Quarters.

After the description of the TARDIS, the Bible devotes five pages to the history of the Daleks, in the form of 'Journal Entries'.[50] This is accompanied by illustrations of Davros, the old and new (a.k.a. 'spider-daleks') in both transformation and fully revealed stages.

The next six pages provide, as is always the case in Bibles, short sample premises illustrating the types of stories that could be told within the series' format.[51] These include:

- *The Pirates* (a.k.a. *The Smugglers* (CC));
- *The Talons of Weng-Chiang* (4S), relocated to New York;
- *Earthshock* (6B), which introduces a more savage version of the Cybermen which are described as 'the pirates of the galaxy, slash and burn marauders from the planet Mondas' and whose accompanying illustration depicts a deadly cyborg version of a Native American-style warrior;[52]
- *The Horror of Fang Rock* (4V);
- *The Celestial Toymaker* (Y);
- *Don't Shoot, I'm the Doctor* (a.k.a. *The Gunfighters* (Z));
- *Tomb of the Cybermen* (MM);
- *The Yeti* (a.k.a. *The Abominable Snowmen* (NN)), with an accompanying illustration of a Neanderthal-looking man; and finally,
- *Ark in Space* (4C).

The Bible ends with a postscript from Borusa, written 'at the end of our travels', after the Doctor has been reunited with Ulysses, had defeated the Master and healed Gallifrey:

I understand now why the Doctor went out in the galaxy. The quest was to find his father . . . to take his rightful place . . . but it was more than this. It was also a journey to the centre of his own cosmos . . .

215

*somewhere under the brilliant yellow sun of the Blue
Planet... and the twin red suns of Gallifrey... It is
said that you cannot know where you're going, if you
don't know where you have been...*

Appendixed are some facts about *Doctor Who* (longest-
running science-fiction series, seen in 88 countries, etc.) as
well as a series of colour illustrations, mostly new, i.e.
created for the Bible (Gallifrey, the interior of the TARDIS,
the new Daleks), but a few others used as pick-up art purely
to illustrate the concepts (the Valeyard, covers of *Witchmark*
and *Birthright*). [53]

Notes

1 The phrase 'in a distant galaxy' appears to be used here
  mostly for dramatic effect (this is, after all, a description and
  not dialogue), since the story clearly states that both Skaro
  and Earth are in the same galaxy, that the Master wants to
  conquer the galaxy, etc. In a memo to Segal, we noted that,
  according to the original BBC television series, Gallifrey is
  located only 29,000 light years from Earth, according to
  information contained in *The Pyramids of Mars* (4G). On
  the other hand, the Time Lords may have moved Gallifrey.
  In *Enemy Within*, the Doctor claims that it is located some
  250 million light years away from Earth. Also see note 13 to
  Denny Martin Flinn's *The Jewels of Time*.

2 Even though the Time Lord Temple is called 'Panopticon' in
  the Bible, it is not referred to as such in the script. The
  planetarium-like visual concept of the galaxy (see note 1)
  eventually found its way into *Enemy Within*, where the
  Doctor could similarly use the 'ceiling' of his TARDIS's
  console room as a giant scanner to check on the cosmic
  state of events.

3 The Time Lords are clearly portrayed here as the ruling elite
  of Gallifrey, i.e. not all Gallifreyans are, in fact, Time Lords.
  There is some ambiguity in the script between the natural
  shapes of the TARDISes and the black obelisk-like
  'Transmats' (like the Time Scoop of *The Five Doctors* (6K)),

which are really gateways into the TARDISes, not the vehicles themselves.

4 In a memo to Segal we stated that we felt that it was a mistake to call this version of the President of the Time Lords 'Borusa', just because it was his name in the original BBC television series. This is, obviously, a different President and in our opinion, calling him Borusa needlessly clashed with the original series. We argued that the character should be renamed, and suggested the name 'Pandak', after the legendary glorious ruler of Gallifrey – a 'Pandak the Third' is mentioned in *The Deadly Assassin* (4P). We have, however, kept the name 'Borusa' throughout this chapter. Alternatively, one may consider the possibility that the Borusa from *The Deadly Assassin* (4P), *The Invasion of Time* (4Z), etc. was another Time Lord named after the Doctor's grandfather – a Borusa the Second. In this scenario, the original Borusa was the first President of the Time Lords to follow Rassilon.

5 The Daleks are clearly introduced here as a new threat, previously unknown on Gallifrey or in the galaxy. Also, it is established that the Time Lords controlled, at that time, a peaceful Dominion, with colonies and peace treaties with other worlds. The use of the word 'Dominion' here predates its use in *Star Trek: Deep Space Nine*.

6 This is a glimpse into early Gallifreyan history, not unlike that of *Star Wars'* Old Republic. The Demat weapons are a continuity reference to *The Invasion of Time* (4Z).

7 Another continuity reference to *The Invasion of Time* (4Z). The Outsiders were actually called 'Outcasts' in the Bible.

8 The Black Hole mythos is consistent with *The Deadly Assassin* (4P). This entire scene indicates that the Gallifrey which is depicted here is indeed one that is still in its early days. (Also see note 12.)

9 We learn here of the existence of a family relationship between Borusa and the Master. The 'Father-Son-Brother' theme is at the core of John Leekley's script, and was influenced by Joseph Campbell's *The Hero with a Thousand Faces*.

10 This is the first time that the name of Rassilon is mentioned in the dialogue. (Also see note 12.)

11 The colour of the Doctor's eyes is an important clue to his origins, as they were first developed in the Bible (see below).

12 The 'Time of Darkness' foretold by Rassilon here is clearly the same as the 'Dark Times' mentioned by Borusa in *The Five Doctors* (6K), also known as the Age of Chaos. The young Doctor depicted in the script is therefore the one who, ultimately, rescued Gallifrey. Also note that Rassilon is described as 'Father of Gallifrey', a subtle reinforcement of the Father-Son-Brother theme. The 'Spirit Guide' is also a Joseph Campbell concept (see note 9).

13 Leekley's description of the notorious 'spider-daleks' was used to create the computer-generated tests and preliminary designs commissioned by Amblin. In this test footage, the Daleks first appear to look like the original Ray Cusick design, with a few minor changes. They then open and unfold to assume the 'spider-dalek' mode. The use of the Daleks in this script was negotiated with, and approved by, Terry Nation, in a separate deal with the producers.

14 The hatred the Master feels for the Doctor because of his half-breed heritage and (as we will soon find out) because of their common parentage, is a powerful theme throughout the script. This does not necessarily conflict with Denny Martin Flinn's *The Jewels of Time*, to the extent that the Young Doctor and the Young Master were obviously unaware of their common ancestry when they attended the Time Lord Academy.

15 This is a continuity reference to *The Deadly Assassin* (4P), which conveniently explains the Doctor's position in Gallifrey. Because of the passing mention of the Prydonians being 'extinct', we would have to assume that other, newer members were later recruited by the Doctor, perhaps to help him in his fight with the Master. Finally, the script uses this opportunity to emphasise several times that this is a *young* Doctor – not one who is 800+ years old with seven regenerations. This is a marked departure from the Bible, and a logical one, in the light of the story's other characteristics.

16 The concept outlined in the Bible is that it is the Doctor's half-human heritage that will help redeem the Time Lords' basic dark, corrupt nature. The notion of the Time Lords being evil had already been mentioned by the Second Doctor in *The Five Doctors* (6K) and the Sixth Doctor in *The Ultimate Foe* (7C); it is further developed here. Leekley seizes it to make it the pivotal conflict in his story.

17 This is the first mention of Ulysses in the dialogue. Ulysses the Explorer – no relation to the historical Greek warrior the First Doctor will meet in *The Myth Makers* (U) – is the Doctor's mysterious and elusive father, whose existence was first postulated by Leekley in the Bible. (We remarked to Segal that the name 'Ulysses' could lead to wrong conclusions.) Since Ulysses is clearly one of the first Time Lords, he could very well be the mysterious 'Other' mentioned in various *Doctor Who* texts.

18 Borusa reveals here the secret of the Doctor's origins for the first time. (Also see the Bible and note 27 below.) For all intents and purposes, Segal's *Enemy Within*, written by Matthew Jacobs, preserved the essence of this stupendous revelation, although future scripts may well modify its details. For example, in Jacobs's script, the Doctor states that he once watched meteor storms with his father 'on a warm Gallifreyan night', which might be construed as a contradiction with Leekley's script. Time will tell.

19 These are additional insights into both the origins of the Doctor, and the rules of Gallifreyan society.

20 The description of the TARDIS is consistent with the early production designs commissioned by Segal for the Bible (see below). A number of these survived the transition to *Enemy Within*.

21 The merging of Borusa's 'soul' into the TARDIS's crystals – while dramatically sound – is perhaps the story's most arguable element. The Bible draws a connection between this process and the Matrix, where Time Lords preserve recordings of their 'life experiences and memories'.

219

22 The notion that Time Lords cannot directly kill other Time Lords without exposing themselves to being cast out and hunted down has sometimes been suggested in the past and is confirmed here. Coincidentally, the same notion is hinted at in *The Jewels of Time*.

23 *Fathers and Brothers* establishes that each TARDIS draws its power from the Eye of Harmony on Gallifrey. This notion will be developed in *The Time of My Life*, and will ultimately become a central plot element in *Enemy Within*.

24 The script makes it clear that this is the Doctor's first visit to Earth, confirming that this story is, in effect, the 'Origin' story. This could be construed as a direct conflict with *The Jewels of Time*, which does provide another story for the Doctor's first visit to Earth. However, it is possible to assume that, first, a fair amount of time has elapsed (by Gallifreyan standards) between the two stories; and second, that the Doctor, having been shaken by the revelation of his half-human ancestry, is now rediscovering Earth with new eyes.

25 It is interesting to note that there is nothing in this script's version of Cheops that contradicts *The Jewels of Time*, which theoretically happens much later in the future. If anything, this would serve as a further justification to explain why the Fourth Doctor entrusted a segment of the Key to Time to Cheops.

26 A clever visualisation of the state of 'temporal grace' supposedly existing within the TARDIS's confines.

27 Leekley introduces the concept of Time Lord regeneration here.

28 Leekley also explains how the TARDIS first acquired the shape of a London police box – the latter being deemed necessary for the benefit of the average viewer previously unacquainted with *Doctor Who*. Technically this would be the very first time the TARDIS took that now-familiar shape.

29 More revelations about the Doctor's origins. We now learn why he was sent back to Gallifrey, and what eventually happened to his mother (who is named in the Bible – see below). Interestingly, the script ambiguously raises the

possibility that this childhood fever may have triggered the Doctor's very first regeneration.

30 Two words foreshadowing the title that Segal would eventually give to Matthew Jacobs's script.

31 It is interesting to note that, freed from the constraints of children's television programming, most 'Nth Doctor' versions of *Doctor Who* entertained the idea of a somewhat chaste and innocent, almost exploratory romance between the Doctor and a female companion. To the extent that Leekley's Doctor is a young Doctor, and that this is his first encounter with an Earth woman, this is even more justifiable in this context. One likes to notice a certain 'book end' similarity between the Doctor's first emotional awakening in *Fathers and Brothers* and his rediscovery of the same emotions (played very much in the same note by Paul McGann) in *Enemy Within*.

32 The descriptions of Skaro are not unlike those of *Genesis of the Daleks* (4E), except of course that the production aimed to present full-scale ruins, etc.

33 In the scenes that follow the script draws a clear parallel between the primitive World War II on Earth, the more advanced Neutron War on Skaro (does the same fate await Earth?) and the ultimate conflict brewing on Gallifrey. Even though these conflicts differ in nature, their causes remain the same.

34 This is, perhaps, the only single direct continuity clash with the original BBC television series, in the sense that the versions of Davros and the origins of the Daleks presented here cannot be easily reconciled with *Genesis of the Daleks* (4E). But then, the latter also conflicted directly with *The Daleks* (B), and it has taken fan scholars such as John Peel and Paul Cornell a great deal of skill to reconcile the two. The easy way out of this conundrum would be, of course, to opt for the 'alternative timelines' explanation raised in *The Discontinuity Guide*, and assume that this is simply a third version of the Daleks' origins, possibly created by future Time Lords' or the Doctor's or even the Daleks' own interference. On the other hand, if one opts for a more 'linear' universe, one may postulate that these

scenes occur after *Genesis of the Daleks* (4E), which clearly takes place during the Neutron Wars, while this story, by its own admission, takes place 109 years later. Davros has somehow survived execution by his first Daleks, stumbled over Aran's survivors, and is up to his old tricks again.

35 If anything some of Davros's experiments would appear to anticipate the gruesome Dalek factory seen in *Revelation of the Daleks* (6Z), which takes place much later. The attempt by Davros to create insect-like Daleks is, in any event, consistent with his philosophy.

36 As Cybermen designs have evolved over the years, because of progress in costume and special effects technology, so would some of the visual effects associated with *Doctor Who*, in this case the appearances of Davros and the Daleks. For all intents and purposes, however, if one chooses not to simply ignore such differences, one could merely hypothesise that Davros later changed his mind about the 'spider-daleks' and the benefits of insect DNA, and reverted to his earlier form.

37. The sonic screwdriver was briefly mentioned in the caves of the Tomb of Rassilon earlier, but this is the first (and only) time it is used in the script.

38 None of this would invalidate the events of *Genesis of the Daleks* (4E), since they took place 109 years before.

39 Continuing our attempts at retrocontinuity, it is obvious that Davros survives the Castellan's murder attempt. He might, after all, have returned in future episodes of the then-planned television series. Ultimately, as mentioned above (note 35), we may believe that he retired to his original lair, returned to his previous, i.e. non insectoid, form and went into stasis, eventually to re-emerge on the *Doctor Who* scene in *Destiny of the Daleks* (5J). As to the 'spider-daleks', most of them were destroyed here. Perhaps it is that very destruction and the knowledge of his actions then which haunted the Doctor and, ultimately, made him choose the way he did in *Genesis of the Daleks* (4E). In any event, it is easy to assume that (a) the 'spider-daleks' were eventually destroyed by the Doctor and the Prydonians during the ensuing 'Time of Darkness', and

(b) that Davros cannot have been pleased that they would have so easily become subservient to the Master, providing additional justification for his return to the more traditional Dalek design.

40 The script makes this the Doctor's very first act of rebellion against Gallifrey, and the beginning of his self-imposed exile from the Time Lords.

41 By this standard, the Doctor, unlike the future Master, is not a 'renegade'. All this, and the assumption that the Doctor eventually restored law and order on Gallifrey after the 'Time of Darkness', helps explain the Time Lords' particularly lenient behaviour towards the future Doctor.

42 Eventually one might assume that the Doctor (and his Prydonian allies?) proved ultimately triumphant against the Master, exposing his villainy and causing his incarceration, from which he eventually escaped to re-emerge in *Terror of the Autons* (EEE). It is tempting to suppose that it was the Master's status as a descendent of Rassilon that saved him from being executed by the Time Lords (including in *The Jewels of Time*), although as *Enemy Within* indicated, the Daleks did not have such scruples. Indeed, the Master may have been executed by the Daleks for his crimes against them, i.e. the entire 'spider-dalek' affair, and not for his villainy towards the rest of the universe.

43 As mentioned above (see note 15), at that time, the Bible still acknowledged the Doctor's previous seven incarnations and his 800+ years.

44 This was an attempt by Leekley to explain away the Borusa of *The Five Doctors* (6K), as if this took place after the original series. As we have just seen, this concept was altered when the script was written.

45 From this point on, the Bible pretty much follows the outline of the script. Variations will be noted.

46 There is more background information about the Doctor's childhood, which did not make it into the script, including – most importantly – the name of the Doctor's mother. 'Annalisse' is the name of Leekley's daughter, a name which he re-used in his recent movie *The Haunting of Annalisse*.

47 In the Bible, this takes place in the Cairo Museum in Egypt, and not the British Museum in London.

48 This was later corrected to six-sided.

49 This was where the Eye of Harmony was located and, combined with the Cloisters, it made the transition into *Enemy Within*.

50 The story retold here is significantly closer in detail to *Genesis of the Daleks* (4E).

51 This probably gave rise to the unfounded rumour that Amblin proposed to remake original television series episodes, while in reality these premises were provided purely as a sample of the types of *Doctor Who* stories that were made and could be made. It was also an easy way of fleshing out the concept to make the Bible – which is nothing more than a sales tool for the proposed show – more attractive.

52 While remaining faithful to the core of the concept of the Cybermen as marauding space scavengers introduced in *The Tenth Planet* (DD) (and not some silver-suited alternative to the Daleks), the visual reinterpretation of the Cybermen, also dubbed 'Cybs' in the Bible, would have undoubtedly been very controversial among the fans. In terms of continuity, it would have been easy to assume that these were Cybermen at a very early stage in their existence.

53 Again, this legitimate and standard-in-the-industry use of various bits of pick-up art was leaked and misconstrued by many fans, who saw them as 'errors' (e.g. 'This is a Charrl, not a Wirrn') instead of sales help.

Review

Fathers and Brothers is a very good script, strong on character, very moving, with great rhythm and pacing, making full use of the TARDIS's abilities and the *Doctor Who* universe.

The Doctor therein is young and charming – he has an endearing Hugh Grantish quality – and his relationship with Lizzie Travis is excellent. There are many good, genuinely emotional scenes between them, and some thought-provoking sub-text as well.

To the extent that Leekley ultimately chose to tell the 'origins' of the Doctor, the script starts with a relatively clean slate. This enables the writer to introduce the characters, the TARDIS, Davros, the Daleks, etc. to an audience presumably unfamiliar with *Doctor Who*. Leekley does this skilfully. The plot always remains character-driven, rather than a series of disconnected incidents.

The *Fugitive*-style format is certainly not new in television, but it is effective; in this case, the Doctor being an exile/outlaw from his powerful, decadent, corrupt home-world is reminiscent of the classics. On the other hand, the 'search for Ulysses' might easily have become stale in the context of a regular, episodic series.

Interview with John Leekley

Question: Why were you hired to write Doctor Who*?*
John Leekley: Philip Segal was the person who asked me to write the script and be one of the executive producers of the show. He was an executive at Amblin, which was located on the Universal lot and their television shows, at that time, were produced in partnership with Universal. I had at that time a two-year overall deal at Universal, exclusive to them for everything in television. I was already a writer/executive producer there. Phil had liked some of the work I had done on other movies, particularly a movie I made for Universal, just prior to this, called *In the Company of Darkness*, starring Helen Hunt.

Q: Had you heard of, or seen any, Doctor Who *before you took the job?*
JL: Yes. My brother, Brian, had seen all of them, and was an enormous fan of *Doctor Who*. He had introduced me to its rather arcane world. I just thought it was so sly and so cool in its essence. So I had learned about the show from my brother in my boyhood.

Q: What kind of research did you do prior to writing the script?

JL: Phil gave me copies of all of the old *Doctor Who* episodes on tape to consider taking the job. I viewed almost all of the existing videotapes. I was impressed in particular by that very first episode of *An Unearthly Child* (A), in which the TARDIS appears in this junkyard, and Susan goes to school and, in her own way, tries to deal with her sense of alienation, of loneliness, of disconnectedness . . . It was a wonderful mythological scene, which illustrates the great potential of *Doctor Who*, either as a television series or a series of movies. It shows how one ordinary person, like the character of Lizzie in my script, is taken on an incredible journey, and it reveals how extraordinary individuals really are in their abilities to deal with adventures like this.

I also read every book on Doctor Who, all of your books, especially *The Universal Databank*. I love all of that stuff. I got a lot of inspiration from it. I find it particularly great that there was that whole universe of characters like the Castellan and Davros and Borusa . . . All these guys were archetypes, which was very useful from a storytelling standpoint.

I mistepped a couple of times. I should not have called the Cardinal Borusa. I'd seen that name and he seemed just one name among the constellation of names in the *Doctor Who* universe, and I thought that I could usurp it; unfortunately, by doing so, I brought along some confusion about that character.

Q: Was it your decision to write the Origin Story?
JL: I had told Phil that I would be very interested in taking the job if, as you put it, I could write the Origin Story of the mythology. I was astonished at the possibilities of the origins of *Doctor Who*, this time traveller who came from the desolate planet of Gallifrey. I very much wanted to reconceive, not as much reconceive but pre-conceive, the mythology of *Doctor Who*, to explain all of the things that came later. All of these things aren't impinged upon by my script. In fact in some ways they are explained. I also wanted to add a kind of visceral reality to it, not unlike some of the great family sagas and mythologies of American cinema, like *The Godfather*, in which these relationships between fathers and brothers carry so much potency.

226

As I looked into all that, I realised I very much wanted to write the script if I could create a world. So I began by writing the Bible, filling it with images that would convey the nature of the world from which the Doctor came: a world of very Earth-like, Greek-like culture, that thrived thousands of years ago. Gallifrey itself is cracking apart. The implications are that it is coming apart because of the split between the dark side, represented by the Master, and the light side, represented by the teachings and the truths of the past, which are still held in these artefacts kept in caves and jars, not unlike our findings of the Dead Sea Scrolls and scraps of the Bible. I was very interested in this split, in showing how a culture can go so wrong and lose its moorings, its sense of enlightenment.

The Doctor stems from a long line of explorers, particularly his father. These are a mythic group of men and women who went out into the universe in an attempt to find the truth, make contact and spread science and light. The Doctor follows in these footsteps. Conversely, the Master, who we later discover is his half-brother, embodies the darker impulses of domination of weaker cultures, the desire to control other people. To me, all this felt like a metaphor that we could identify with, in terms of our own dark impulses as human beings.

Q: Why the name Ulysses for the Doctor's father?

JL: I chose that name because I wanted to imply that his father was an archetype, from the kind of storytelling that western culture has passed down from the Greeks. It was not intended to be confused with the real Ulysses, or Odysseus, or any past story of *Doctor Who* [*The Myth Makers* (U)].

Q: Whose idea was it to come up with the concept that the Doctor was half-human, which had never been established before?

JL: Mine. In the original BBC television series no one ever seemed to ask themselves why Earth? Why was the Doctor so passionate about this place and these people? There was some implication that he loved the humanness of the human races and was very attracted to their qualities, some of which he shared, such as adventuresomeness and that certain sense of boundless curiosity. I was very interested in the fact that, with him being half-human, he was being called, almost in the way the moon can pull the ocean, by the Blue Planet. It gave a reason, a significance, for his attraction to Earth. I was very attracted to the idea that that call from the Blue Planet brought him here. It called him back to that place which turns out to be the home of his mother. It brought him back to all this classic culture of Earth, which in turn informs on where he comes from, in a storytelling way.

Q: Were you purposefully inspired by Star Wars *or Joseph Campbell in your handling of the archetypes and the relationships between the protagonists?*

JL: Yes. *The Hero with a Thousand Faces* has been a great source of inspiration to me. I loved the idea that the Cardinal was a Guardian or a Spirit Guide. He was the Joseph Campbell character, the one teaching the Hero what is important, truthful and necessary for his own kind of evolution, his path, his redemption. I liked the idea that the death of the Spirit Guide was necessary for the birth of the Doctor. The propulsion of the Doctor into the world and into the work necessary for him to do could only happen upon the death of the Cardinal. In retrospect, I suppose it would have been compared to Obi-Wan Kenobi from *Star Wars*, but that is exactly where George Lucas got his inspiration from.

I loved the fact that these two brothers both had a father of such extraordinary quality. For the Doctor, the search for father was a search for self, and it could have been continued throughout a regular series. In my opinion, one of the most important, moving things about *Star Trek* is Spock's search for his father, for his heritage. Spock, too, was half-human. There was always a tug in him between the Vulcan and the Human sensibilities. To control our passions and ferocious desires of the Id when, in fact, for Humans, the Id is so morally dangerous to be set free. I liked those themes, which were very important to me.

I thought that the most powerful thing about *Doctor Who* was not just the origins of his world, but what was the cause of his Search, his Quest. Curiosity alone was not strong enough of a motive for me. The search for father, i.e. the search for self, could have been carried on. Depending on how the part of his father was cast, say, with someone like Sean Connery, it would have been fantastic and carry great potency.

Q: Were you told to have the Daleks in the script or was it your own idea?

JL: I was required to put the Daleks into the story. Phil, Peter Wagg and I spent a fair amount of time in London talking to the folks at the BBC, mostly Alan Yentob and Michael Waring and we were told that the Daleks had to be in it. So I was hoping to make them more frightening and less unintentionally funny than mere tin cans rolling around. I was hoping to create something, using the facilities of Amblin Imaging, extraordinarily scary and effective. I wanted to reconceive them, using the original shape but then opening it up. That took a huge amount of my time, explaining what I wanted to the designers. They were all extremely talented and very patient, and they generated a seemingly endless number of designs before we got it right. From my perspective, it took a long time to arrive at something that I was happy with.

Q: Had you had any discussions or meetings with Terry Nation about the use of the Daleks?

JL: No, I never met with him, although I admire his work. I heard a lot of good things about him.

Q: Were you given any other elements that had to be included in the script, or did you have carte blanche?

JL: One element that I was very interested in was the Outsiders, the people who lived in the wild on Gallifrey. In a funny way, to me, they represented the keepers of the flame, the heart and truth of the ancient culture. In my concept they were relentlessly hunted by the Time Lords. I wanted them to look like a sort of quintessential primal people, like the American Indians or the Australian Aborigines, and they had the same kind of primal powers that these people have.

Another area which interested me was the redesign of the TARDIS. Since its interior could be any shape or size, I thought it would be kind of cool if it had the mythic quality of an old ship at sea.

Q: How would you have envisioned the continuation of the series?

JL: The Doctor would have been full of passion, full of life. I was very much taken with Paul McGann, who had all these qualities. Swept up in his charm, his world and his adventures would be an ordinary person, as Lizzie is in my script.

Q: I was led to believe that your approach to Doctor Who *was ultimately deemed to have been maybe too serious, maybe too cerebral, by Steven Spielberg, and that another 'take' was called for. Any comments?*

JL: We were already into pre-production . . . We had gone to England to cast Paul McGann, then Segal, Wagg and I had travelled through the American west, Utah and Colorado, looking for locations for Gallifrey . . . It was a thrilling and exhausting adventure. We were loaned the plane of the Governor of Utah and flew all over the state, landing places and exploring . . . The day we'd just hired a production designer we were told that Steven Spielberg had decided not to proceed with the script after all. Even though he had seen the Bible, been given everything, including the drawings and the earlier drafts . . . It was a mystery to me. I was later told that he was in the editing room working on *Schindler's List* when he decided that he didn't want to make a serious, dramatic *Doctor Who* and preferred a much lighter version. Which they later attempted to do with Robert DeLaurentis.

I had felt that the Bible and script presented a world people would have embraced, in terms of visceral qualities and mythology. I think both fans and newcomers would have enjoyed it, and I was sad to see it end. Some of my concepts and designs seem to have survived in the new movie. I wish them well, because I very much would like to see *Doctor Who* return to the screen.

7

THE TIME OF MY LIFE

by

Robert DeLaurentis

Background

For a variety of internal reasons the John Leekley script was eventually shelved by the co-producers – Amblin, Universal and BBC Worldwide – before it got 'out of the gate'.

Unlike what was said in some of the rather distorted rumours that surfaced at the time, this was due not (as some fans preferred to believe) to matters pertaining to *Doctor Who* history and continuity but to a complicated mix of factors, some having to do with business differences between Leekley and the producers, others relating to the general direction the producers wished to give the new show. In simplistic terms, Leekley's script was deemed in some quarters to be too serious and cerebral, and another 'take' was called for.

As is standard practice in Hollywood, Segal then decided to hire a new writer, Robert DeLaurentis (no relation to producer Dino DeLaurentis). DeLaurentis's credits include scripts for such series as *Mann & Machine* and *South Beach*. The writer delivered his first draft in December 1994 to enable Segal to pitch it to the Fox Television Network in early January 1995.

Even though the script was officially entitled *Dr Who?*, DeLaurentis, when offered the opportunity, chose the more distinctive title *The Time of My Life*.

[To be concluded at the end of this chapter.]

Story

TEASER

We open on a far-away, desert-like planet, lit by six moons, located on the edge of a distant galaxy. A TARDIS, in its natural shape of a black pyramid,[1] rematerialises. The DOCTOR and his companion, SHERMAN, come out of it.[2]

The Doctor is described as the 'legendary cosmologist, philosopher and explorer . . . dressed in a dazzling array of mis-matched clothing.' He wears carbonite goggles which also give him various digital readouts. Sherman is a heavy-set, gluttonish man, wearing red shoes. He is munching on a sandwich.

According to the readouts, the date is 1 January 2395 (Earth Time).[3] They have been drawn off-course from their exploration journey by an unknown force, which turns out to be a neighbouring, mysterious 'boomerang black hole' – an extremely rare cosmic phenomenon.

The Doctor uses the TARDIS 'key' and, pointing it at the TARDIS, activates its chameleon circuit, causing it to assume the shape of a sand dune.[4] He then asks Sherman to take some soil samples, while he investigates the black hole with various scientific instruments. He also advises the Earthman to watch out for VOXYLS. A few seconds later, a shadow falls across the now-camouflaged TARDIS, while we hear an ominous 'clanging' sound.

Meanwhile, the Doctor has identified the six moons as the Moons of Ardor.

> **Doctor** *They say if a man and a woman are joined under their glow, their union is forever blessed.*

While the Doctor is measuring the black hole, Sherman comes across a Voxyl, a fierce-looking sand-rat which has been drawn to Sherman's sandwich. The Earthman discards the sandwich in a hurry. The Doctor tells him they have bigger worries . . .

He has finally figured out where they are – but too late. Suddenly they are captured by DALEKS, a new type of Dalek, 'MODELS X-7', humanoid in shape, 'composed of living tissue fused to a shiny platinum-like exo-skeleton'.[5]

They are taken to the MASTER – a man with piercing blue eyes – who welcomes them to . . . SKARO.[6]

ACT ONE

We cut to GALLIFREY, a planet located 29,000 light years from Earth.[7] The TIME LORDS, who have 'harnessed the power of the Black Hole', live in huge, domed cities.

We move into the Temple where an emergency meeting is being chaired by CARDINAL BORUSA,[8] President of the Time Lords, who wears the Sash of Rassilon, symbol of his rank. At his side is his wife, VARDA. The CASTELLAN, Chief of Security, has called the meeting because there have been new reports of recent attacks on Gallifreyan 'outposts' by a 'new breed' of Daleks. He urges the President to take action, claiming to have received an urgent report from the Master. Borusa questions the Master's absence. The Castellan replies that the Master chose to stay behind to help the outpost.

> **Borusa** *I was not aware that the Master has such an altruistic streak . . .*
>
> **Castellan** *We're all aware of your ill health, Cardinal. In the absence of your son and rightful successor, the Sash might fall . . .*
>
> **Borusa** *. . . To the Master? Is that what this is about? He seeks to become President of the Time Lords?*[9]

The Castellan tries to reassure the Council as to the Master's intentions, until Borusa cuts him short, saying the Master should be here to defend himself.

At that very moment a black pyramid TARDIS rematerialises. The Master has arrived. He also urges war, but Borusa wants peace and sees no reason to alter the Time Lords' traditional policy of non-interference.

> **Borusa** *Non-violence has been the heart of our philosophy ever since we harnessed the power of the Black Hole.*
>
> **Master** *A record for which we can all be proud. But if history has taught us one lesson, it is that war, however venal, is inevitable.*[10]
>
> **Borusa** *If history has taught us one thing, it is that war merely produces more war.*

Borusa refuses to yield to the Master's entreaties. Instead, he proposes to send an emissary, his own grandson, the 'only man I know devoted exclusively to the truth', the Doctor, to investigate.

At this point, the Master signals to two GUARDS and unveils the allegedly recently-discovered body of the Doctor, seemingly killed by the Daleks. Borusa collapses under the shock.

Cut back to Skaro. In a cell, the Doctor and Sherman discuss the new Daleks.

SHERMAN *I thought Daleks were supposed to be much smaller.*
Doctor *This is apparently a new incarnation.* [11]

The Master shows up and tells him that the new Daleks are his creation but remain just as deadly as the old model.

Master *Unlike the old version, the X-7s also have assault capability. The new exoskeletons are made from a remarkable alloy, impervious to conventional weapons. You'd be quite surprised at some of the new tricks I've taught them.* [12]

The Master then tells the Doctor about what has happened on Gallifrey, and how the report of his death caused Borusa's collapse. Soon, in the absence of the Doctor's father, he plans to assume the Presidency of the Time Lords. However, he would like to enlist the Doctor's help in his plans to conquer the universe.

The Master takes the Doctor and Sherman on a tour of the huge underground facility located under the Crater of Wyq. He reveals his plan: after nearly a century of research, he has managed to locate a boomerang black hole near Skaro, and now plans to duplicate Rassilon's great work and harness it to power a fleet of 'warships' – TARDISes independent of Gallifrey. [13] These 'warships' will be staffed by armies of new Daleks and sent to conquer the universe.

However, the Master still needs the Doctor's help with some of the time engineering involved – the Doctor being one of the best Time Engineers on Gallifrey. The Master wants him to install a giant Time Rotor, which will then control and channel the black hole's immense energies. Naturally, the Doctor refuses.

Doctor *Sorry, I don't grovel well.*

The Master activates a switch, a digital doomsday clock, which means that the black hole will be powered up in 72 hours, without any possibility of turning back.

While the Master returns to Gallifrey to wait for news of Borusa's death, the Doctor succeeds in outwitting the Daleks. They have been instructed to keep the Time Lord and his companion alive, but the Doctor confuses his captors with orders to kill them instead.

Since the Master's base is protected by a deadly force field, the Doctor and Sherman escape through a ventilation shaft. The Doctor uses his sonic screwdriver to overcome various obstacles and, eventually, manages to disable the force field. Unfortunately, as they are about to reach the outside, they become separated in the ventilation shaft. Sherman is killed by Voxyls, while the Doctor barely escapes with his life.[14]

The Doctor returns to Gallifrey just in time to have a last conversation with Borusa, who is happy to find out that his grandson is not dead after all. The Doctor's story confirms the Master's villainy. The dying President tells the Doctor that their only hope is to find his father, Borusa's son.

> **Borusa** *You remind me of your father. Nothing gave him pleasure like being off in the great unknown.*[15]
> **Doctor** *I wish I'd known him.*
> **Borusa** *You will. You must.*

Borusa takes the Sash of Rassilon and gives it to the Doctor. The Doctor's father is the one person who can be its undisputed inheritor. Otherwise, the Master, who already has the Council in the palm of his hand, will succeed in getting himself appointed President and will take over Gallifrey. With the powers of both Gallifrey and the Daleks at the Master's command, the universe would be gravely endangered.

However, the Doctor does not know where, or even who, his father is. When the Doctor was raised on Gallifrey, his father was already a legend. Borusa tells him that he is the only one who knows the secret of the Doctor's father.

> **Borusa** *Not gone, stranded. You were an infant when his TARDIS was brought to me, supposedly abandoned. For that reason, I hid the TARDIS, knowing that this day would come . . .*[16]

The dying Borusa gives the Doctor a small silver button and the key to his father's TARDIS. The button was found inside the TARDIS when it returned, alone, to Gallifrey. He instructs him to look for his father in San Francisco, on Earth, a planet the Doctor knows well and of which he is very fond. Then Borusa dies before he can reveal anything more. [17]

ACT TWO

Following Borusa's instructions, the Doctor locates his father's TARDIS in the Temple. It is 'an old Type 40', looking like a dull and battered grey cabinet. A stencil on its outside reads 'Loose Lips Sink Ships'.

He enters the TARDIS, whose console is covered with dust. The last co-ordinates in its memory banks are London, 6 March 1944 – World War II. The Doctor decides to first go there and leaves – unaware that his movements are being secretly tracked by the Master and the Castellan.

Master *No use risking a confrontation here, when we can safely take him on alien territory.*

Inside the TARDIS, the Doctor takes a closer look at the silver button. It bears the insignia of the US Army.

The TARDIS rematerialises on Oxford Street in 1944 LONDON. The Doctor steps out of the TARDIS, pulls his key and aims at the time machine, causing it to assume the shape of a neighbouring Police Box. [18]

Looking for clues to his father's whereabouts, the Doctor visits a police station where a SERGEANT suggests that he call in the American Military Intelligence office in Grosvenor Square.

Meanwhile, a Black Pyramid rematerialises near the Doctor's TARDIS. The Castellan and two Daleks emerge. The Daleks suck the life energies of two passing MPs and assume their human shapes, while retaining their non-human behaviour, and making a metallic noise when they walk.

At the OSS building we meet young American WAC, JANE McDONALD, her pet bulldog, WINSTON, and her British superior, the pompous CAPTAIN SANDERS. Jane is very devoted to her job of tracking down missing persons; Sanders somewhat less.

The Doctor arrives and immediately develops a good rapport, first with Winston, then with Jane.

> **Jane** *(. . .) I'm Private McDonald, Jane to my friends . . .*
> **Doctor** *And I'm the Doctor . . .*
> **Jane** *Doctor Who?*
> **Doctor** *Just the Doctor.* [19]

The Doctor explains that he is looking for his missing father, who was travelling under the name 'John Smith',[20] and shows Jane the button. He claims to be from San Francisco, which is how we learn that Jane is from Boston. The Doctor starts reminiscing about Paul Revere, then catches himself. Jane eventually promises to do the best she can, and they agree to meet later in the park across the street.

Meanwhile, the Castellan and his two Dalek/MPs, now driving a stolen military jeep, are using a tracking device to monitor the Doctor's movements.

The Doctor returns to his TARDIS, where he uses the computers to check on Jane's past history.

> **Computer** *Jane Agnes McDonald, born 6:47 a.m. 7 December 1922, at St Anne's Hospital, Boston, Massachusetts, to Joseph, a detective with the Boston Police Force, and Jane, homemaker, who dies in childbirth at 11:59 p.m. of same date . . .* [21]

In the filing room of the OSS, Jane finally finds the information she was looking for. It is cross-referenced with something called 'Operation Black Cross'. Her jaw drops.

Telling Sanders that she is taking Winston out for a walk, she goes to meet the Doctor at their appointed rendezvous. There, she tells him that his father was part of a very secret mission, 'Operation Black Cross', a special OSS team dispatched to assassinate Hitler. But someone informed the Germans, and the men were captured. The Doctor asks her to find out where he might be held. Jane agrees, and tells the

Doctor to wait for her at her place. She also entrusts him with Winston.

The Castellan and his two Daleks have been watching the scene and request instructions from the Master.

The Doctor reaches Jane's flat and decides to take a short nap, using a small white capsule (a 'Z-Cap') that releases a harmless sleep vapour.

At OSS headquarters, Captain Sanders surprises Jane while she is looking through classified 'Operation Black Cross' files. She tells him what she is looking for, and why, but he suspects the Doctor of being a Nazi spy. After all, how could his father be only twenty-five years old, as mentioned in his file?

Jane's confidence is shaken. Borrowing Sanders's service revolver, she returns to her flat, where she confronts the Doctor.

> **Jane** *You said you were a Doctor. Doctor of what?*
> **Doctor** *Many things. Astronomy, cosmology, temporal engineering . . .*
> **Jane** *Temporal engineering?* [22]

A confused Jane tells the Doctor what she has found out about his father's age. The Doctor then decides to tell her the truth, which naturally she finds hard to believe.

> **Doctor** *I come from a planet at the edge of our solar system. Our people discovered the secret of time travel. My father left and never returned. (. . .) There's a man from my planet, called the Master, who wants to take over the universe. He's like your Hitler, only with greater power at his disposal . . . I know it sounds far-fetched, but it's the truth, I swear . . .* [23]

The Doctor finally convinces Jane by telling her the information about her that he found in the TARDIS computer; even then she remains doubtful. As a final proof of what he is saying he offers to take her to the TARDIS. She agrees. But, once outside, they're arrested by Captain Sanders and two MPs.

Sanders takes the Doctor aside. His face morphs into that of the Master.

ACT THREE

The Master/Sanders attempts to dismiss Jane. He claims the Doctor is a famous Nazi spy who was only after their classified files. But Jane insists on talking to the Doctor. The Master cannot find a credible reason to stop her without exposing himself.

In his cell, the Doctor again tells Jane the truth, including the fact that Sanders is the Master.

> **Doctor** *He has the ability to take on a person's physical appearance.*
>
> **Jane** *And how exactly does he do that?*
>
> **Doctor** *It's a highly evolved form of mass hypnosis. He's the only one to ever master it. Hence his name . . .* [24]

Something in the Doctor's voice appeals to Jane. She finally tests her superior by mentioning Winston. Previously, Sanders hated the dog; now, he tells her that he loves him. That clinches it for Jane. She leaves, convinced that the Doctor is indeed telling the truth.

Alone with the Doctor, the Master again tries to seduce him to his side. He reveals that he is the one who betrayed 'Operation Black Cross' to the Germans, so that he would be rid of the Doctor's father, thus clearing his path to the Presidency. He even tempts him with the lure of the beautiful Jane McDonald. But the Doctor retains his faith in the ultimate superiority of good versus evil, which he calls the 'Great Moral Dialectic'.

> **Master** *You're a man of science, surely you don't believe that gibberish about the primal power of good.*
>
> **Doctor** *For a true scientist, the soul is just as appropriate for investigation as the test tube. Evil does have its flaws . . .* [25]

Having failed, the Master leaves the Doctor behind, alone in his cell.

Later that night Jane returns to the OSS office. In the

basement where classified files are kept, she locates the Doctor's father's file, which shows that he is being held prisoner in Dachau. She then discovers Sanders's dead body.

She rushes home but, when she gets there, she finds the Master/Sanders and his two Dalek/MPs waiting for her; however, Winston enables her to get away.

Meanwhile, the Doctor uses the sleeping vapour Z-Caps to escape from his guards. He steals a jeep and arrives just in time to rescue Jane from the Dalek/MPs.

The Daleks pursue them. One of them manages to leap onto the back of the car, but the Doctor manages to get rid of him by making a hard U-turn.

Jane then tells the Doctor about having located his father in Dachau. Since he cannot go there safely, the Doctor suggests that they 'skip the war' and travel directly to 1946.

Meanwhile, the Master/Sanders is now giving chase in a Bentley. Jane offers to stay behind to divert him, but the Doctor does not want to place her in danger, and instead takes her to the TARDIS. She looks at it, sceptical.

> **Jane** *That's a police box.*
> **Doctor** *No, just a cloaking device for camouflage . . .* [26]

After she walks inside, she is astounded by its size.

> **Jane** *How can it be so small on the outside, and so big on the inside?*
> **Doctor** *It's transdimensional engineering. I'll give you the tour later. You might want to take a seat.*

The Doctor then sets the co-ordinates for San Francisco, 1946, and they dematerialise.

But the Master now pursues the Doctor into the Vortex in his own TARDIS and attempts a Time Ram. [27] The Doctor escapes by boosting his TARDIS, but this means that they will overshoot their destination.

ACT FOUR

The Doctor's TARDIS rematerialises at the top of the Transamerica Pyramid in San Francisco. [28] They have

241

indeed overshot their destination – by fifty years. It is now 1995.

The Doctor and Jane step out of the TARDIS. Because of the Time Ram, the Doctor's key doesn't work and his TARDIS is now stuck in the shape of a London police box.[29] Its Time Rotor is also damaged, and they're stuck there until the Doctor can fix it.

While eating breakfast in a coffee shop, the Doctor decides to go looking for his father. When Jane objects that he might have died, the Doctor explains the concept of regeneration.

> **Doctor** *You see, a Time Lord doesn't die, in the conventional sense. He 'regenerates'.*
>
> **Jane** *No wonder you were so calm around those Daleks.*
>
> **Doctor** *Oh, I can still be killed, if there's damage to both hearts.*[30]

Eventually, the conversation returns to the whereabouts of the Doctor's father.

> **Jane** *What makes you think that your father hasn't 'regenerated'?*
>
> **Doctor** *The fact that he hasn't shown up on Gallifrey leads me to assume he hasn't finished his current timestream. (. . .) The duration of a life is called a timestream. It's like a destiny. You have to finish one before you start another.*[31]

Meanwhile, the Master's TARDIS rematerialises nearby. The Castellan and the Daleks step out. The Daleks kill and take the shape of two local SFPD policemen.

Thanks to information contained in the San Francisco Public Library computers, the Doctor is able to trace his father's post-war career through a series of scientific papers published under the name of John Smith by Princeton, Chicago, Brown University, Duke and, finally, UC Berkeley – in 1970, twenty-five years ago. He and Jane decide to go to Berkeley and investigate.

Outside, the Castellan is tracking their movements on his monitoring device.

We cut to a campus bar in Berkeley called 'Mad Joe's'.

The Doctor asks the owner, MAD JOE, about Dr John Smith. He tells them that Smith was a radical, anti-nuke professor nicknamed 'Doctor Doom', who got himself fired after building a small A-bomb, just to demonstrate how easy and dangerous it could be. He suggests that they track down Smith's former research assistant, a woman he had nicknamed 'Q-Star'. Later, the Doctor explains the meaning of that name to Jane.

> **Doctor** *When a Q-star burns energy, it creates Quad Magnetism . . . The most powerful magnetic force in the universe.* [32]

The Doctor and Jane, still followed by the Castellan and his two Dalek/Cops, go to the campus. In the Physics Department Chairman's Office, they meet Professor ANNE BAKER, an attractive woman in her mid-fifties, who first inquires about their motive. The Doctor tells her that he is looking for his father.

> **Professor Baker** *His son? Of course, I remember now. His first wife died in childbirth and the child was sent to live with his grandparents.* [33]

Professor Baker tells them that 'Q-Star' used to be her roommate, but she left to work in Eastern Europe. As to Dr Smith, he disappeared. She believes he has become a science-fiction writer. She offers to make a few phone calls on their behalf. The Doctor and Jane agree to return later.

Once outside, they decide to spend some time in the local shopping mall. In a bookstore inside the mall, the Doctor finds copies of sci-fi novels by Dr John Smith, featuring a time-traveling hero named 'The Traveller'. The author's photo on the jacket shows a handsome and vibrant man in his sixties.

Suddenly, the Doctor notices the Castellan and the two Dalek/Cops tailing them. The Doctor then realises that they're being tracked through the old army button, which contains a hidden transmitter. He crushes it. He then manages to temporarily disable the Daleks and they escape.

Back at the campus, Professor Baker tells them that John Smith passed away three months ago.

ACT FIVE

Because of some minor contradictions in her story, the Doctor suspects that Professor Baker lied; they decide to follow her.

We cut to Skaro. There are only 36 hours left to go on the Doomsday Clock. The Master is furious at the Castellan for losing the Doctor in San Francisco. The Castellan shows him a copy of the paperback with Smith's photo. The Master remarks that he aged hideously, and blames it on Earth's lifestyle and pollution. He then orders the Castellan to be taken away to the Surgery Room and converted into a Dalek.

Master *The truth is, you'd be better off as a Dalek. No thinking to do.*

The Castellan is dragged away, screaming.

Back in California, the Doctor and Jane have succeeded in following Professor Baker to her rustic house in the hills of Sausalito. There he discovers what we had suspected all along: Professor Baker herself is – was – 'Q-Star', and the Doctor's father is not dead but living with her.

At first, Dr Smith is concerned that the Doctor has been sent by Gallifrey to return him home, which he does not want to do, which is why he instructed Professor Baker – his second wife – to lie.

Over lunch, the Doctor tells his father about Borusa's death and the Master's plan. But even knowing all this, Dr Smith still refuses to return, because he feels that his 'mission' on Earth is still incomplete. Each Time Lord incarnation has a specific 'timestream', or destiny, which must be fulfilled before he can move on. His is on Earth.

Dr Smith *As my son will attest, there is no greater sin for a Time Lord than to quit one's destiny before its natural conclusion.* [31]

He tells the Doctor that his mother – unknown, but obviously an Earth woman – died while he was still an

244

infant. Dr Smith decided to send his baby son back to Gallifrey and Borusa, because he could not care for him alone on Earth,[33] and because he was planning to enlist in 'Operation Black Cross'. He has spent many years on our planet; he has visited Copernicus and Newton, befriended Leonardo and Einstein, always trying to steer our world away from war and destruction, on the path of peace and progress – what he calls the Great Moral Dialectic.

Dr Smith *It's what you call God.*

Doctor *It states that the moral universe refines itself towards goodness just as the physical universe keeps expanding.* [25]

Dr Smith admits to having been misguided in his attempts to try and prevent World War II by killing Hitler. In any event, 'Operation Black Cross' failed. After the war he came to the United States and met Anne Baker, whom he later married.

Dr Smith (to Jane) *It takes a special woman to be involved with a man from another planet.*

Jane *Oh, but we're not . . . involved.*

Dr Smith *Not yet. But you're in his timestream. From here on, even if you're separated by a million miles and a thousand years, you'll always be connected.* [31]

Dr Smith tells the Doctor that he and Anne have a child; in effect, the Doctor has a half-sister.

Dr Smith *She's a great girl, quite grown herself. You must meet someday. But for now, it'll have to wait.* [34]

Eventually, the Doctor accepts that his father has a different destiny. The job to stop the Master is his, and his alone. Dr Smith helps him repair his Time Rotor with the help of some nitro cellulose (nail polish), and they say goodbye.

As they leave they hear the doorbell ring. They look back to see a YOUNG WOMAN with a four-year-old child. The LITTLE GIRL jumps into Dr Smith's arms. The Doctor departs, feeling both sad and happy at the sight of the family he never knew.

He and Jane prepare themselves for the trip to Skaro. The Doctor is still unsure about embarking on what may be a desperate mission, but Jane's confidence in him helps to make up his mind.

> **Jane** *Like your father said, I listened to my heart.*
> **Doctor** *Well, mine are equally divided.*
> **Jane** *Can I listen?* (**She puts a hand over each side of his chest, then leans her head against him.**) *That's not what I hear.*

When they arrive at the Transamerica Pyramid, however, they are again chased by the Daleks, now in the shape of two punks, and discover that the TARDIS has vanished.

ACT SIX
Surprisingly, Dr Smith shows up and reveals that he fixed the chameleon ('cloaking') device. He has decided to accompany them to Skaro after all. They install the repaired Time Rotor.

> **Dr Smith** *The installation is very delicate. The receptors have to be lined up perfectly with the actuators.* [26]
> **Doctor** *A Time Rotor is empowered with the energy of a black hole. One false move unleashes that power.*

They successfully complete the installation, then dematerialise just in time to escape from the Daleks.

Cut to Skaro. They rematerialise on the Newbon Plateau, near the Crater of Wyq. The Doctor again reminisces about the fact that the planet used to be a magical place where lovers of many cultures used to get engaged, under the six moons of Ardor. Then it was destroyed by the savage Neutron Wars which lasted two hundred years.

> **Dr Smith** *The radiation reduced the people to mutants. Science offered them new life . . . as Daleks.* [35]
> **Doctor** *By the time they realised the price of their salvation was merely another mutation, it was too late . . .*

246

The Doctor would like Jane to remain safely behind in the TARDIS, but naturally she refuses. They share a moving, emotional moment. Then the three of them go out in a sandstorm, determined to infiltrate the Master's base and sabotage the Master's giant Time Rotor.

They cut their way into a ventilation shaft, and use honey the Doctor took from the San Francisco coffee shop to keep the Voxyls at bay. They come across Sherman's skeleton and, finally, infiltrate the Master's base.

Once inside, they pass the Surgical Room where loud screams tell them that New Daleks are being made. Jane asks if there is anything they can do.

Doctor *Once they've grafted living tissue onto the exoskeleton, it's too late.*

Eventually, they reach the black hole control room. There the Doctor discovers that the Time Rotor is not yet properly installed.

Behind him 'Dr Smith' tells him that it has been waiting for him, then morphs into . . . the Master.

ACT SEVEN

The Doctor and Jane are in a holding cell. The Doctor knows that he will refuse to help the Master, and tells Jane that he is sorry that he dragged her into his timestream. To the sight of the moons through the window, they exchange traditional vows; they manage to share a brief kiss, just before the Daleks come and snatch the Doctor away.[36]

In the control room, only ten minutes remain on the Doomsday Clock. Dalek armies are entering the warships, which only await power from the Black Hole to depart and conquer the universe. The Master watches, the Dalek/Castellan by his side.

Master *The moment has finally come. You have the privilege of leading the most magnificent army in history. You must feel very honoured.*

The evil Time Lord then orders the Doctor to finish the installation of the Time Rotor, but the Doctor replies that, even if he was willing to do it (which he isn't), it wouldn't work because the Master's installations are not strong enough to contain the immensely powerful energies of a boomerang black hole.

Doctor *Even if I were willing to install your Rotor, it wouldn't work. It violates the Unified Field Theory.* [37]

Master *People who invent theories, people like your father, can't know what will work because they don't have the nerve to test their ideas . . .*

The Master obviously disagrees with the Doctor's assessment, and orders Jane to be turned into a Dalek unless the Doctor obeys. In spite of Jane's spirited readiness to sacrifice herself, the Doctor reluctantly agrees to do what the Master wants. However, the Master says that he will not rescind his order until the Rotor is installed and fully operational.

There are now only five minutes left on the clock.

Jane is taken to the Operating Room, where a team of Surgeons start prepping her. Meanwhile the Doctor works feverishly on various super-scientific machines.

There are now only three minutes left on the clock.

Just as Jane is about to be operated on, the Doctor finishes his engineering work. The Time Rotor is installed. The black hole is about to be tapped and harnessed.

But the Master refuses to release Jane; worse, he pulls a bowie knife and advances towards the Doctor, intent on killing him once and for all, by removing both his hearts.

Master *I have what I wanted with time to spare. In fact, I have time for one final pleasure before we launch . . . The sight of your quivering hearts, lying at my feet . . .*

Doctor *Even if you kill me, I'll be back to stop you in another life . . .* [38]

Master *But you'll carry the memory of this pain forever . . . The imprint of my blade as it enters your flesh, fuelled by the power of my hatred.*

The Doctor appeals to whatever humanity may be left in the transformed Castellan, and just as the Master is about to plunge his blade into the Doctor's chest the Castellan grabs the knife and plunges it into his own heart.

The Doctor escapes and rushes towards the Operating Room. On his way he starts a fire alarm, which stops the surgery. He rescues Jane.

There are now only thirty seconds left on the clock.

The Doctor fools the Daleks that have been sent after them by having Jane wear the exo-skeleton into which she was to be fused. This enables the Doctor to disable them.

As the Doomsday Clock ticks its final seconds, the Doctor and Jane face the Master again. He believes he has just triumphed.

Master *So much for your father's theory . . .*

But the Doctor is proved right after all, as the energies of the black hole can't be contained by the Master's Time Rotor. Everything begins to fall apart.

Doctor *You've unleashed the power of the Black Hole. In a few moments, you won't have any ships or an army . . .*

Master *But I'll still be alive, somewhere in the time corridor, to haunt you! The present may be yours but the future is mine!*

The Master then summons his own TARDIS and escapes.

The Doctor and Jane manage to make it out and to the TARDIS just in the nick of time before the planet explodes in a huge fireball. From the TARDIS they take a last long look at the six moons before returning to Gallifrey.

Back on Gallifrey, the Doctor persuades Varda to replace Borusa and assume the Presidency.

Doctor *Like my father, I was not meant for the office. It deserves a person whose destiny is tied to Borusa to finish his work . . . As heir to the office, I exercise my right to pass on the Sash to the person of my choosing . . .*

Varda *But no woman has ever held the office of President.*

Doctor *Then it's about time.* [39]

The Doctor then takes Jane back to London, 1944, where she is happily reunited with Winston.

The Doctor is happy that his father found his destiny, and he knows that his is to continue to fight evil, such as the Master and the Daleks, throughout the Universe.

Doctor *With all my heart, I must dedicate my life to tracking down the Master . . . As for my other heart, that will always belong to you. (. . .) The Master's already got a head start on me. I'm afraid time is of the essence . . .*

Jane *Where will you find him?*

Doctor *I'm not exactly sure, but I have a strong hunch . . .* [40]

The Doctor gives Jane his watch which is somehow connected to the TARDIS and will always tell her when/where he is. In return, she gives him her red/white/blue WAC scarf. They kiss and he leaves.

Later she notices the watch clicking to another space-time date: Germany, 1 September 1939, the day World War II began. [41]

She steps outside. A Bobbie asks her if she saw a stranger lurking about. She replies that that was no stranger, that was the Doctor. 'Doctor Who?' says the Bobbie. 'Exactly,' replies Jane.

Notes

1 The natural shape of a TARDIS is described here as pyramidal, a slight variation on the obelisk of *Fathers and Brothers*. Note that the TARDIS used by the Doctor is not, at this stage, the old Type 40 in the classic shape of the police box.

250

2 In terms of continuity, *The Time of My Life* presents several problems. First, and obviously, the story was intended from the start to replace the previous script, *Fathers and Brothers*. Consequently it incorporated a number of elements from the older script, and some events were duplicated. This makes the co-existence of both scripts problematic, and any history of *Doctor Who* including one would almost have to exclude the other.

Second, if one assumes that *The Time of My Life* had been produced as intended, the question remains as to where, and how, it would have fitted within prior *Doctor Who* continuity. When the story opens, the Doctor has obviously been a space-time adventurer for a long time: he is well familiar with Earth, even has a human companion named Sherman, and he has encountered the Daleks before. Unlike *Fathers and Brothers*, it cannot therefore be considered as a 'past' (i.e. pre-Hartnell) *Doctor Who* story.

Could it then be a 'future' *Doctor Who* story, like *The Jewels of Time*, taking place in some hypothetical future, like *Last of the Time Lords*? This is also difficult to accept, because *The Time of My Life* shares certain 'origins' characteristics with *Fathers and Brothers*, such as the introduction of the TARDIS-as-a-police-box, the revelations about the Doctor's father (who only left Gallifrey fifty years before the story begins), and the role of the Master as a trusted servant of the Time Lords and not yet a wanted criminal.

So, if *The Time of My Life* is not a 'past' or a 'future' *Doctor Who* story, what is it? We finally came to the conclusion that it was an 'alternative' *Doctor Who* story, or more precisely an 'alternative future' *Doctor Who* story. Furthermore, one must keep in mind that, since it was intended to be the pilot of a new television series, had the series been made, the continuity differences between the original BBC television series and the new one would have grown increasingly greater. This is why we eventually came up with the premise *The End of Time* (see Appendix), with an eye towards reconciling these two potentially divergent universes.

3 In the original *Doctor Who* universe that date would place the future part of this story before the Second Dalek Wars, according to the chronology outlined in *The Terrestrial Index*.

4 The TARDIS key also serves here as a kind of security lock which activates the chameleon circuit.

5 The Daleks used in this script are materially different from the computer-generated 'spider-daleks' depicted in *Fathers and Brothers*, as well as markedly different from the original BBC television series Daleks. Robert DeLaurentis takes great pains to explain that these are a new type of Dalek ('Models X-7'), and that they are probably the result of the Master's own genetic engineering, not Davros's creations. In *The Time of My Life* one is left with the impression that, in some undetermined future of that alternative universe, the Master purely and simply took over Skaro and the Daleks for his own nefarious purposes.

The X-7s are basically Terminator-like humanoid cyborgs with the ability to assume human shapes. Since these new Daleks are given more screen time than in *Fathers and Brothers*, and yet they spend that screen time in various human guises, one is tempted to see this change as motivated by cost-savings. Certainly, the cost of making the pilot was an issue with Fox, and computer-generated imagery is notoriously expensive.

Even though one might have argued that these Daleks are, to some extent, not too different from the mysterious Dalek/Policemen introduced in *Resurrection of the Daleks* (6P), we pointed out to Segal that such a change might be deemed too far a departure from the established Dalek concept, and suggested using other names (including that of 'Ogrons') for the same creatures. Alternatively, we also discussed incorporating into subsequent rewrites – this was, after all, only a first draft – the notion that the Master has allied himself with the 'real' Daleks (ruled by Davros or by a Supreme Dalek), who would have loaned him some Daleks and allowed him to turn them into his personal stormtroopers in his bid for universal conquest. One further presumes that, if the Daleks had indeed allied themselves with the Master, it would have been with the intention of using him and then getting rid of him later. In any event, there would not have been enough room in the script to cover this, although it may have been developed further had the series been produced.

6 The use of the name 'Skaro' is consistent with DeLaurentis's approach to the relationship between the Master and the Daleks. We also suggested changing that name (offering 'Kembel' as an alternative). It is interesting to note that the idea of opening the movie on Skaro was ultimately retained in *Enemy Within*. Even though the circumstances outlined in *The Time of My Life* are different from those of *Fathers and Brothers*, they both lead to the conclusion that the Master was indeed tried for his crimes against the Dalek race, and not necessarily the rest of the universe.

7 The galactic location of Gallifrey is consistent with the data offered in *Pyramids of Mars* (4G), but different from the various locations offered up in *The Jewels of Time*, *Fathers and Brothers* and *Enemy Within*. The description of the planet, however, is very similar to that proposed in *Fathers and Brothers*.

8 We again suggested not using the name 'Borusa' here to avoid confusion. See note 4 in the *Fathers and Brothers* chapter.

9 This scene is very similar to the one in *Fathers and Brothers*. The major differences are that the Master is clearly not Gallifrey's Minister of Defence, and no longer Borusa's heir, i.e. the Doctor's half-brother. In this version he is an influential member of the Time Lords who is plotting to betray his people.

10. While neither *Fathers and Brothers* nor *The Time of My Life* provides an exact indication as to how much time elapsed since the days of Rassilon, the latter implies that more time has gone by.

11 Another indication that these are 'new' Daleks. Also see note 5 above.

12 And this is one more indication that the X-7s are the product of the Master's technology.

13 The notion that the Eye of Harmony on Gallifrey powers all TARDISes originated in *Fathers and Brothers* (see note 23 in that chapter), and eventually became a major plot element in *Enemy Within*.

14 Sherman joins Adric, Katarina and Sara Kingdom in the list of Companions to have died in the course of their association with the Doctor.

15 While there is nothing in *The Time of My Life* to conflict with the 'Ulysses/Cheops' version of the Doctor's father, nevertheless one is led to the conclusion that they were not intended to be the same character. At one point the script states that the Doctor's father has been missing for only fifty years. Also, later, 'Dr Smith' (the Doctor's father) states that his first trip to Earth was to research the Unified Field Theory – visits to Copernicus, Newton and Einstein are quoted. The Master mentions that Smith 'aged hideously' while on Earth but appears to refer to the fifty years the latter spent on Earth between the 1940s and the 1990s. All this seems very different from the Ulysses character. Also see note 33 below.

16 As in *Fathers and Brothers*, the Doctor's TARDIS turns out to be his father's old Type 40. Interestingly, the Doctor's 'origins' remain somewhat similar – in both cases he was born on Earth but sent back to be raised on Gallifrey. Also see note 33 below.

17 In this version Borusa's spirit does not reincarnate in the TARDIS. See interview with DeLaurentis below.

18 DeLaurentis retained Leekley's explanation for the TARDIS's original assumption of the police box shape. But since this Doctor travelled before, met the Daleks, etc., this is also one more argument in favour of the 'alternative universe' theory. Also see note 29.

19 A seemingly almost compulsory introduction . . .

20 'Dr John Smith' is, in this script, the alias of the Doctor's father. This is, clearly, a reference to the alias used by the Second and Third Doctors. This homage was carried over into *Enemy Within*.

21 While Jane McDonald shares certain similarities with *Fathers and Brothers*' Lizzie Travis, she comes across as stronger, spunkier, more sophisticated and determined.

22 Conversely, Robert DeLaurentis's Doctor is more intellectual and wiser than the younger, brasher version presented in *Fathers and Brothers*. His scientific knowledge of temporal engineering is, after all, the reason why the Master is after him in this story.

23 This may be the only time a writer identified Gallifrey's location within its own star system. The analogy between the conflict on Gallifrey and World War II on Earth is carried over from *Fathers and Brothers*.

24 An interesting explanation of the name 'Master', as well as a logical extrapolation of the Master's hypnotic powers.

25 DeLaurentis's script introduces a moral dimension to the Doctor's adventures. His destiny, or 'timestream' (see note 31 below), is no longer random, but serves an overall purpose. This concept is emphasised throughout the script.

26 The terms 'cloaking' and 'chameleon' appear to have been used through *Fathers and Brothers*, *The Time of My Life* and *Enemy Within* in an interchangeable way. Some of the words connected with time travel 'science' (such as 'Time Rotor') are also employed in an arguable manner. On the *Star Trek* series writers often use the abbreviation 'tech' in their scripts to indicate that the correct bit of *Star Trek* 'science' must be inserted; technical consultant Michael Okuda then contributes the appropriate terminology. There is no doubt that these minor discrepancies would have been ironed out in later rewrites. The 'Z-Caps' used by the Doctor are, for instance, similar to the 'Q Capsules' used in *The Sunmakers* (4W).

27 The mechanism of the Time Ram described here is similar to that used in *The Time Monster* (OOO).

28 Even though *The Time of My Life* skipped the trip to Ancient Egypt (*Fathers and Brothers*), Robert DeLaurentis nevertheless managed to incorporate its pyramid imagery by making use of a famous San Francisco landmark.

29 This is DeLaurentis's explanation for the London police box shape of the TARDIS. As evidenced in *Enemy Within*, it was eventually felt that it was not necessary to explain to

the uninitiated American viewers the reason why the TARDIS looks like a London police box. Also see note 18 above.

30 An interesting variation on the concept of Time Lord biology and regeneration. Would a Time Lord survive if both his hearts were cut out? A later comment by the Doctor (see note 35 below) would indicate that he might.

31 The concept of an individual 'timestream', or destiny (also see note 25 above), is introduced by DeLaurentis as part of his attempt at providing an overall moral dimension to the story.

32 A possible reference to *Arc of Infinity* (6E).

33 In this version of the Doctor's origins, we learn virtually nothing about the identity of the Doctor's mother, other than that she was human, probably British, from the 1940s, and died in childbirth. (In *Fathers and Brothers*, the Egyptian 'Annalisse' died from fever.) Also, the Doctor's father sent his son to be raised on Gallifrey for what seem to be here reasons of convenience – to not be burdened with a baby – rather than to save his child's life. The story of the Doctor's half-human ancestry would eventually be reduced to mere hints in *Enemy Within*. Also see notes 15 and 16 above.

34 The major revelation of *The Time of My Life* is that the Doctor's father had another child, a daughter (the Doctor's half-sister, unnamed), from his second wife, Anne Baker, and that that daughter had, in turn, a daughter (the Doctor's half-niece, also unnamed). The script remains secretive about these characters and it is very likely that they may have been given greater exposure had a television series been commissioned. See interview with DeLaurentis below.

One would be tempted to draw a parallel between the Doctor's half-niece and the character of Susan from the original BBC television series. Some fascinating questions remain: has the Doctor's half-sister inherited their father's Gallifreyan (Time Lord?) biology, i.e. two hearts, etc.? What about her child, who would be a quarter Gallifreyan? These are questions which must remain unanswered.

35 Other than the fact that, in *Genesis of the Daleks* (4E), the Neutron(ic) Wars are said to have lasted a thousand years, this portion of Skaro's history is more or less in accordance with the previous continuity. However, in this universe, it would seem that the Master happened to take over the pitiful remains of Skaro to create his own armies.

36 As was the case with *Last of the Time Lords*, *The Jewels of Time*, *Fathers and Brothers* and, ultimately, *Enemy Within*, the Doctor is romantically drawn to his Companion. While the BBC has always exhibited concern about preserving the 'purity' of the character (e.g. objecting to the use of illegal drugs in the Golden Gate Park scene in *The Jewels of Time*), it has nevertheless recognised the necessity to relax the standards once applied to what was then deemed to be a children's show.

37 This is another example of 'tech' language (see note 26) that would almost certainly have been polished in later rewrites.

38 In *The Time of My Life*, the rule against Time Lords killing each other (*Fathers and Brothers*) has obviously vanished. The Master depicted here exhibits a violent, sadistic streak not previously displayed.

39 The character of Varda is not unlike that of Chancellor Flavia who was deputised as President by the Fifth Doctor in *The Five Doctors* (6K). This is otherwise a clever use of the promotional blurb, 'it's about time'.

40 One wonders, had the show gone to series, if the argument of the Doctor pursuing the Master through time and space would have been enough to sustain a regular series. Probably not. But then, we have the 8th season of the original television series to prove us wrong.

41 A hint that the Master may have been behind the events leading to World War II – the war was officially declared on 3 September.

Review

The Time of My Life is a well-written script, strong on breakneck pacing and relentless action. It is somewhat reminiscent of a *James Bond* story, with the Doctor a more mature yet dashing hero, the Master a sadistic, despicable villain, and a countdown-to-destruction plot with big special effects of the K-BOOM nature at the end.

The Time of My Life is undoubtedly – and this is certainly not intended as a criticism – the most 'American' of all the 'Nth Doctor' scripts, in the sense that it is the one which most consciously and closely fits the formula of an action/adventure television story.

The relationship between the Doctor and Jane is romantic, in a traditional fashion; that between the Doctor and his father is rich and textured, and is a highlight of the script. The moments of self-doubt plaguing the Doctor and the reinforcement of his belief in his special destiny are well handled and a welcome addition to the psychology of the character.

While *The Time of My Life* would have represented a significant departure from the style of the original BBC television series, it nevertheless retained its basic premise and would have stood well on its own merits.

Background

In January 1995 the series division of Fox Television Network, under the direction of John Matoian, turned down *Doctor Who*, not because of the script, as has been wrongly alleged in various fan magazines, but because they thought *Doctor Who* was not enough of a 'mainstream' concept and, furthermore, because they deemed it too expensive to produce on a regular basis. (With no standing sets, and major special effects required every week, either in the form of monsters or opticals, the budget would have probably been in the $1.5–$2 million range.)

Philip Segal was forced to retrench and, once again, to rethink his approach. Some entreaties were made to other networks, in particular UPN, but they too turned down the concept.

Salvation for the show came in the person of Trevor Walton, yet another British expatriate, and head of the Fox Television Network's made-for-TV feature division. Walton not only supported the concept of *Doctor Who*, but was prepared to order a feature, which could then be used as a 'backdoor pilot' for a possible series. He also enthusiastically supported Segal's plans to make that feature closer to the original BBC television series, including the vital decision to open the movie with a regeneration sequence, for which Sylvester McCoy would be rehired to play the Seventh Doctor, thereby providing a link with the past.

Clearly one more script had to be commissioned, if only because a new set of executives was now in charge. While Terrance Dicks was seriously considered to write it, the other candidate, Matthew Jacobs, another British-born writer, was ultimately hired because of his feature film and American network television credentials (which included *Young Indiana Jones*).

The final hurdle that the budding production had to overcome was the folding of Amblin into DreamWorks SKG, a new entertainment company created in the summer of 1995 between Steven Spielberg, former Disney executive Jeffrey Katzenberg and music mogul David Geffen. Segal, who had always been the prime mover of *Doctor Who* at Amblin, was fortunately able successfully to disentangle the project from Amblin/DreamWorks and produce it alone with Universal and BBC Worldwide.

Matthew Jacobs delivered the first draft of what was to become known as *Enemy Within* in August 1995. Paul McGann, who had already been on the producers' wish list since *Fathers and Brothers*, was hired to play the Eighth Doctor (Segal also liked Liam Cunningham from *Little Princess*), and the production was finally on its way.

By then our job of 'fan liaisons' was superseded by Universal's and, later, Fox's efficient publicity departments and, with other work requiring our attention, our involvement with the new *Doctor Who* had come to an end.

Interview with Robert DeLaurentis

Question: How were you hired to write Doctor Who?

Robert DeLaurentis: I was hired to write *Doctor Who* after the draft of a previous writer (John Leekley's) was deemed unworkable by the studio. I had a relationship with Philip Segal and Amblin which dated back to discussions on an earlier project (*Earth 2*), and since I had done a science fiction series for Universal (*Mann and Machine*), the thought was that I might have an affinity for the Doctor (I did). In addition, there was very little time – one week for a new story, and six weeks for a two-hour script.

Q: Had you heard of, or seen any, original Doctor Who *before you took the job?*

RDL: I was a fan of the original series through an English friend, and over the years had seen many episodes.

Q: What kind of research did you do prior to writing the script?

RDL: I did very little research other than to read the standard *Doctor Who Programme Guide*, the *Doctor Who Handbooks*, etc. My feeling about research is that it should be approached very cautiously to avoid the classic trap of 'writing' the research. I tried to find a personal connection with the story first, and added the research later for authenticity.

Q: What type of story were the producers specifically looking for?

RDL: The producers were looking for a story with a lighter touch and more romance, and one that had action elements.

Q; Who made the decision to keep what elements from John Leekley's script?

RDL: There were a few elements of John Leekley's script that the producers felt were necessary: the backstory of the Doctor's life on Gallifrey, how he came to occupy his TARDIS, the Master and the Daleks.

Q: For instance, why was the backstory of the Doctor's father and mother changed?

RDL: The backstory was changed in order to create a connection to contemporary Earth. As we live in the nuclear age (the discovery of nuclear energy being perhaps the most formative event of current history), it was also important to me to intersect that great scientific moment. Equally important was to try and reveal the negative ramifications of the nuclear discovery, through the Doctor's earthbound father, as well as his attempt to struggle with the most powerful personal forces in creation, human love and propagation. Finally it was important to choose an earthly connection to the Doctor that would not only reveal the past (as in John Leekley's Egyptian history), but also propel the story forward in time.

Q: Why was the concept of Borusa as a 'Spirit Guide' taken out?

RDL: The concept of Borusa as a Spirit Guide was very interesting to me. But with the zero-sum restrictions of time and page count, it was sacrificed for a more 'present' and accessible character, i.e. Sherman.

Q: And why were the 'spider-daleks' changed?

RDL: The 'spider-daleks' were changed to be consistent with a newer, more modern tone, less Gothic and more action-capable.

Q: Had you had any discussions or meetings with Terry Nation about the redesign of the Daleks?

RDL: I had no discussions, in large part due to restrictions of time, with Terry Nation about the Daleks.

Q: What motivated you to give the Doctor a half-sister? Is it something that you'd have liked to explore further, had the pilot gone to series, or was it more a throw-away sort of thing?

RDL: I gave the Doctor a half-sister because I wanted a real genetic connection to contemporary human life, not to mention the ability to explore the unique convergence of the two life forms. In that way I hoped to say something about the nature of human life as well, what we might be missing, where we might be heading in an evolutionary way. In a series, I would have explored not only the Doctor's relationship with his half-sister, but also her children, in particular an only male child who becomes a future Time Lord renegade.

261

Q: Unlike Leekley's script, which was like an 'origin' story/a prequel, your script is clearly intended to be more like a 'reboot' of the original series. Can you explain how this came to pass?

RDL: Science fiction, including the original *Doctor Who* BBC television series, is notoriously male-oriented. One was faced with the choice of making a valentine to a wonderful classic, or evolving the original elements, while remaining true to the spirit of the Doctor. I felt very strongly that any new incarnation of the show must appeal not only to a global audience, but also to women.

My feeling was that since the primary mission of a new *Doctor Who* script was to introduce him to a new generation of viewers, with all the historical baggage of the original series, I felt it was imperative to establish a new connection for this new audience, allowing them to 'begin' his adventures with him.

Q: How would you have envisioned the continuation of the series? What would have been your vision of Doctor Who – *the series?*

RDL: In the short term, I envisioned the series as the continuation of the Doctor's adventures in the contemporary world, initially America, exploring the issue of how the past and future shape events in our world, a kind of warning about where our technological society is headed, with its loss of humanity and destruction of the planet. I saw the Doctor himself as a character at the centre of these events, with a unique perspective on past and future, essentially a lone hero trying to resolve monumental, historic issues.

I subtitled my script *The Time of My Life* with the intention to put a 'frame' around the Doctor's personal history, somehow to connect his current existence to the personal forces at work in his past and future, to provide a character analogue to the history and adventure story. That, to me, was the single most critical element in presenting a new *Doctor Who* to a new audience.

Q: What do you think led the network to pass on the series?

RDL: I think that, in order for the network to order a new series, they needed to see the new prototype connect in some fundamental way with a new audience, as well as clearly articulate the possibilities of future adventures. The network were clearly concerned that *Doctor Who* had been a 'cult' show, and that any new incarnation would have to bridge the gap, cultural and economic, to new global programming requirements.

Q: Any comments or statements you'd like to make?

RDL: I still feel very strongly that *Doctor Who* is out there, waiting for the proper moment to return. I have no doubt that, if properly introduced, a whole new generation of viewers would embrace the character and his world view. But in network television, as in most things, time is of the essence.

APPENDIX

As a self-indulgent appendix to this book, and at the request of a couple of friends (yes, you, Chris!) I have decided to present here two documents, of the type known in Hollywood lingo as 'premises', which Randy and I wrote during the time of our collaboration with Philip Segal.

None of these should be construed as 'official' in any way, shape or form, since they were not commissioned or paid for by the production; however, I believe they may provide an interesting insight into the creative process that takes place during the creation of a television series.

These premises were written after a number of informal, brainstorming discussions with Segal, during which he would bounce around ideas about the format and contents of the new *Doctor Who*. We wrote them purely as an attempt to find ways to reconcile two conflicting requirements: (a) the necessity of pleasing the network, and (b) Segal's genuine desire to make a *Doctor Who* that would fit within the tapestry of the original BBC television series.

It must again be stressed that these premises were never intended to be anything more than springboards for further discussion and thoughts, not actual to-be-produced material.

The End of Time

The first premise was written in late 1994, after we had read Robert DeLaurentis's *The Time of My Life*, and before John Matoian (the head of Fox Television series' division) had initially passed on the project.

As mentioned above, Segal always wanted, from the beginning, to connect the new series to the original one, and also to bring back a previous incarnation of the Doctor – which one would depend on actors' availability, although McCoy and Tom Baker were leading contenders. Considering that, for all intents and purposes, *The Time of My Life* presented us with an 'alternate' Doctor, these goals seemed rather difficult to achieve, at least while maintaining a certain amount of fictional coherence.

The parallel universe device – of the type used in *Inferno* (DDD) or *Star Trek*'s 'Mirror Universe' – having already been done, it was preferable to find something less ordinary. The inspiration for *The End of Time* came from my friend the comic-book writer Marv Wolfman's classic series, *Crisis on Infinite Earths*, in which the DC Universe was 'rebooted' from its very beginnings.

Fans will pick up on the references to Deva Loka from *Kinda* (5Y), Dalios from *The Time Monster* (OOO) and, of course, the Terrible Zodin, mentioned in *The Five Doctors* (6K). The entire first episode was actually based on an outline for a New Adventure submitted to Virgin, featuring the real-life Order of the Golden Dawn secret society, which Bram Stoker, Arthur Machen, etc., belonged to. Coincidentally, we later found that the sinking of the *Titanic* was one of Segal's favourite themes. The similarities with *The Jewels of Time* are totally coincidental.

The End of Time was written to show Segal how the two proverbial birds could be killed with a single stone. It was also a way of 'retconning' the new and the original *Doctor Who*, and explaining the differences between the two universes. Finally, it would also have made an effective cliff-hanger for the last episode of a hypothetical first season (like the return of Spock in *Star Trek: The Next Generation*'s famous *Reunification* episode).

Episode 1: 'The Terrible Zodin'

We open on the planet DEVA LOKA, home of the peaceful, native-American-like KINDA.

The alien villainess ZODIN steals the fourth segment of the mythical, all-powerful KEY TO TIME after killing its guardian, the Kinda's HIGH PRIEST.

She then uses the segment and her psychic powers to trigger a volcanic eruption which destroys many of the natives. Like a psychic vampire, she feeds on the spiritual energies released by her victims' deaths.

She then activates a sub-space tunnel which will take her to the location of the next Segment, EARTH.

Meanwhile, the WHITE GUARDIAN takes control of the TARDIS and warns the DOCTOR about ZODIN.

By looking through ancient records dating back to the days of RASSILON, the founder of the TIME LORDS, the Doctor discovers that the Guardian is the Incarnation of Life, one of the two forces (Death being the other) which make up the Universal Balance.

The TARDIS takes the Doctor to LONDON, in early April 1912.

At the British Museum, he meets ANN MANSARD, a young woman who belongs to the Adepts of Eleusis, an esoteric society. She is trying to translate an Atlantean palimpsest, the SCROLLS OF DALIOS, which her 'magus', SIR ALASTAIR MACHEN, brought back from a dig in Crete. The Doctor's curiosity is piqued when he fails to decipher it.

Zodin is also looking for the Scrolls, because they contain the location of the Key's fifth segment. She kills Machen, but fails to find the Scrolls. When she spots the Doctor and identifies him as a Time Lord she hits on another plan.

The laws which the White Guardian must obey forbid him from directly helping his champion, but he can offer hints. These eventually lead the Doctor to understand what is at stake. Zodin serves the BLACK GUARDIAN, the Incarnation of Death. If she succeeds in gathering all six segments of the Key to Time (she already has four), she will then destroy the entire universe and recreate it in her own image.

After the Doctor and Ann discover Machen's death, they seek his killer among the other members of the Adepts' Inner Circle; but Zodin is murdering them, one by one.

The Doctor finally learns enough to decipher the Scrolls and locate the fifth segment at [depending on location]. However, DeVRIES, one of the Adepts who had been helping the Doctor and Ann, reveals himself to have been secretly working for Zodin, who tempted him with promises of supreme power. Zodin and DeVries kidnap Ann and steal the segment. But Zodin can't leave Earth without a massive sacrifice. She and DeVries embark upon the *TITANIC*, Ann still their prisoner.

The Doctor uses his TARDIS to rematerialise aboard the

Titanic minutes before the fateful crash. He fights with Zodin, but DeVries threatens to kill Ann. In order to save her, the Doctor releases Zodin and rushes DeVries. This allows Zodin to use the Key and her psychic powers to cause the crash with the iceberg. The villainess absorbs the waves of fear and panic spreading across the ship. She tells the Doctor he played into her hands. She knows where the sixth and final segment is located, but in order to go there, she needed a TARDIS – his TARDIS.

The sixth segment is, in fact, on GALLIFREY, home planet of the Time Lords.

The Doctor leaps at Zodin, but DeVries pulls out a gun and shoots him. Zodin uses the power of the almost-complete Key to break into the TARDIS. As she and DeVries step into it, Zodin tells the Doctor that she plans to kill all the Time Lords in a final sacrifice which will herald the Death of the Universe. Then the TARDIS dematerialises, leaving a wounded Doctor and Ann aboard the sinking *Titanic*. Ann believes all is lost. The Doctor, however, reveals that this is not so. He suspected DeVries, and had the TARDIS manufacture a simulacrum of the fifth segment – which is what Zodin stole. So her Key is flawed.

The Doctor pulls the real segment from his pocket. Ann asks how that will help. The Doctor smiles mysteriously. He says that this moment has been prepared for . . .

Suddenly, a familiar noise is heard. A blue police box appears. Ann wonders if Zodin is returning. The Doctor tells her no. The police box's door opens. The SEVENTH DOCTOR steps through, inviting them in.

Ann asks who this man is. Both Doctors reply, smiling, 'Me'.

[We added a note here to the effect that, if for cost reasons, the London 1912/*Titanic* background, which was dear to Segal's heart, could not be used, a viable alternative would be San Francisco's 1906 Earthquake. The beats of the story would have remained basically the same. We also pointed out that the story could easily be changed to accommodate a companion other than Ann.]

Episode 2: 'The Eye of Harmony'

We open inside the TARDIS – the Seventh Doctor's TAR-DIS. The White Guardian reveals (again) that he, like his counterpart, the Black Guardian, is bound by natural laws and must allow his champions to fight alone. However, laws are subject to interpretation. Since the Doctor clearly needed help, and had managed to gain one of the segments of the Key to Time on his own, the Guardian could pull another version of the Doctor from the infinity of timelines to come to his rescue. This, as we shall discover, is not the truth, but it is what the characters believe at this point.

The Seventh Doctor's TARDIS lands on Gallifrey. But it is a Gallifrey which appears to be suffering from a power blight. The Time Lords and their machines appear equally affected, as if they have all been drained of their energy. The Doctors guess that this is, somehow, caused by Zodin, but they don't know how. In order to discover what has happened they must locate the hidden sixth segment of the Key to Time.

During these scenes we will play on the Seventh Doctor's reactions to a Gallifrey which is not his own.

They eventually learn the answers from the Doctor's old teacher at the Time Lords' Academy, CARDINAL BORUSA. The sixth segment is one of the vital control elements of the EYE OF HARMONY, the black hole captured millions of years ago by RASSILON, and which powers the entire Time Lord civilisation, including their bodies, whose regenerative capabilities are triggered by nanomachines powered by the black hole.

The Eye of Harmony is the moon in orbit around Gallifrey, or rather it is a moon-size ship, the very ship built by Rassilon for the task. Obviously Zodin has already begun tampering with the Eye. Since the Seventh Doctor's TARDIS is the only one operational – since it comes from another universe, it isn't bound by the physical realities of this one – it is up to our heroes to stop her.

Borusa insists that they must be accompanied by one of his students, a young energetic Time Lady-in-training,

ARIEL, who knows the Eye of Harmony and the legends surrounding Rassilon like no one else – except for the Doctor, of course.

The TARDIS rematerialises inside the Eye. The Doctor goes with Ariel, looking for Zodin and the segment. The Seventh Doctor goes with Ann. They encounter some of the strange and wondrous robotic GUARDIANS protecting the Eye. Ann is wounded by one of these.

They finally arrive in the vast transdimensional machine rooms holding the Black Hole captive behind its controlled event horizon, all powered by devices beyond human comprehension.

To get to Zodin, they must first battle DeVries, who has been given control of some of the most deadly of Rassilon's guardians. They eventually defeat him and move forward.

Zodin has already been to work at dismantling the control panels in her efforts to secure the sixth segment. They are too late to stop her. She succeeds. She pulls the segment.

On Gallifrey below all grows dark, and the older Time Lords begin to collapse.

Zodin believes that she now has the full, complete Key, but her triumph is short-lived. She immediately realises something is not right. She understands what has happened when the Doctor pulls out the fifth segment, which he had earlier replaced with a simulacrum.

Zodin tells the Doctors that she is planning to do nothing more or less than what Rassilon himself did to save his people. When he saw that the Time Lords were waning, and that he himself was dying, he found and used the Key to Time to destroy his universe and recreate a new one in its place. The Seventh Doctor comes from that very same universe which was destroyed by Rassilon.

[Alternatively, we might choose to reveal that the Seventh Doctor himself was forced to use the Key and 'reboot' the universe to prevent it from falling under the Black Guardian's control. In this version, he himself was stored by the White Guardian inside the Key to act as its future 'Keeper', should another doomsday scenario occur.]

Reeling from the shock of this news, the Doctor is thrown

off-balance, and unable to react quickly enough when Zodin rushes forward and grabs Ariel.

She threatens to throw the young Time Lady beyond the event horizon and into the Black Hole if the Doctor does not give her the missing fifth segment.

The Doctor has no choice but to obey.

Zodin now holds all six segments. The Key to Time is complete and assembled. The universe is placed in a state of temporal grace.

The Black and White Guardians appear, as they must.

Zodin prepares to use the Key to destroy the universe, but the Doctor rushes her. They fight.

Zodin, still holding the Key, falls beyond the event horizon and into the BLACK HOLE. If the Key is not recovered, not only Gallifrey but the entire universe will be destroyed. But stepping beyond the event horizon means certain death.

However, the Seventh Doctor now realises that his body, like his TARDIS, does not belong to this physical universe. (This is why his TARDIS was the only one to work.) He crosses the event horizon and, after a final battle with Zodin, gains possession of the Key.

He returns with the Key, while the villainess is crushed by the unfathomable forces of the Black Hole.

The Seventh Doctor hands the Key to the Doctor, who is wondering what he should do.

The Seventh Doctor tells him that since it is his universe, it is his choice. Like Rassilon, he can choose to scrap it all and start all over again or break the Key apart, an action that will automatically scatter its six segments to the far corners of the universe, thereby dooming Gallifrey.

The Doctor hesitates.

The Black Guardian, in a Mephistophelian gesture, tempts him with the same offer he had made to Zodin. Even Ariel argues that Gallifrey must be saved at all costs. But the Doctor looks at the wounded Ann, shakes his head, and scatters the Key.

The universe is saved. Life goes on.

The Black Guardian howls in rage and vanishes, threatening to have his revenge on the Doctor.

The White Guardian smiles, tells the Doctor that he has made the right choice, and picks up the discarded simulacrum segment.

He imbues it with some of his own power, and tells the Doctor that, although it will not last as long as the real segment, it will still give the Time Lords a few billion more years of energy. He vanishes as well.

The Seventh Doctor congratulates the Doctor, and tells him that this universe is in good hands. He steps into his TARDIS and dematerialises.

The Hand of Omega

The second premise was written around the time that Trevor Walton (the head of Fox Television movies' division) first indicated his interest in bringing *Doctor Who* back, and before official discussions began with Terrance Dicks and Matthew Jacobs.

Segal had told us that Walton favoured a reintroduction of the concept like the first episode of *An Unearthly Child* (A). The two shows were to be linked; however, the decision to have a regeneration scene featuring Sylvester McCoy had not yet been made.

The challenge here was to introduce *Doctor Who* to an American audience, presumably unfamiliar with the character, and yet simultaneously to do it in a fashion that would follow logically from the original BBC television series.

The idea of starting with an amnesiac Doctor had the merit of enabling the viewer to discover the Doctor's universe at the same time as the hero, and through his eyes. The Doctor as a rebel against a Master-controlled Gallifrey obviously originated with *Fathers and Brothers*, and the University of Berkeley alias of 'Dr John Smith' came from *The Time of My Life*. The similarities with Johnny Byrne's *Last of the Time Lords* are totally coincidental.

The Master as a mysterious US Government agent in charge of the notorious 'Men in Black' harks back to the same field so successfully tapped by *The X-Files*. In a related discussion we suggested that the Daleks could be reintroduced in the same fashion, as mysterious aliens who mutilated cattle and abducted humans for genetic experiments.

The Hand of Omega is borrowed from *Remembrance of the Daleks* (7H), while the journey back through time to San Francisco's Chinatown in the early 1900s is equally inspired by *The Talons of Weng-Chiang* (4S) as well as a dream I had (which also included the construction site scene).

I would like to think that some of the rough ideas which are presented here were somewhow instrumental in helping Philip Segal define and sell the new show.

Story

We open on the prestigious University of California, BERKELEY, CA, the Department of Physics.

Through PAM HENDERSON, a young Teacher's Assistant, we meet the charismatic DOCTOR JOHN SMITH, who's been teaching a very successful class in advanced physics.

Dr Smith has an unpleasant encounter with the Head of the Physics Department, the rat-like DR JARVIS, who's obviously jealous of his popularity and of the notoriety he's gained in such a short time (he's been teaching there for only two years).

Dr Smith and Pam share a drink together after class. She drives him home to a modest house located in the Berkeley suburbs.

The home has been broken into and ransacked!

Dr Smith doesn't know why. Nothing's been stolen, he's got nothing to steal. His head starts throbbing with a bad headache . . .

Outside, in the darkness, we see a couple of mysterious MEN IN BLACK (MIBs) watching the house . . .

The next day, Dr. Smith is called into the DEAN's office. The Dean introduces him to the dark, sinister-looking MR MAGISTER, who claims to be an agent of the National Security Agency; he is accompanied by two tall, ugly, silent MIBs.

The jealous Dr Jarvis has dug into Dr Smith's past; it turns out that all his papers and credentials are false! He wasn't born in Essex, didn't go to university in Cambridge, etc. His name may not even be Smith. As the university does secret government research, the well-meaning Dean had no choice but to call in the government, which sent Agent Magister to investigate.

Dr Smith protests that he is what he claims to be, but in the face of seemingly incontrovertible evidence his faith begins to crumble.

The Dean suspends him and gives him two days to prepare a defence.

Dr Smith grabs his file and leaves.

From the window, Magister watches him cross the parking lot.

MIB *Do you think it's HIM, Master?*
Magister *Perhaps. If it is, he's regenerated again. But in case Dr Smith really is the Doctor, let's follow him. He'll lead us to the HAND OF OMEGA . . .*

Later Dr Smith shares a drink with Pam. They've looked through the file. It's darn convincing.

Doctor *But if I'm not Doctor John Smith, then who am I? Doctor WHO?*

The only clue they have is the university file. Calling on BILLY, one of Pam's ex-boyfriends, a computer wiz who works on the university computers, the Doctor and Pam are able to access and download the original software that was used to create Dr Smith's file. Billy whistles in admiration, because it looks like the work of a master-hacker, rerouted halfway around the world, to hide its origin.

Meanwhile, they haven't noticed that they've been watched most carefully by a cat which leaves and, once out of sight, morphs back into one of the MIBs!

Back home, Dr Smith and Pam study the software file. The Doctor's prodigious mind finds a hidden message, encrypted within the software itself. That message, once decyphered, leads them to a mailbox shop, located in one of the seedier parts of San Francisco. Inside the box, waiting for them, are a slip of paper with an address, a strangely-shaped key-like pendant, and a cylindrical object wrapped in brown paper.

As they leave the mailbox shop, Dr Smith spots the MIBs. They try to lose them in Pam's car, with Pam doing the driving. They think they have succeeded.

They eventually reach the address on the slip of paper. It's a vacant lot stuck between tall buildings, protected behind a wooden fence. They enter the gate. The lot is totally empty, except for a small abandoned trailer.

Suddenly, the MIBs are right there. They morph into savage man-wolves who aggressively move forward towards Dr Smith and Pam! There's no way out.

The trailer?

Dr Smith throws the cylinder away saying 'fetch!', the man-wolves run after it. We hear Magister's voice:

Magister *After him, you fool! He's escaping!*

Meanwhile, Dr Smith and Pam have run to the trailer. Alas, it's locked. Dr Smith pulls out the strangely-shaped key-like pendant and tries it. It works. The door opens . . . They go inside . . . And step right into the impossibly large space of the TARDIS!

Outside, the MASTER – for it is he! – unwraps the cylinder and discovers what looks like half a tuning fork.

Master *The Hand of Omega, at last . . .* (**Snarling**) *What did he do with the other half?*

Enraged, the Master points the Hand towards the trailer. A coruscating wave of deadly artron energy blasts the shed, which mysteriously remains intact.

Inside the TARDIS just as the Doctor and Pam are slowly coming to grips with their surroundings – things are beginning to come back to the Doctor's mind – the ship is shaken by the force of the Master's attack.

The TARDIS dematerialises, seemingly of its own volition, plunging into the Space-Time Vortex. Outside, the Master sees the trailer shimmer, morph, then vanish, accompanied by the well-known groaning, wheezing sound FX.

Master (to MIBs, who've returned to human shapes)
He's gone. Let's follow him in my TARDIS.

While in the Space-Time Vortex, fragments of the Doctor's memory begin to return, boosted by the TARDIS's empathic neuron nets. He shares this information with Pam. He belongs to an incredibly advanced race of people who have dubbed themselves 'TIME LORDS' – from the planet GALLIFREY, located near the centre of the galaxy. The Time Lords have the ability to travel through time and space in their TARDISes. They constantly scan the cosmos. Very little happens in the universe about which they don't know.

The Doctor fled from Gallifrey after stealing a very powerful artifact, a stellar manipulator called the 'Hand of Omega'. He stole it to hide it away, because it was too powerful a weapon to be allowed to fall into the wrong hands – the hands of the Master.

Pam asks who the Master is. The Doctor tells her that he is the Master of Records of the Time Lords. He is the Dark Eminence behind an ageing and increasingly feeble President. The Master wants to take over the Council of Time and become President himself, which would be a very bad thing because, like Hitler, he would then steer the Time Lords back into the war-like policies abandoned before. The Master is opposed by a group of young Time Lord rebels who call themselves SHOBOGANS. The Doctor was one of their leaders. He stole the Hand, intending to hide it on Earth.

Pam asked him how he ended up an amnesiac in San Francisco.

But the Doctor shakes his head. That is still hidden in the folds of his memory.

Meanwhile the TARDIS has arrived at the location where the Doctor hid the first component of the Hand.

The TARDIS has rematerialised in London, in the 1920s. It assumes the shape of a blue police box.

There the Doctor and Pam become involved in a Fu-Manchu-like adventure, which takes them into the fog-shrouded opium dens of the Limehouse district. Eventually they discover that, during his earlier visit, the Doctor entrusted the first component of the Hand to a wise Chinese PRIEST, who may or may not be a Time Lord living in secret exile on Earth.

During the course of the story, the Doctor discovers what really happened to him. After he stole the Hand from Gallifrey the Master pursued him. The evil Time Lord eventually caught up with the Doctor after the latter had already disposed of the first component in 1920s London, but before his intended stop in San Francisco.

Trapped by the Master's more advanced TARDIS, the Doctor was willing to sacrifice himself to destroy the Hand and prevent it from falling into evil hands.

He chose to 'Time Ram' the Master's TARDIS.

The Master thought him dead in the ensuing conflagration.

In reality, the Time Ram had left the Doctor, his body racked with artron energy, dying in San Francisco. Knowing that he was about to regenerate, he barely had time to hide the Hand's second component and set up a secret identity for himself.

What he hadn't foreseen was that he would lose his memory!

Eventually one of the Master's agents on Earth alerted him when the 'John Smith' paperwork was forwarded by the university, and the Master came to investigate personally.

Finally all the plot threads lead to a dramatic confrontation between the Doctor and the Master and his morphing henchmen (OGRONS?).

The Doctor and the Master fight, each holding one component of the Hand of Omega. We should see what the Hand is capable of doing – causing a star to go nova – in order for the threat to Planet Earth (or its sun) as well as to the Doctor, to be real. Also this final confrontation should use the TARDIS's resources in full and display the Doctor's ingenuity. In effect it should be a replay – a successful one this time! – of the earlier battle.

In the end the Doctor eventually succeeds in outwitting the Master and in destroying the Hand. The Master either departs swearing revenge, or is believed dead in his TARDIS' destruction. We then return to San Francisco, 1995.

Damaged by the Hand's energies during the final confrontation, the TARDIS now appears to be stuck in the police box shape. The Doctor shrugs. He likes it that way.

The Doctor is now a fugitive from his own people, wanted for stealing and destroying the Hand. Only the Shobogans can aid him in his fight against the Master (or, if the Master is believed dead, the High Council).

The Doctor is a new man, in a new body. But there are still huge chunks of his memory missing. He doesn't remember who may be a friend or a foe. Or his real name, for instance. He is still – Doctor WHO?

Pam either joins him, or watches him dematerialise in the TARDIS.

THE HANDBOOK: THE THIRD DOCTOR

David J Howe & Stephen James Walker

Jon Pertwee burst on the scene as the new man-of-action Doctor in January 1970. Immediately, the series, now in full colour, took a whole new direction. The Earth-bound Time Lord, backed by the hugely popular UNIT team, soon became a household favourite as the show's traditional strengths were blended with elements of James Bond and the star's own dynamism and charisma.

This book is an in-depth study of Jon Pertwee's tenure as the Doctor, including a profile of the actor, a critical summary of each story in which he starred, an extensive feature on DAY OF THE DALEKS which saw the return of the Daleks to the series after almost five years away, and much more. The authors have established their reputation with best-selling books such as THE SIXTIES and THE SEVENTIES, and their acclaimed work on the four previous books in the handbook range.

ISBN: 0 426 20486 7

DOCTOR WHO
A HISTORY OF THE UNIVERSE

Lance Parkin

At last, the complete timeline of the DOCTOR WHO universe, from Event One to its final destruction tens of billions of years in the future.

This essential reference work reveals the full story of the Daleks, the Cybermen and the Time Lords. It also includes a comprehensive history of Earth, charting the rise of humanity from a primitive tribe on the African plains to a race of galaxy-spanning conquerors.

Containing a wealth of behind-the-scenes information, much of it revealed here for the first time, A HISTORY OF THE UNIVERSE is an indispensable guide to the worlds of DOCTOR WHO.

ISBN: 0 426 20471 9